THE SHELL COUNTY GUIDES

edited by JOHN BETJEMAN *and* JOHN PIPER

CORNWALL *John Betjeman*
DORSET *Michael Pitt-Rivers*
THE ISLE OF WIGHT *Pennethorne Hughes*
LINCOLNSHIRE *Jack Yates and Henry Thorold*
NORFOLK *Wilhelmine Harrod and C. L. S. Linnell*
SUFFOLK *Norman Scarfe*
WORCESTERSHIRE *J. Lees-Milne*

*

Edited by JOHN PIPER
DERBYSHIRE *Henry Thorold*
ESSEX *Norman Scarfe*
GLOUCESTERSHIRE *David Verey*
KENT *Pennethorne Hughes*
LEICESTERSHIRE *W. G. Hoskins*
NORTHUMBERLAND *Thomas Sharp*
SHROPSHIRE *Michael Moulder*
MID WESTERN WALES *Vyvyan Rees*
NORTH WALES *Elisabeth Beazley and Lionel Brett*
SOUTH-WEST WALES *Vyvyan Rees*
WILTSHIRE (third edition) *J. H. Cheetham and John Piper*

*

NORTHAMPTONSHIRE *Juliet Smith*

*   *   *

THE SHELL PILOT TO THE
SOUTH COAST HARBOURS *K. Adlard Coles*

*

A Shell Guide

DEVON

A Shell Guide

DEVON

by Ann Jellicoe and Roger Mayne

Faber & Faber   3 Queen Square   London

First published in 1975
by Faber and Faber Limited
3 Queen Square London W C 1
Printed in Great Britain by
Butler & Tanner Ltd
Frome and London
All rights reserved

ISBN 0 571 04836 6

To Katkin and Tom

Illustrations

All the photographs in this book are by Roger Mayne.
Those in the gazetteer are in alphabetical order.
Photographs not in the gazetteer are listed below (bold type indicates gazetteer entry).

Acknowledgments

In preparing this Guide we referred constantly to Prof. N. PEVSNER's *The Buildings of England, North Devon and South Devon* (Penguin). A monumental work embracing the totality of architectural history with meticulous accuracy and austere wit. Faults and omissions in Pevsner are rare indeed and when we found one we regarded it as an occasion for some self congratulation. W. G. HOSKINS is probably the greatest of Devon historians and his *Devon* is a rich and rambling survey of the county, particularly its history. These two books, with Brian WATSON's earlier *Shell Guide to Devon*, were always in the car as we travelled through the county.

Other books which we found of great value were (in alphabetical order): Joyce CAREW: *Dusty Pages* (*privately printed*) with the author's memories of Castle Hill, Clovelly Court and Hartland. B. F. L. CLARKE: *19th Century Church Builders*. COX & FORD: *The Parish Churches of England*. CROSSING's *Dartmoor* (reprint *David & Charles*) an old and authoritative book by a man who knew every inch of the moor. Dartington Amenity Research: *Industrial Archaeology in Devon*. Devon County Council: *The Challenge. The Motorway into Devon*. Two further books by W. G. HOSKINS: *Old Devon* (*David & Charles*) and *English Landscapes*

(*BBC publications*). George P. R. PULMAN: *The Book of the Axe* (*Kingsmead Reprints, Bath*). A. E. TRUEMAN: *Geology and Scenery in England and Wales*. As well as countless Town Guides, Church leaflets and National Trust brochures, we consulted the transactions of the *Devonshire Association* in the Exeter City Library, and the *Goodhart-Rendel* file of Victorian churches in the RIBA library.

We would like to thank the many vicars and custodians of churches who gave us much time and help; we have been charmed by the eager enthusiasm of many vicars for their church buildings. We would specially like to acknowledge the kind assistance of the following: Mr Simon Clements for his suggestion that we explore the Devonport Leat and for his first opening our eyes to the appreciation of Butterfield. Mr Peter Cox, Principal of Dartington College of Arts, for his help and hospitality. Mrs L. Ridler, librarian of Newton Abbot, whose researches led us to ascribe the hospital there to Gilbert Scott. Mr Laurence Whistler, who drew our attention to Way Barton and thus confirmed the significance of the old trackway from Crediton to Bideford. Lastly Mr John Piper for his unfailing kindness, knowledge and tact.

A.J. and R.M.

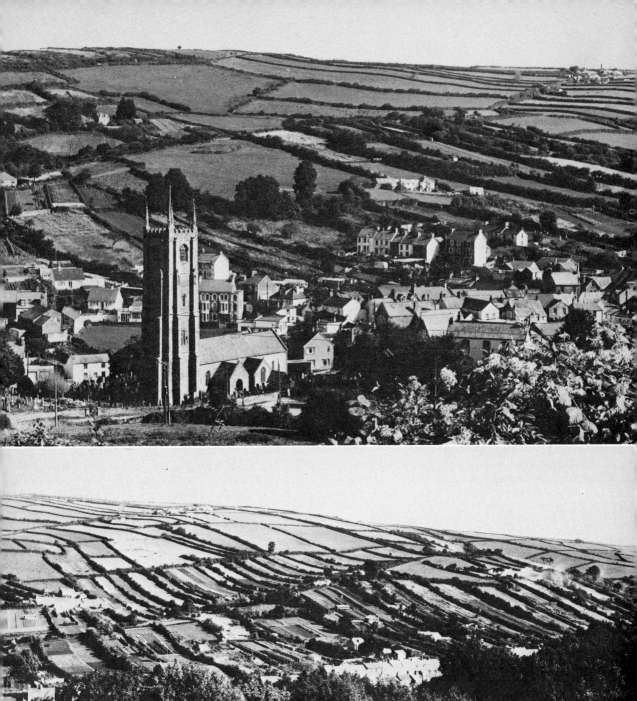

Introduction

Two great roads lead into Devon, converge on Exeter and then divide and thus they define the county. The A38 curves south irrigating the prosperous and popular coast and linking the two great urban centres: Exeter and Plymouth; south of Dartmoor the rich, red soil has always meant fat farming and the French facing coast rich trade and busy naval defence. The A30 skirts the granite mass of Dartmoor and runs on through Okehampton to Cornwall. But no great road runs north. Here the poor culm soil lies in a band 15 or 20 miles deep from Holsworthy to Bampton; and the coast, rocky, precipitous, wooded, offers no proper harbour west of Bideford and, exquisite towns though they are now, Barnstaple and Bideford deferred to Bristol in trade.

Yet poverty has brought its compensations. The small villages and churches north of Dartmoor are little restored and built over; there are more ancient screens in the north, and no county is richer in screens than Devon, more old carved bench ends. The south has nothing to match the tiny church of Honeychurch preserved because it stood in a parish so small and poor that no one could afford to restore it.

The north coast is exquisite and almost unspoiled. You drive into Devon skirting Exmoor; on your left long, narrow, wooded valleys finger their way deep into the moor. At Lynmouth comes the first of those thrilling plunges to the sea. If you take the minor road along the cliff top past Woody Bay and Trentishoe you may see the panorama of South Wales across the Bristol Channel. From Combe Martin to Ilfracombe the road is a true *corniche* winding along beside the sea. Then south past Woolacombe Sands and Saunton Sands, long, clean and inviting, the best beaches in Devon, marking the entrance to the Taw and Torridge Estuary. Behind are Braunton Burrows and Northam Burrows: wastes of rough hillocky sand and grass magnificently open to the sky. A little inland from here are villages of 17th-century and 18th-century cottages still standing on the Saxon plan, Sheepwash perhaps or Shebbear still with its Norman doorway and 17th-century Devil's Stone Inn. Here too you will begin to notice the farm bartons so characteristic of Devon and almost entirely confined to this county. The high barton walls, often of cob roofed with a ridge of thatch, link the farm buildings and enclose the farm yard. Built to shelter and confine cattle the barton shows the Devon bias to dairy farming.

Returning to the coast you pass the curious Victorian resort of Westward Ho! where the cliffs begin to rise and soon the land is cut away steep and precipitous, no beaches here only a tiny haven at Clovelly and the stupendous prow of Hartland where the massy Atlantic breakers burst upon glistening black rocks. Here at the Cornish coast is the unknown quarter of Devon: few roads or villages; but Stoke (Hartland) church rivals, and perhaps surpasses, Ottery St Mary as the most beautiful in the county. Going south along the Cornish border you reach the band of culm near

◁*above* **Combe Martin**
below Field pattern at
Combe Martin

The north coast ▷
p 8 Woolacombe sands (**Morthoe**)
Looking towards **Combe Martin**
p 11 **Hartland** Quay

7

Holsworthy and here indeed the land is barren, chilly and scraggy.

At Okehampton Dartmoor begins. You will find views of the moor in an arc west to north-east of Okehampton and occasionally a double view of Exmoor as well. Dartmoor, the great granite mass of central Devon, is here at its highest point and now starts to slope south. At Lydford on its west edge the poor culm soil begins to disappear and you get the first spectacular landscape since Hartland. Now you begin to meet the deep gorge of the Tamar marking the border just west of Tavistock and to the east the Cleaves of Dartmoor. Here by the road are seen gaunt skeletons of early 19th-century mines, one of the last great industries in the county.

The south coast from Plymouth to Paignton is essentially a plateau sliced by valleys. Plymouth Sound is a great creek, and going east is a curious creek-breached shore with no resorts and few roads to the sea. The climate here is so mild that oranges and lemons will ripen in the open air. At Bigbury is a good beach. And then from Bolt Tail to Start Point is coast scenery grand and bleak pierced by the exquisite Salcombe Estuary: sheltered, south facing, luxuriant and balmy. The main road cuts across from Kingsbridge to Torcross and has cut off the coastal area too so that again it seems to have its own character—less defined than Hartland but still individual. From Torcross to Dartmouth is a *corniche* passing beaches of coarse red sand and unspoilt fishing villages. South-east of Dartmoor you find many handsome church towers modelled on Ashburton, the earliest; Totnes is a fine example.

Now you reach the Dart valley, a ravishing stretch from Dartmouth to Totnes, the towns themselves both beautiful and historic and the waterway in between one of the prettiest in the country. A remarkable similarity of Norman fonts here: red sandstone, bowl shaped, decorated with palmettes and saltire crosses; such as Buckfastleigh to the west and Paignton to the

◁ **Dunchideock**

pp 12/13 Near **Swimbridge** ▷

Dartmoor: *above* Grimspound
opposite Hound Tor
below Devonport Leat

east. Going east, within easier reach of London and the Midlands, comes the resort area. First Brixham, still a fisherman's town and full of character and then, less happily, Paignton: seaside development at its blindest and seediest, and then Torquay, conscious Queen of resorts. Plenty of coarse sandy beaches here and at Dawlish and Teignmouth. At Exmouth the sand is finer, the town less interesting. West of the Exe estuary is an area particularly rich in screens with painted wainscots, e.g. Kenton, Ashton,

Bovey Tracey. Beyond the Exe valley the coastline changes, becoming more like Dorset, i.e. less of a plateau, the hills and valleys coming right up to the sea. Heathy country behind Budleigh Salterton, until you reach exquisite Regency Sidmouth, whole areas of the town perfectly unspoiled.

The red earth country continues up the Exe valley through steep, hilly country until it reaches Tiverton where the landscape becomes gorge-like. Farther into central Devon the sheltered east edge of Dartmoor around Chagford, Moreton Hampstead and Bovey Tracey is pretty, fertile and well wooded, the upper Teign valley and the Bovey valley being particularly

The south coast:

◁ Looking towards **Sidmouth** from Beer Head

Dawlish

attractive: steep and tree clad. Here are nestling moorland villages, perfectly peaceful and pretty.

The earliest Devonians lived in Kent's Cavern, Torquay, about half a million years ago during the Old Stone Age; some remains from this period were also found in caves at Brixham and Plymouth and in gravel pits near Axminster. The first farmers built Hembury Fort about 2500 BC and about 700 years later the Beaker Folk crossed from Spain and Brittany. Most of the prehistoric remains on Dartmoor date from the Bronze Age. In AD 43 the Roman invasion of Britain began but the Romans never penetrated deep into Devon. Uplyme on the Dorset border had a handsome Roman villa. Exeter was founded as a Roman city, *Isca Dumnoniorum*, and still has its Roman plan and walls. After the arrival of the Saxons the population increased rapidly and the religious and trading structure of the county was laid down: the See of Devon and Cornwall was founded at Crediton in 909, Bideford received its first charter in 930. Danish raids caused the removal of the See to Exeter in 1050. There are not many Saxon remains left in the county: crosses at Colyton, Dolton, Copplestone, Exeter; fonts at Hatherleigh and Spreyton, a crypt at Sidbury. Braunton Great Field is still farmed on the Saxon strip system. The Normans confirmed Exeter as chief city by building Rougemont castle and supporting it by a string of lesser forts and castles, e.g. Totnes, Plympton, Barnstaple; but the most durable Norman work has proved to be church building. Even where all the Norman fabric has disappeared the font is often retained.

Church restoration has always been a continuing process, a way of demonstrating religious fervour, conspicuous expense for attracting favourable attention from the powers that be. Certain periods were more prone to restore: the Normans built, but within 200 years their churches were too small and there was a surge of rebuilding during the first half of the 14th century: single-minded, exuberant, sublime, far outstripping the domestic architecture of the period;

◁ Regency Gothick at **Sidmouth**

Dartington, palace of the Dukes of Exeter, simply does not compare with Exeter Cathedral in terms of grandeur, size and finish. These churches are palaces for God and they speak for the power of the clergy and the wealth, anxiety and ambition of the people. Later in the 14th century the Black Death reduced the population by a third and there was little need for enlargement for many years. By the 16th century the mediaeval churches were still in good repair, but the population had increased again and you now find aisles being added, and splendid they are, e.g. the Dorset aisle at Ottery St Mary and the Lane aisle at Cullompton. By the mid 18th century the fabric of the mediaeval churches was beginning to deteriorate. How much the Georgians restored is now not easy to say since the Victorians swept so much away, beginning, naturally enough, with the unfashionable work of their immediate predecessors. The few remaining Georgian interiors charm us by their simplicity and there is some Georgian work in markedly urban and polished taste, e.g. St George's Tiverton and the reredos at Morchard Bishop. But by and large the 18th century was not a time of great religious fervour and restoration was a matter of enlarging windows (which the Victorians later recut) and refurnishing, and when it came to slicing across a mediaeval pillar to fit in a set of box pews the Georgians were as brutal as any later church architect.

But by the 19th century the mediaeval churches were in real need of restoration and, coinciding with a period of great commercial expansion, abundant self-confidence and a parallel moral self-condemnation, the Victorians went to work with a will. We bitterly blame them for what they destroyed, but recent experience has shown that we, with all our knowledge and experience, can be as stupid. They meant well. How can we altogether blame an enthusiastic bishop for failing to save a 14th-century carved screen in bad repair? The philosophy which created screens, the separation of the body of the people from the celebration of a mystery, became suspect during the 19th-century religious

Early fonts:
opposite above **Marystow, Spreyton**
opposite below **Buckfastleigh, Honeychurch**
above St Mary Steps, **Exeter**
right above Stoke, **Hartland**
right below **Dolton**

21

Bench end carvings:
upper row **Braunton, West Worlington,
Marwood, Alwington**
lower row **Countisbury, Lewtrenchard
High Bickington, Marwood**

Next page Stoke, **Hartland** ▷

Details of painted screens: *above* **Ashton, Kenton** *opposite* **Kenton**

revivals and many screens were swept away. But the Victorians could also create: Ottery St Mary is probably due as much to Butterfield as to its mediaeval builders and the Victorian churches of Torquay demand a study in themselves.

Certain things tend to survive restoration: Norman towers could still serve; the naves were too small but the towers immensely solidly built. An odd item that often remains is the south door;

it is hard to say why, but there are countless ancient doors 600 years old or more. The list is enormous and idiosyncratic: Paignton has a dog door, Chagford is hinged, Powderham shot up by Roundheads, Honeychurch patched, re-patched and remounted.

The mid 18th century saw the beginning of that Industrial Revolution which still moulds our landscape and thinking. Devon has never

Font by Butterfield; **Ottery St Mary**

◁ Pulpits at **Dittisham, Swimbridge** and **Bovey Tracy**

next page Cob and thatch at **Dawlish** ▷

been heavily industralised, but a network of communications was woven which spread over the county and decided the pattern of future prosperity. In 1780 the first road was opened across Dartmoor, built by French prisoners of war. In the early 1830s new roads (now A377 and B3220) were built linking Exeter, Barnstaple and Bideford. Before the new turnpikes were built the older road, now an unnumbered white road on the map, ran from a point across the river from Old Ford House, Bideford, to Crediton (the old see). This in turn covered an ageless trackway. The road system south of Dartmoor was improved. Exeter had its first canal in 1563–6, but during the canal mania of the 18th century several were cut, of which the most successful was at Morwellham. Then in 1843 Brunel began to extend his Great Western Railway from Pad-

dington to Exeter, continuing on to Plymouth in 1846 but using the new atmospheric system. By this method the trains were drawn along by a vacuum created by pumping stations; unfortunately (for at its best it was a uniquely smooth ride) the leather flanges regulating the vacuum perished along the entire rail. This setback by no means stopped the railway and Brunel's grand stations still survive. By the 1880s the county was threaded with major lines and the last decade saw the seaside branches which were to serve the rising tourist trade so well for the next fifty years.

In the last fifty years have come urban sprawl and our love–hate relationship with the motor car. Our cars at first only needed petrol stations, now they demand new roads and an over-

South Molton and *opposite* **Plympton St Maurice**

The museum at **Tiverton**

abundance of signs which litter our streets and mask the buildings in country towns. But there have been good things too: quite recently two minor but very real improvements in the rural scene. One is the Countryside Act 1968, which lays a responsibility upon local authorities to signpost public footpaths, and this work, in Devon at least, has been taken seriously. A signpost opens up the countryside: it makes you want to explore. The second development is the new popularity of local folk and industrial museums. Almost all the collections we saw have been opened recently, usually by local amateurs, for this is a field where enthusiasm is possibly more important than academic knowledge. As often as not these museums celebrate some inland industry: the Finch brothers' foundry at Sticklepath or the Centre of Industrial Archaeology at

34

Morwellham Quay, and, perhaps best of all, Exeter Maritime Museum.

The obvious places in Devon: Torquay, the Dart Valley, Clovelly, and many more, are deservedly famous. But in preparing this guide we each day looked forward to some surprise or unexpected pleasure, and this never failed. In the course of exploring each day a few parishes in some detail it was delightful to come across things which we didn't know were there, or which were placed so quietly and modestly that their almost secret existence added to the fun of finding them. Exeter Cathedral is magnificent, we all know of it, and few will fail to admire it. But to discover, for yourself, the early 19th-century Quaker Meeting House near Culmstock is a different kind of thrill. The county is amazingly rich in beautiful things, and most of them are to be found one by

Exeter Maritime Museum

one in village churches or small houses: the 18th-century font cupboard at Plympton St Maurice, for example, or the plaster ceiling in the Royal Hotel at Bideford, Laurence Whistler's carving at Dolton. The same is true of the countryside and landscape. Take to the minor roads and you will find the unexpected pleasure: Hartland Quay, the view of South Wales from above Combe Martin, Wembury churchyard poised above the sea, the moorland around Gidleigh. Anyone who explores this county will create their own contour of its geography, art and history. The possibilities are endless and limited only by your own taste and nature.

Devon Landscapes: ▷

p 36 On **Aylesbeare** Common and near Sidmouth
p 37 **Honiton, Colyton** and **Chulmleigh**

Gazetteer

The number after the place name refers to the square on the maps, pp. 172–6, where the place is to be found. Those with an asterisk are too small to actually appear on the map.

Abbreviations: century c. circa *c*, and points of the compass. *Italics* draw attention in the text to certain houses, places and sometimes churches in each parish. Generally the place headings are parishes; there are a few exceptions such as Sheldon (now under Teignmouth) and principally Dartmoor.

Abbot's Bickington [5*] The Abbot of Hartland held a court here at the Barton just by the church. *St James* has a low 13c tower; ceiled wagon roof, crib-like in so small a church; some 13c windows with a little 14c stained glass.

Abbotsham [5] Undulating plateau gently sloping towards Bideford bay. *St Helen's* church has a fluted Norman font; old bench ends; original ceiled wagon roof with carved angels; nave higher than chancel with two Tudor windows above chancel arch.

Abbotskerswell [31] Old town centre has several enviable Tudor and Georg-

ian houses but is ringed by large-scale contemporary building, overspill from Newton Abbot. Church has a most unusual statue of the Virgin, very large and badly mutilated but still kindling the imagination with a ghostly presence; discovered 1884 when the church was restored by Butterfield. The restoration is surprisingly anonymous for this architect, but the pulpit is clearly his.

Alphington [17] Noisily near Exeter; two main roads stream together below the church and there is much modern building between the old cottages. Above the church S porch a notice reads: "Please remove your pattens";

those little wooden platforms, early galoshes, must have made a racket. Fine Norman font: arcading below and above a pattern of strapwork circles with soldiers, an archer, beasts, flowers etc; screen with original painted wainscot; Jacobean carving in tower arch screen with painted coats of arms; original W gallery; parish chest of 1753; floor set with many old tombstones. Nearby is the *Rectory* of 1609 with decorated plaster ceilings. *Double Cocks Inn* is early Georgian with Dutch influence.

Alverdiscott [5] Pronounced Alscott. Scattered village. *All Saints'* church

Tuckenhay (*see* **Ashprington**)

stands high with wide views. Its most striking feature is tucked away behind the organ: a monument to Thomas Walshe, d 1639, boy of ten dressed as a cavalier and lying on a tomb chest, his head a little to one side as if asleep, tender and life-like; Norman font and behind it the piers of the N aisle, 19c but Norman in feeling and sympathetic to the font; they support a wooden entablature of 1863; Jacobean font cover; old Barnstaple tiles in S porch.

Alwington [5*] N Devon coastal parish but little means of reaching the sea except at *Portledge House*, now an hotel, 16c building altered 19c, the older parts can still be seen at the rear where there are glimpses of the sea towards Clovelly; Portledge was the home of the oddly named Pine-Coffins. Jacobean carving from old Portledge house went to make the large family pew in Alwington church. Indeed the church is stuffed with bits of carving, mostly old bench ends, some very fine, put together to form reredos, pulpit etc. N transept: an attractive little raised stone plaque of a kneeling lady in horned head-dress holding a scroll, said to be from the chapel of Yeo Vale (which was licensed 1408). *Yeo Vale House* 1 m E of Alwington church, now ruinous; square Georgian with Gothick windows, built around the gate house of a mediaeval mansion.

Appledore [2] Pretty, sleepy, unspoilt: fishing boats lie parked along the streets. The wide front looking over the estuary is edged with quiet, handsome houses, Georgian and Early Victorian: solid abodes of wealthy merchants and ships' captains; they face the sea at Appledore bar lapped by the tinkling of Instow bells across the water. Behind the front are streets of fishermen's cottages: bow windowed, late 18c and early 19c. These streets are too narrow for cars and a whole area of the town, full of life and colour, is much as it must have been 200 years ago. Higher up the river are thriving ship yards. Relatively large ships can berth here. Perhaps it is this local industry that gives the back streets their air of prosperous contentment. *See also* Northam.

Arlington [3] *Arlington Court*: Regency house renovated in high Victorian and movingly filled with the personality of its last owner, Miss Rosalie Chichester, "the last of the Chichesters of Arling-

Methodist chapel, **Ashburton**

ton" says her epitaph in the church. She died in 1947 over 80 years old, having preserved her home almost as it was when she was a girl. She left it to the National Trust who have arranged its public showing with much tact. A Chichester family seat since 1534, the present house was built 1820, severe and plain, its only ornament a semi-circular Doric porch. In 1864 Sir Bruce Chichester, who entertained lavishly, added a new wing and stable block. Sir Bruce, an Edwardian before his time, loved splendid hospitality and conspicuous expense; for 30 years he ran Arlington in spanking style. When he died in 1881 his heir was his daughter Rosalie, then 15 years old. She inherited a magnificent house and ruined fortunes and devoted the rest of her life to paying off her father's debts.

The plain exterior doesn't prepare for the glitter within. Downstairs is a magnificent Regency saloon divided into three by shallow arches, it can be used as a single 70 ft room; furnished with French and English furniture. Next, a boudoir hung with Spitalfields silk in red and gold. Also downstairs, the dining room, dark and splendid with mahogany, twinkling with glass and silver. Upstairs, you may walk into Miss Chichester's bedroom, and it seems an intrusion so vivid is her presence: her parasol leans against a chair, a white lawn nightgown lies ready folded on the bed. All around the room are intimate mementoes of a long life. In her girlhood Miss Chichester collected endlessly monograms, stamps, letter headings—and arranged them artistically in albums. A pleasant, laborious, genteel occupation, so gratifying to a young lady in that one was not idle and yet not actually *working*. These albums give immense pleasure today to visitors who appreciate their careful ingenuity. In later life Miss

Chichester persisted in her habit of collecting pewter, snuff boxes, old ship models etc., and these collections are on display all over the house.

Possibly the single most valuable object in the house is really the only thing quite out of sympathy with it. This is a water colour by William Blake, "The Vision of the Cycle of Life and Man" 1821, in the White Drawing Room. It was found after Miss Chichester's death on top of a cupboard. It had been bought, probably directly from the artist, and so fresh are its colours, it was surely never displayed, but put away and forgotten.

The *Stable Block* has an engrossing collection of 19c carriages. The *church*, 15c but restored, has Chichester family monuments including one to Miss Chichester herself, designed by John Piper and erected by the National Trust.

Ashburton [31] Small market town, unspoiled and of great character, lying in a side valley of the Dart. One of the original stannary towns and with later prosperity coming from serge; the good times lasted until the mid 19c, old warehouses in Kingsbridge Lane still give the feeling of a wool town. The main East and West Streets wind up and down lined with modest 17c, 18c, and 19c houses, many slate hung; some, very old, have been washed over with concrete to hold the slates together and keep out damp; it looks like ragged fleece. Many pretty Georgian details and a few good Victorian shopfronts, e.g. *Sims*, butchers in East St; *Pollock*, baker in North St. Few exceptional houses, although *The Hall*, 1803, at the E end of the town is demure and pretty above its smooth lawns, with busts of Scott and Byron in the façade. Along East St is the early 18c *Golden Lion Hotel*; just beyond that, on the left is St Lawrence Lane. Here is the nucleus of the old town. *St Lawrence Chapel* is disused and behind it is the *Grammar School*, founded 1314 and near by the *Old Court House*. In North St *Victorian Market House*, 1850. Up West Street; the *Methodist Chapel*, 1835, the whole front framed by an Ionic portico. Just beyond, set back from the road, are the early 18c gates to *St Andrew's* churchyard; you are fetched up close to the S façade of the church, and it makes a rich effect. The tower is steep with plain pinnacles and sensitive moulding adding

to its appearance and height. Inside, restored by G. E. Street c. 1880, is less riveting; fine roofs with carved beams and bosses; two 18c candelabra; other furnishings are mostly Victorian. It is said that during an earlier restoration in 1840 the dried hearts of Ashburton men who fought abroad during the Middle Ages were found urned up in the chancel.

Ashbury [8] A row of cottages, a barton and a prettily placed Victorian church look across the valley to Dartmoor. The landscape, tranquil and parklike, belonged to *Wadlands*, 16c Manor House pulled down about 1965.

Ashcombe [29] Church, vicarage and a house or two in a tight fold of the hills above Teignmouth. A few old bench ends remain in the dull church, restored 1824–6; the vicarage, probably of the same period, is more attractive.

Ashford [2] Village clings to a steep slope above the Taw estuary. Church interior restored: a jumble of chopped up Jacobean woodwork. In the vestry a small, multilated 14c sculpture of St John.

Ashprington [31] Hilly setting above the Dart: well-kept stone houses with sparkling white paint. Two fine mansions: *Sharpham*, rebuilt 1770 by Capt. Pownell out of prize money, on a ridge above the creek with gardens by Capability Brown using the magnificent situation, and *Painsford* with chapel licensed 1400 used until the 18c but now in ruins; house built by John Pellew 1687. Memorials to both builders in the church, *St David's*, which stands at the top of the village. Fiendishly complicated bolt to lychgate. Inside large Norman font decorated with cable and saltire crosses; two doors remain of 15c screen; small brass by S door to Wylliam Sumaster, d 1589. Church owns a famous chalice, in constant use since 1275 and probably the oldest in the country.

Tuckenhay. Mr Tucker tried to found an industrial complex in 1806 and slowly failed. Lying 1 m S of Ashprington up a side creek of the Dart with quays, warehouses and even a gas house. Deserted but evocative.

Ashreigney [6] Featureless village in poor and unvisited country N of Okehampton; it stands on a plateau cut by

two pretty wooded valleys. Church has a 15c wagon roof with angel corbels.

Ashton [16] Above the Teign valley: steep little hills and peaceful outlook so quiet you can hear a voice 100 yds away and *cowbells* from across the valley. Small village of knarled and crooked cottages, at the bottom Place Barton, partly 14c. *St Michael's* Church, set high on a rocky spur, has exceptionally fine painted panels on parclose screen and back of rood screen: free, broad and confident, quite unlike any other screen in the county; archbraced roof, screen, font and pews all of about 1476; Jacobean pulpit, square-sided with tester and hour glass stand; altar rails 17c; wall monument of painted wood to Sir George and Lady Mary Chudleigh, d 1657.

Ashwater [8] Village grouped around a triangular green, most of the cottages are late Victorian. The church, *St Peter in Chains*, has a splendid 13c wagon roof, exceptionally broad; massy Norman font, one of the largest in Devon, with free and lively carving; tomb chest with recumbent effigies of a knight and lady said to be Thomas Carminow, d 1442; old bench ends; plaster coat of arms of Charles I 1638 (how could something so fragile survive the Commonwealth?).

Atherington [6] Wonderful views across Exmoor from the churchyard. Village set around the remnants of a green: thatched cottages with great chimneys, stout and knobbly as tree trunks, set against the walls. Distinguished church with remarkable and beautiful rood loft, unique in Devon, rising above the slender branches of the screen, thrillingly top heavy, like a castle in an illustrated manuscript; unusual crocheted bench ends probably 15c; early monuments: sensitive 13c knight wearing a thin tunic over his chain mail, legs crossed; 14c knight and lady lying on a tomb chest; Tudor brasses of c. 1530—all in the chancel.

Aveton Gifford [27] Pronounced Orton Jifford. Church received a direct hit during the second world war and for years only the shell remained; restoration is now nearly complete with the bold solution of building altar and pulpit in brutal contemporary style; ex-

Atherington: the rood loft

quisite 13c S porch and doorway remain from the old church. On the Kingsbridge road is a mediaeval causeway across water meadows nearly $\frac{3}{4}$ m long.

Awliscombe [18] In a tributary valley of the Otter not far from Honiton. Above the village is St Cyres hill, one of the old naval telegraph stations between Plymouth and London; fine view; on a clear day you can glimpse Exeter Cathedral. The church, *St Michael*, has a simple, rather sturdy screen in Bere stone. *Awliscombe House*, standing in its park, can be seen from the Honiton by-pass.

Axminster [36] The A35 snaking through has imposed bosomy serpentine frontages to many of the main buildings, mostly Georgian and early Victorian. A busy little town—no fewer than three markets are held here on

Thursdays, the pubs are open all day and the narrow pavements seethe and heave. Traffic laps at the edges of the churchyard, which is raised some 5 ft above the market place and the main road.

The church, *St Mary*, has carved parapet, two-storey porch and crossing tower, Norman doorway at the E end. Inside: 14c piscina and sedilia with steep elegant gables; two effigies in the chancel in poor condition; pulpit and reading desk 1633; 17c bust in the W wall with defaced inscription.

NE of the church (on your right as you face the market) is the old Axminster carpet factory, large and charmless. Devon still has some very fine Axminster carpets made by Thomas Whitty, founder of the firm. Two are at *Saltram*, near Plymouth, in the Adam saloon and the dining room, both carpets mirror the ceiling decorations; the carpet in the saloon cost £126 in 1768.

Another Axminster of 1790 is in the music room at *Powderham Castle* near Exeter.

A bookshop S of the church has as its entrance an archway reputedly removed from Newnham Abbey. In the market place the memorial to Queen Victoria's Jubilee was originally the town pump, given a face lift and removed to its present position; you can see it in its original state in an early Victorian print in the church vestry.

Set on a curve, following the line of the main road, is *Victoria Place*; a row of 19c buildings with a continuous balcony on the first floor. Further along is *Castle Hill* with a good late 18c house at the top and Shaw's sackworks at the bottom—the latter romantic and decrepit 19c industrial, *Chard Street*: early 19c shop front. On the same side is the *Congregational Chapel*, austere, but it grows on you. *Oak House*, 1758, now town offices, is further up left; a hand-

41

Barnstaple

some little mansion in brick with quoins and Venetian window.

Newnham Abbey. 1 m SW, a few remains of a Cistercian Abbey.

Clocombe House, 1732, looks up the lush water meadows of the Axe Valley.

Weycroft Hall and Manor. 1 m NE, 15c, the latter visible from the road and very pretty.

Axmouth [36] Until the 14c the Axe had a broad, navigable estuary, and Axmouth marked the point where the Fosse Way reached the river; it was thus a place of some importance. Then the river silted up and the village fell asleep; today it's almost unspoilt with thatched cottages and a 14c inn.

The church, *St Michael*, has a good deal of Norman work, with a large S door in fine condition. S aisle, added 13c, has low rounded arches and small trefoil windows. 14c priest's tomb in chancel. Two 15c paintings S side of the nave.

Stedcombe House, 1695, $\frac{3}{4}$ m NE on a hillside overlooking the Axe. Square William and Mary; interesting solution to the chimney problem. Can be seen from the main A3052.

Dowlands Landslip: spectacular scenery, and rough walking. This coast E to Lyme Regis has always been liable to slipping, the greatest of all was at Dowlands Farm on Christmas Eve 1839. Millions of tons of earth and rock slipped and left a chasm $\frac{3}{4}$ m long by 300 ft wide by 150 ft deep. There is a dramatic coast walk here from Lyme Regis to Seaton.

Aylesbeare [17] *Aylesbeare Common* is a spreading hilltop of scrub and heathland with tremendous views of the coast between Sidmouth and Budleigh Salterton; good for picnics and children. Village proper is uninspiring. *Truants* is thatched with 17c canopy over the door and a tiny 12c round-headed window.

Babbacombe. *See* Torquay.

Bampton [14] Narrow Exmoor valleys begin to broaden here. Small town, mostly Georgian built of stone from the local quarries. The church is big and not very interesting except for details: small sculptured panel, figures in niches below a canopy; fragments of 15c tomb carving in the chancel; 15c screen to tower room; wagon roof; 16c pulpit. In the S porch the base of a Saxon cross decorated with cable pattern; on the exterior S wall a scratch sundial dated 1586; on the W wall copy of a tablet of 1776:

"Bless my little iiiii
  Here he lies
  In a sad pickle
  Kill'd by icicle."

On the A396 $1\frac{1}{2}$ m SW are the lodge cottage and gates to *Stuckeridge House*, late Georgian. The cottage is quite elaborate with thatched colonnade; also an iron chain bridge.

Barnstaple [3] Georgian in feeling,

42

reflecting the last great period of prosperity in the wool trade. An ancient town (and still the principal market town of north Devon). The *Oxford Dictionary of Place Names* defines "Barnstaple" as "a post to which a warship was moored" or "Bearda's post". The town grew at the point of the river which was lowest fordable and highest navigable. It was granted its first charter in 930, one of the earliest in the country; it had a mint at about the same time. The first bridge was built in the 13c, the present one of 16 arches is *c.* 1437.

A bustling town of narrow streets, thundering traffic and insouciant jay walkers. It has a tranquil centre: the church *St Peter and St Paul*, *St Anne's Chapel* and the 17c *Horwood's Almshouses and School* are all grouped together in a quiet, green churchyard which lies between three seething shopping streets. The church, originally 13c but restored, with 17c broach spire, is large and gloomy. Five wall tablets in a pose that caught the local fancy: half figure with head supported by one hand while the other toys with skull or book. Exquisite 15c chasuble on display in the S aisle: embroidered angels with bare legs and feet and short, feather skirts. St Anne's Chapel 15c, later used as Grammar School for 400 years until 1908. John Gay, who wrote *The Beggar's Opera*, was taught here.

W of this oasis is the High St; almost every house worthy of notice above the shops and traffic, mostly Georgian but some later. *Butchers' Row*, N of the churchyard, has modest little 19c shops, booth-like and mostly butchers, oddly enough. Opposite the shops is the *Pannier Market*, late Victorian, with iron pillars and glass roof; magnificent iron fanlight. Corner of High St and Butchers' Row: the *Guildhall*, severest Georgian almost unadorned; civic portraits inside. Facing S end of the High St, but actually in Boutport St: the *Royal Fortescue Hotel* and the *Westminster Bank*. To the outside view they are a matched pair of Georgian houses, with rhythmical curves to the bow windows, the hotel slightly Victorianised; the bank was formerly the house of the Spanish merchants and has an ebullient 1620 plaster ceiling, very rich and elaborate. Across the road: *North Devon Dispensary, c.* 1835. Down by the river, *Queen Anne's Walk*, 1708, the Exchange, surmounted by a statue of the Queen, its colonnade decorated with a chaste profusion that speaks volumes for the substance and self confidence of the Barnstaple wool merchants, as no doubt it was intended to do. Here is the *Tome Stone*, over which bargains struck by word of mouth were rendered binding. The old quay was originally near by; five Barnstaple ships sailed from here to join Drake against the Armada in 1588.

There is much domestic Georgian architecture scattered through the town. *Trafalgar Lawn* is one of those matched compositions of five houses, the central one being rather more elaborate than the other four, in front: a pleasant sward of grass and trees. *Union Terrace*, overlooking the river: balconies and fretting. *Priory Cottage*, 10 Boutport Street; shell doorway. These are perhaps the outstanding Georgian buildings but there are many more.

Besides Horwood's two other foundations of almshouses: *Salem*, 1834, Trinity St and *Penrose Almshouses*, 1627, Litchford St, one of the best things in the town, with colonnade of stocky granite pillars. Beyond is a cobbled court and well, the almshouses grouped around.

Also in Litchford St, the *Pottery showrooms*, designed by C. H. Brannam: late Victorian much influenced by William Morris, a kind of imitation Tudor highly decorated with fruit, flowers and animals, very attractive. Barnstaple was a centre for the manufacture of mediaeval tiles, many of them still to be seen in churches around.

In Vicarage St, now a rather muddled and crummy area, is the 16c former *Vicarage*, somewhat mucked about now but castellated, and fretted, a rather amazing survival. You may guess the limits of the old Vicarage garden by the names of the streets running off.

See also Pilton.

Beaford [6] Village in the centre of N Devon, which would be of little interest but that the Beaford Centre was started here in 1966. Sponsored by the Dartington Arts Trust, the Arts Council and, significantly, by many N Devon town councils, the Beaford Centre is trying to activate the life of N Devon with excitement and pleasure by means of art. It is less of a centre to which people come than an energy point from which theatre, music and poetry surge out as far W as Bude, as far E as Minehead. It is housed in a large, ugly, pleasant house by the church.

All Saints is over-restored 15c: but there are interesting 17c slate wall tablets. John Syng, d 1667, has an exceptional verse, Shakespearian in its ease and polish: "We spring like flowers for a daye's delight at noone we flourish and wee fade at night" etc.

Beaworthy [8] Darkest Devon. The embankment of the old LSWR (Southern) railway, recently closed, thrusts its massive level banks above the parish roads; how the Victorian navvies must have frightened the neighbourhood. But now the place is so quiet that turkeys peck in the middle of the road. *St Alban's* church has two Norman capitals, moustached faces, by the S door.

Beer [18] Pretty and popular fishing village in a combe sloping down to an open bay. The steep white cliffs are topped by a rippling coverlet of grass and crossed by pleasant walks. The famous quarries, from which stone has been taken since Roman times, lie at the approach to the town: through the high slit-like openings, you can glimpse great curtains of raw stone, not at all unlike the cathedrals that Beer stone has gone to build.

There is a good walk from Bovey House following a stream down into Beer, where it runs into an open stone channel and rustles freshly on through the town, traversed at two points by stone conduits with pagoda tops, *c.* 1700. The *Almshouses* and *Charity School* were endowed by Lady Rolle in 1820.

Bovey House. 1 m N of Beer. 1592. A storey was removed during the 19c and it now has a rather hard, squat skyline. After the last Mrs Walrond died in 1786 the house was left unoccupied and became a centre of smuggling—helped no doubt by carefully put about tales that it was haunted. Now an hotel, it has some good Jacobean carving in hall and dining room, also plastered coffered ceiling in the *King Charles' Room*. This was put up after the Restoration and celebrates the King's hiding in an oak tree after the battle of Worcester.

Belstone [21] On the side of Dartmoor, cattle graze on common land just W of the village and beyond are the reeling

hillsides of the moor. A few old thatched houses in the village but mostly Victorian which has weathered to look Scottish; some new buildings E along the fringe of the view.

The church, simple, almost barbarous, shows how remote and primitive this village must once have been: low granite pillars, quite plain; a few early 18c tombstones in the floor but so crude that they look like 16c work.

Bere Ferrers [23] The word *bere* comes from Saxon and means "spit of land", and the village is perched on a remote tongue of riverside where the Tamar and the Tavy meet just above Plymouth to form the Hamoaze. It's a strange place, remote and inaccessible; the river is so broad at this point that the village seems to be standing at the edge of some peaceful lake. The churchyard lies directly by the river and the silence is broken only by the occasional

Calstock viaduct
(*see* **Bere Ferrers**)

Bere Ferrers

sound of creaking rowlocks across the water. Some of the tombstones state laconically: "*Cholera 1849*," with no name. The church itself, although it has been given a thick coat of pebble dash outside, and of plaster inside, is otherwise little altered. There is a tomb *c.* 1300—a knight and his lady lie under a high cusped arch, sensitive carving: exquisite heads at the cusps, fragment of a child's hand on the lady's shoulder.

Near by are mysterious old quays at *Wier Quay* and *Hole's Hole*: originally built for shipping minerals from the Dartmoor mines, they have lain unused for fifty years. A few interesting houses; one by the water's edge is crudely dated 1648; another, *Cleave*, is 18c.

Bere Alston. On a high plateau between the Tavy and Tamar, once an important village but now smothered in bungalows. School porch has a carved stone over it dated 1665. This is an area of small, intensively cultivated market gardens and N of Bere Alston the hillsides are covered with neat strips and patches of daffodils, early potatoes

and so on, precise yet variegated like samplers. At *Calstock* the gorge dividing Devon and Cornwall is traversed by a magnificent viaduct carrying a single track line. You look across to Cornwall and see dozens of commercial greenhouses basking on the S facing hillside.

Berrynarbor [3] The lilting name is a combination of Old English *byrig*, a fort, and Nerebert, the name of its 13c owners. It lies in a steep combe just inland. There are glimpses of the coast along the road W of the village, and a good many bungalows share the view. But the village itself is old and pretty.

Remains of the old Manor House stand behind the church, the home of the Berrys, with initials HB carved above the windows; later it became the village school. Church monuments are interesting: Richard Berry, d 1645, Tudor family piece; Jane Spence d 1815, classical and pretty: grey and white marble urn and lozenge side by side; also a folksy coloured slate with wings, flowers and scrolls, 1811. Little

Bicton: the ruined church

niches crenellated like sea foam: two on a pillar inside the church, one outside halfway up the tower.

Watermouth Castle. On the coast road Gothick, castellated, *c.* 1825; now a museum and show piece of a nearby camping site and beach.

Berry Pomeroy [31] Small village with pleasant view from the church. *St Mary* has vaulted S porch with good bosses. Screen stretches the breadth of the church and is exceptionally fine, still keeping much of its original carving; early 17c Seymour monument: three recumbent figures above each other; Royal coat of arms of William and Mary; having landed at Brixham, Wil-liam is said to have held his first council at Langcombe farm, now called *Parliament Cottage.* E of the church is *Berry House,* 16c but with a Georgian façade.

Castle: romantic of an aspect, most castly of castles, perched on top of a beetling cliff and girt by deep woods. Built by the Pomeroys it passed to the Seymours in 1548. Guardhouse, *c.* 1300, is linked to corner towers, the walls are riddled with narrow staircases and small chambers; within the keep is the vast shell of the Seymours' 16c house. A thrilling place.

Bickington [31] High hilltop village on the edge of Dartmoor with a distant view of Haytor rocks from the church-yard. Church itself much restored 1884, but there remains a 16c priest's door in S chancel and a 17c font cover, octa-gonal, side panels carved with primitive heads and formalised foliage.

Bickleigh (Nr Plymouth) [23] A large army camp is here and some of the bosky dells of the Plym are given over to assault courses. The army has pre-sented the church with some woodwork—"modern ecclesiastical" would best describe it—panelling in the chancel and a new pulpit. Also a new altar and altar rail in granite, brutalist and odd looking in a 13c church. Norman font with a little primitive carving round the rim, unearthed in the churchyard in 1909.

Bickleigh (Nr Tiverton) [14] The Exe valley, still broad and wide, begins to narrow here, and the wooded hills rise, close and warm, above the water-side. A well known beauty spot with an old post bridge and picturesque cottages with manicured thatch; the sign of the *Trout Inn* even has its own thatched awning. Across the river the old Victor-ian railway station stands like an abandoned toy, its lacy bargeboarding beginning to fray. The more workaday part of the village is on the hill beyond with the Early Victorian Rectory, which enjoys a wide view across the valley. The church has an entertaining collection of 17c Carew family monu-ments; the faces bearing a family resemblance, including Bamfylde Moore Carew b 1690, who became King of the Gypsies.

Bickleigh Castle stands ½ m down river on the W bank. It consists of a massive Norman gatehouse in sand-stone closed by exquisite 18c wrought-iron gates, grouped round with Tudor buildings. Opposite is a Norman chapel.

Bicton [18*] Once the home of Lord Rolle, the house, Georgian and neo-Georgian, is now a college of agricul-ture. The gardens are open to the public. They are claimed to be designed by Le Notre, but it seems unlikely since Le Notre visited England in 1662, and the present house at Bicton was built *c.* 1730. The gardens do have a very formal look, with water courses, ter-races and parterres. There is, too, an

The gardens, Bicton

Bishopsteignton: detail of the tympanum

avenue of monkey puzzle trees, charming 19c greenhouse, miniature railway with tunnel, pinetum (plantation of varieties of pine), and tea room.

In the SW corner of the grounds, by the main road, are the church, by Hayward 1851 (porch corbels being portraits of Victoria and Albert, otherwise uninteresting), and *mausoleum*. This was by Pugin, also 1851, one of the few of his designs actually built; it joins up with the ivy-covered ruins of a much older church and looks very romantic. Inside the mausoleum is small, dark and high with floor of yellow and blue tiles, and ceiling richly decorated, arched and coffered, Moorish in feeling. There are two tombs: a 17c Rolle sarcophagus with recumbent figures in black and white marble, very handsome. Opposite is the monument to Lord Rolle (in whose memory all this was built) who, according to his epitaph, was "the last representative of one of the most ancient and opulent families of Devon". The rest of the tablet is superbly Victor-

ian: a self-confident, unquestioning statement as to the role of the aristocracy in supporting the Creator, the Queen and the Conservative Party.

Bideford [5] Market town on the broad Torridge, spanned here by a long mediaeval bridge which is the essential feature of the town and its focal point. Two other special characteristics: the broad Quay, tree lined, with shops and houses set back across the road from the water; and the sharply rising ground behind the Quay with narrow twisted streets where old houses rise above each other.

The bridge, which links the town with its suburb "East-the-Water", was first built *c*. 1250 of timber with 24 irregularly spaced arches; about 1460 the timber was clad with stone. The bridge, particularly the superstructure, has been altered many times since but the haphazard arch span was always retained so that when the bridge was widened in 1925 pieces of the original

timber were found inside the stonework. Model showing the phases of construction in the library reading room. At the S end of the town *Old Ford House*, an interesting building in itself marks the older point of crossing before the bridge was built; this was the end of an ancient trackway which was at least pre-1050 since it led to Crediton (not Exeter). Later the old turnpike picked up the route; it is now a minor road having been superseded by the new turnpike in 1835 (now B3220). The old trackway crossed with another at *Way Barton*; this second trackway probably linked Great Torrington and South Molton.

Bideford was immensely prosperous during the last quarter of the 17c and the first half of the 18c, mostly due to trade with the American colonies, especially tobacco. *Bridgeland St* climbing up from the Quay was laid out during these good years, planned as a whole by Nathaniel Gascoyne about 1690, much remains today.

To the period of high prosperity belongs the chief, though wellnigh secret, glory of the town. This is an exquisite plaster ceiling: a delicate, daring riot of flowers and foliage in elegant arabesques, probably one of the finest examples of this kind of work to be seen. It is in the Royal Hotel. East-the-Water, built around the remains of a merchant's house of 1688. Another room in the hotel has a similar ceiling but the central medallion has gone. Of the same period is the wainscotting and the grand staircase.

The church was rebuilt 1864 by Ashworth; the few points of interest are all preserved from the earlier church: fine Norman font with cable moulding and three carved panels; pieces of Elizabethan and Renaissance carving from the old screen now in the tower arch; tomb of Sir Thomas Graynfyldd, d 1513, behind a good stone screen.

From the Quay, with many fine old façades above the shop fronts, there is a walk along the riverside to Appledore; it passes a Georgian *mill*, now the Devon concrete works, skirts Northam at *Cleave Houses* (at the end of Limer's Lane) and passes several small, pebbly anchorages; much of the land is National Trust.

Bigbury [27] In three scattered parts: $1\frac{1}{2}$ m inland a village with a few cottages, one with Royal coat of arms let into an exterior chimney wall. Down by the sea is a suburbanised enclave with much post-war building; this overlooks a fine view E to the rock stacks at the mouth of the Avon estuary; W is *Burgh Island*, conical and linked to the mainland by a tidal causeway.

The church, 2 m back on a plateau above the sea, has 14c sedilia, piscina and tomb recess in chancel; pulpit, brought from Ashburton in the early 18c, with goblet stem; eagle-lectern; two early 15c brasses and remains of a third; large slate wall tablet with crude figures to John and Jane Pearse. She d 1589 he d 1612; it has a long verse with a complicated 16c conceit:

thus Pearse being pierced by death doth peace obtaine oh happey pierce since peace is Pearses gaine

Behind the church is *Bigbury Barton*, plainish, early 19c, slate hung; earlier buildings to the side were once the original house.

Bishop's Nympton [13] Its first charter was AD 974 "Granted to his faithfull thane Aelfhane three hides of land at Nymet". Nymet was the old name for the river Yeo; this land was later given to the church, hence the Bishop's. Long, sloping village of mossy, thatched cottages. Tall and graceful church tower, a landmark for miles around. Interior restored but with original wagon roof, Norman font, fine 16c tomb chest in N chancel wall; figure, possibly 14c, in the wall above the vestry.

Bishop's Tawton [3] Large village with some ancient thatched cottages. Church has an octagonal crocketed spire, very pretty and unique in Devon. From the W end you can look across the water meadows to *Tawstock Court* and church embowered in trees. Inside the church, among some unremarkable monuments is one to an infant girl: the tiny baby lies swaddled at the base of a plaque in the S chancel. At the end of the S aisle is a memorial, proudly headed "*Trafalgar*" with crossed flags, to Lewis Rooke, who died in his bed in 1870 aged 82.

Bishopsteignton [32] On the N bank of the Teign, you walk up through the village, the view unrolling below. Church has a fine Norman W door with still crisp carving; in the S wall a remarkable Norman tympanum: the three Magi approach the Virgin with small palm tree above; style and dress recall the Norman connection with Sicily.

$1\frac{1}{4}$ m NE, in a tight fold of the hills, the site of Bishop Grandisson's summer palace, 1332; only a massy wall remains, pierced by ogee arches and thick with creeper.

From the Haldon Hills N of the parish there is a panoramic view of the estuary and coast to Sidmouth, and inland to Dartmoor. The hills are traversed by B3192 Exeter–Teignmouth road.

Bittadon [3] An enchanting group to be seen across the valley from the main B3230 road: ivy covered *Bittadon Barton* with farm buildings and the little *St Peter's* church.

Blackawton [34] Large, little visited village a few miles inland from the coast. Used as a battle training area by the Americans in 1944, the inhabitants

having to leave their homes. 14c church: fine Norman font in red sandstone with cable pattern and palmettes; screen with carved pomegranates, emblem of Catherine of Aragon; Jacobean pulpit; large brass in nave floor to Nicholas Forde, d 1588, and wife; slate wall tablet in chancel to Grace Stuer with verse acrostic; tomb chest to Richard Spark, d 1700. He left money for the annual distribution of bread, a bequest still honoured. Church door similar to Ugborough and there dated 1731.

Ruins of *Oldstones* 1 m NE, large Georgian house surrounded by mediaeval ruins of an earlier building.

Black Torrington [8] Featureless village above the Torridge. The church has some engaging, naïve slate tombstones of 1722 and 1751; two panels of the old reredos now form an organ screen. Pulpit, 1907, exactly similar to Tetcott, Georgian sounding board above.

Bondleigh [9] Hamlet on a side road above the Taw: a few thatched cottages with trim Georgian details and a farm barton. Church has Norman tympanum above S door, lamb with flag and two eagles. Also Norman is the font. Two broad and richly carved capitals in E wall of N aisle. Many extremely primitive old bench ends (as at Honeychurch). 15c tomb recess in chancel with a breadth of style and lack of fussy detail unusual for the period.

Bovey Tracey [31] Divided by the river Bovey and rising up the hillside; the church is at the top on the N bank and steals most of the thunder since, although it is a pleasant little town, there are few houses of great interest. A few Georgian buildings at the top of East St; 16c *Manor House* opposite; down in the town is 66 and 68 Fore St, Tudor with two-storey porch and original door.

St Thomas of Canterbury is exceptional because of its 15c furnishings, the structure also generally 15c. S porch with fine 15c bosses, central boss has four heads: King, Queen, Bishop, Burgher, many others inside. Screen 1427; pulpit of similar date; 15c brass eagle lectern; three misericordes in choir, one showing fox carrying off a duck. In the chancel two 17c monuments: Nicholas Eveleigh tomb 1620 with flat damask-like carving; his

Bradninch: part of the painted screen

widow married Elizeus Hele as his second wife and their monument of 1636 was erected in their lifetime. A brave eccentric, James Forbes, was vicar here 1628–65; he hid the lectern, chalice and registers during the Commonwealth and, when it was over, hung up notices proclaiming his disgust; these are now beneath the Tower arch. Outside by the S chancel wall is his wife's peculiar tomb of 1655: barbaric and odd-fangled box.

Over the river is *St John's*, 1852, by Carpenter: Victorian Gothick at its most mediaeval and high church: sombre, rich, twinkling, mysterious. Reredos with mosaics by Salviati.

Bow [16] Long, sleepy, dusty village which grew up as a market centre along what used to be the main road from Crediton to Okehampton; the parent village, Nymet Tracey, lies 1 m SE and Bow church is there, a smart step along from the village. (Odd that no chapel of ease was built.) *St Bartholomew's* has traces of Norman work: crowned head above S door, remains of a Norman arch below. Church was enlarged in the 13c and it shows in the clumsy arrangement of two Norman capitals in the N wall removed from elsewhere; original wagon roofs; rood screen with a little original colour; altar rails 1680; 18c pulpit; pews, obviously dating from

restoration of 1889–90, appear to have utilised 18c box pews; stuffed barn owl over vestry. *Nymet Barton* close by church: thatched Tudor house; a pretty glimpse through the archway of the ancient barton.

Bradford [8] "Commercial centre" of the parish is the hamlet of Hole Moor, set around an ancient oak. The church, 1 m N, has a Norman S door with restored carved capitals. *Dunsland House*, known for its magnificent Tudor ceilings, was burned down 1967. The park remains tranquil and beautiful, leased by the Caravan Club from the National Trust.

Bradley Manor *see* Newton Abbot.

Bradninch [17] Set amid the rich and rounded hills above the Exe valley, its main street, wide, sleepy and tree-lined, meanders up and down a hill top. The houses are of different styles with a few Georgian doorways to lift the whole above mere seemliness. *Comfort House*, Hen St, 1681, is thatched with a two-storey portico. The *Manor House*, 1547, rebuilt two hundred years later, still has some fine Jacobean wood and plaster work.

The town has known greater things: a borough, with mayor, for 700 years, its annual income in 1835 was £64. 10. 0, of which the mayor and corporation spent £32. 5. 0 on giving themselves a feast (*Hoskins' Devon*). One of the town's great annual fairs (there were several) was that of St Dionysius, and the parish church was named after him; since restoration in 1881 it has been more primly known as St Disen. The church's pride is the 16c rood screen extending right across the chancel with painted panels (retouched) showing Adam and Eve, the Expulsion from Paradise, Ladies Holding Instruments of the Passion, etc. The Royal coat of arms below the tower is that of Edward VIII, commemorating a visit here, and one of the few mementos of his short reign.

Bradstone [20*] The manor house has a splendid early 17c gatehouse with pinnacles and flaunting weathervane. Glimpsed through the Tudor arch the house still has two Tudor windows, the rest having been replaced by Georgian work. A large farmyard, attached to the house, is enclosed by barns and stables in beautifully weathered granite.

The church of *St Nonne*, a Cornishman, has some Norman work, and there is a holy water stoup, of three primitive stones. In the churchyard an undistinguished modern slate tomb to William Henry Wood ARCA (d 1939) has inscription:

"Life without Industry is Guilt,
Industry without Art is Brutality."

Bradworthy [4] Remote village neatly grouped round a large open square on the Saxon plan. Small friendly houses mostly 18c but in no way showy. *St John the Baptist* church stands back from the square. It has an early 18c pulpit with open balusters and 18c communion rail.

Bramford Speke [29] Pretty, but incoherent village of many thatched 18c cottages.

Branscombe [18] The village follows the contour round a hill, on either side are two steep and wooded valleys which then join before going down to the sea at *Branscombe Mouth* ½ m away. The shore is unspoilt and now belongs to the National Trust. *Great Seaside Farm* is a sprawling Tudor house overarched by a venerable holm oak. A good walk across the cliffs to Beer starts here.

Branscombe itself is a pretty village with a picturesque creepered pub; ½ m W are the old village bakery, and opposite, the smithy. The great blackened forge was reputedly built in 1580 and is still in use. The church, W at the farthest end of the valley, is exceptionally interesting. It has a Norman crossing tower, with stair turret and narrow Norman windows on the N side, also an unusual exterior staircase leading to the gallery. The inner wall of the tower may be Saxon at the base, the nave is Norman. Wagon roof 15c; fragment of 15c wall painting on the N wall of the nave; W gallery is Jacobean, as are screen and altar rails; splendid 18c three-decker pulpit. There are some handsome monuments. *Jane Wadham* has her two husbands kneeling opposite each other and flanked by their several offspring. (The Wadhams lived at Edge Barton and founded Wadham College, Oxford.) There is also a collection of slate tablets to the *Bartlett* family, the latest recording the death of H. N. Bartlett in 1922 at the age of 103 years 6 months. Opposite the church is the 16c *Living House*.

Edge Barton has been continuously occupied since the 12c. It was the home of the great Bishop Branscombe of Exeter (1258–80) and there are many traces of monastic stonework of this period inside the house. A small room in the W wing betrays its use as a nursery: scratched in the stone window arch are drawings of a lady in Elizabethan dress, a sailing ship, dogs, horses etc.—they speak vividly of succeeding generations of children pent up on wet days.

Bratton Clovelly [8] Remote and pretty village in a magnificent situation looking over the valley of the Thrushel to Dartmoor; the colour and aspect of the moor constantly change as light and weather alter. A shock on entering the church: the floor was lowered at some time and the church seems as high as a cathedral. Good Norman font; some primitive heads in the arches of the N windows and traces of wall painting on the N wall. N of the parish the B3218 Holsworthy to Okehampton road offers motorists fine views of Dartmoor.

Bratton Fleming [3] Large upland village. Seemly Baptist chapel 1850. Church restored and without interest except for a set of old bell clappers.

Braunton [2] Claiming to be the largest village in the country, now almost a suburb of Barnstaple. The Middle Ages seem very near: *Braunton Great Field*, still farmed on the strip system, calls to mind the background in so many early paintings and illuminated manuscripts. The parish church is 13c and enormous showing how important Braunton must then have been. The old part of the village, E of the main road, has plenty of village Georgian and some houses a good deal earlier. 28 Church St has a band of Perpendicular carving; 36 Church St is early 19c with pretty iron balconies and pilasters; just E of the church is the old schoolroom with double external staircase leading to its upper room and on into the churchyard.

The first church was built by St Brannock, who is buried here. Present building very high and wide. Ancient benches in chestnut which time and Sunday best have burnished to an exquisite hue (they are massive, three or four inches thick, adze cut, all with carved ends); Norman font with 13c carving; Jacobean panelling in chancel, 1593, with angels, flowers and castles picked out in gilt; Jacobean carving to gallery, 1619; altar rails early 17c; candelabra, 1833, elaborately wrought floating stars and arabesques, a very Christmassy effect with the painted and gilt bosses in the roof; Lady Chapel has a brass palimpsest (the panel turned round so that the reverse may be used) of Lady Elizabeth Bowcer with, on the other side, the head and shoulders of a knight in chain mail; also a 16c

Portugese chest with fiendishly complicated lock.

Braunton Great Field lies SW and is probably best seen from the road to Lobb NW of Braunton. The view is wide including the meeting of the Taw and Torridge as they flow to the Atlantic. Further west are *Braunton Burrows*, strange, lumpy and lunar. The Great Field is one of the few remaining examples of the open strip system still farmed as such, dating back to Saxon times. It is about 350 acres in size. The original strips were about a furlong wide—the distance a heavy Saxon plough could comfortably be drawn. The strips were separated by a foot or so of unploughed turf. During the last thousand years the strips have been bought or exchanged so as to create more compact plots, and the intervening "landshares" were then ploughed out. There were originally at least 700 strips, today there are less than 200. You can get a fair idea of the original layout by imagining all the broader pieces subdivided to match the surviving half-acre strips. (Sellman: *Illustrations of Devon History*)

Brendon [10] The toplands are rough and bare but the valleys are thickly wooded and from above the trees appear to surge up from the deep clefts like foam. The whole area is wonderful for walking, much of it National Trust with well marked footpaths. The Brendon valley is on the very edge of Devon, next Somerset, fingering deep into Exmoor. It's at its steepest and most spectacular W towards Lynton (see *Watersmeet* under Lynton). *St Brendon Church* has a Norman font, and a second font, or font-like object: three separate pieces of stone forming a chalice; the base probably came from a Norman pillar, the stem has Norman, or perhaps Celtic carving, the bowl is Norman, richly carved with birds, foliage, abstract patterns. This is Doone country: *Lorna Doone*, with its exquisite feeling for the countryside, is well worth re-reading, especially if you are in the area.

Brentor [20] A highly dramatic volcanic rock rears up—you keep on getting glimpses of it as you drive round the area. From the top there are magnificent views of Dartmoor, E, Bodmin moor lies W beyond the hills above the Tamar valley; on a clear day you can

see Plymouth Sound. The church of *St Michael de Rupe* is perched on the very pinnacle of the tor, its tower only a few feet from the beetling face. Tavistock Abbey (to which the church belonged) established an annual fair here in 1232, but there is evidence that this extraordinary site was used much earlier. If you make the steep climb you may record your achievement in the church visitors' book.

Bridestowe [8] The church is hopelessly restored. A Norman arch with carving on the capitals was removed and placed as a gate arch on the main road. It's better than anything left inside the church.

Bridford [28] High (800 ft) on a hilltop in country dimpled with wooded valleys. *St Thomas Becket* has an early 16c screen with lively little carved figures in wainscot instead of the more usual paintings. Initials above rood stair said to be those of Walter Southcote, rector 1508–50, who gave the screen. Fragments of mediaeval stained glass collected in E window, N chancel chapel.

Bridgerule [7] Dullish village on the Tamar. Church has a handsome tower of ashlar granite. Image niche above the S porch converted to take an 18c sundial; inside the porch are the village stocks and a free-standing holy water stoup, "about 1500 years old" says the note above, but the pillar on which it stands looks Norman and the top might be the capital of a colonnette as at Holsworthy. Other Norman work inside: primitive font of a block of granite hollowed out and slightly waisted; doorway in N transept leading now to vestry but probably originally to the rood loft; blocked off arch in S chancel; open wagon roofs. Otherwise a plethora of rich, dark Victorian carving and a stupendous 10 inch key on the back of the S door.

Brixham [35] Workmanlike fishing town which greatly adds to its interest as a seaside resort. Fishmarkets line the Quay, the harbour is filled with smacks and trawlers, fishermen eye the girls and add to the local colour. An ancient settlement: *Berry Head*, the cliff S, takes its name from the Celtic and had an Iron Age fort later covered by a massy defensive rampart built during the Napoleonic wars. William of Orange

landed here in 1688, and his statue is down by the harbour.

Few houses of particular merit, but stepping down the steep cliff sides to the harbour are decks of seemly houses, painted in fresh pale colours. Most available sites were filled in by the first world war and later suburban buildings (and there are a lot) had to spread inland behind Berry Head. The *Berry Head Hotel* was built as a military hospital in 1809. Local museum is housed in an old sail loft and two fishermen's cottages: intimate and affectionate in feeling, strong on boat building, sail making etc.

St Mary's, Upper Brixham, is one of those windswept, clifftop churchyards. Exceptional S porch with kerne vaulting and boss of the Trinity; N transept is set behind low, late 18c panelling and a wooden arcade with Corinthian pilasters; wall monument to Mrs Compton-Smith, d 1862 but 100 years earlier in style.

Brixton [27] Now a sizeable suburb of Plymouth, but round the church is the old village centre, ancient and decayed. The Green, with line of chestnuts, lies E and all about are mouldering 16c and 17c cottages.

Broadclyst [29] An exceptionally large parish; the actual village lies athwart the main Exeter–Taunton road. Church has a richly decorated tower similar to Cullompton but here more austere, being all grey stone. Interior also notable for carved stone, mostly 15c: the arches, decorated with fleurons, spring from angles carrying shields except by the S door where they are replaced by grotesque heads; 14c sedilia; two Jacobean monuments: Sir John Acland d 1613, figure in arched recess surmounted by infinitely elaborate carving; pillars, plinths, crests, cartouches, obelisks and achievements, almost colourless, looking like icing sugar; another to Francis Drewe d 1675. By the S door a fragment from an ancient mass showing music and words, rescued from an account book of 1581 where it had been used to mend the binding. This copy of the mass was probably made by a monk from *Prior's Court*, now the vicarage but once a religious cell; the front part of the house is

Branscombe

52

18c, the rear ancient. Near the church is *Broadclyst House*, large, clumsy Georgian.

Columbjohn, 2 m NW of the church. The gatehouse of an Elizabethan mansion built by Sir John Acland. The family moved to Killerton in the early 18c and in 1778 built a mansion there.

Killerton Gardens, 2 m N of the church, is a Devonian Kew with rare trees and flowering shrubs, laid out by Sir Thomas Acland after the Napoleonic Wars, now owned by the National Trust and open to the public. The gardens lie up the slope of Dolbury Hill: the lawns, smooth as baize below, grow wilder as you climb with ever widening views of the Clyst valley. At the top of the hill is *Killerton Clump*, remains of Iron Age earthwork. In the gardens is a folly, *The Hermitage*, built about 1840, a tiny thatched cottage of split tree trunks lined inside with wicker, the ceiling decorated with pine cones, the floor made from slices of tree trunk. Another tiny room even quainter: floor of knuckle bones of deer, ceiling (and possibly the whole room at one time) lined with deerskin. At one dark end a "lancet" window glowing with fragments of apparently genuine 15c stained glass including some fine heads. The window is surrounded by what appears in the room to be stone carving but at the rear of the cottage you see the trick: branches with the twigs lopped off short so they strongly resemble 15c crockets.

The Chapel of 1841 stands in the park, built by Cockerell in Norman style on the plan of a college chapel with choir and apse but no nave. Carving of bird nesting in the rose window: a swallow nested there during building and work was halted while she hatched her eggs.

Broadhembury [18] An early estate village, pretty and well kept, the broad street lined with terrace cottages roofed with continuous thatch; there are no front gardens, and the thatched porches give directly onto the street with roses, clematis and fuchsia twining neatly up the frontages. *Drewe Arms* is 15c, low and broadspreading with Tudor wood and plaster work. Great chestnut trees lead past up to the church.

Bridford

St Andrew's has the same broad, but not heavy, look as the inn; the tower is decorated with stone blocks of contrasting texture; two-storey porch with three elaborate image niches and Jacobean gate; porch roof vaulted. Inside is a perpendicular font with carved figures, unusually plain for the period: early 17c Drewe Monument in the chancel: wall tablet with delicate raised plaster work of flowers and arabesques.

The Drewes first acquired *The Grange* in 1603, an attractive house with 17c profile and 18c windows, $\frac{3}{4}$ m S of the village, good view of the S front across rhododendron lawns; the gardens behind are bounded by magnificent yew hedges. The house has exuberantly worked plaster ceilings and fireplaces, carved wood grand staircase and Oak Drawing Room.

Broadhempston [31] Church has an idiosyncratic collection of 17c black stone wall tablets. Largest is the Robert Warryings, *c.* 1656, and wives, decorated with charming naked angels and verse expressing an original thought.

Broadwood-Kelly [9] On a hillside above the Okement valley with views S to Dartmoor. In the church an unusually complete stained glass window dated 1523 in delicate colours of white, blue and irregular yellow; S door dated 1695 with name Robert Wollan.

Broadwoodwidger [8] A remote village with a blissful situation on a spur of hills above the river Wolf and looking across towards Dartmoor. The few houses cluster around common land where cows graze; the village stocks are kept handy beneath the church. *St Nicholas* is partly 13c but additions from time to time have made a weird confusion of arches. There are a number of fine 16c bench ends. The wagon roof was sensitively restored in 1966.

Brushford [14] A remote little church in a pastoral setting on a hilltop. Very plain Norman arch; screen with tracery so fine and delicate that some of it has simply not survived; 17c pulpit.

Buckerell [30] View across the hills beyond Honiton. 15c church, *St Mary and St Giles*, not large and inside the more intimate because of cramped fur-

niture. Good rood screen brought here from elsewhere and cut to fit, the top half is original, the bottom mere joinery. 18c box pews and W gallery. Memorial to Admiral Graves of the Boston Tea Party, who lived near by. *Deer Park*, an early 19c mansion, now an hotel, restrained pillared portico and well proportioned bow windows.

Buckfastleigh [31] Early industrial centre, the town having many old mills and workshops. *Museum* of early farm machinery. Across the 15c Dart Bridge is the *Dart Valley Railway Station*, reopened 1969 and itself an industrial curiosity: spick and span rolling stock in the GWR livery of chocolate and cream and a charming country station complete with advertisements from between the wars and bookshop. The single track line runs to Totnes through exquisite countryside. *Holy Trinity* church stands N high above the town. It has a red sandstone Norman font with cable pattern and palmettes and 19c box pews. E of the churchyard is a 13c ruined chapel.

Buckfast Abbey, 1 m N of Buckfastleigh, founded by Canute, 1018, became Cistercian, 1147. At the Dissolution the land passed to private owners; in 1882 it was bought by French Benedictines, who became an autonomous community in 1902. The brothers began to rebuild the abbey with their own hands in 1907 to a design by F. A. Walters, it took them 25 years. The E *Chapel of the Blessed Sacrament*, designed by *Dom Charles Norris* O.S.B., was added 1966. The abbey is in Norman style, built of Bath stone, the interior providing a strong contrast with most churches in that it is not the home of centuries of clutter, but has been furnished by a simple, energetic taste.

The surrounding village, quiet and pleasant, is clearly organised to feed and entertain thousands of visitors.

Buckland Abbey. *See* Buckland Monachorum.

Buckland Brewer [5] Village stands high with a wide outlook. Church has a Norman S door arch, finely carved: a row of human and birds' heads, the beards and beaks spread over the arch below as over a counterpane; Norman image niche above the font of 1771.

Orleigh Court 1 m NE, and visible from the Bideford Road travelling NE, is a Tudor house of 1580 with additions and alterations *c.* 1700.

Buckland Filleigh [5] Pastoral setting in rich parkland looking S to Dartmoor. No village, but a careful composition of manor house (1810 in grand classical manner), church, and ornamental lake beyond. The house is now a school. Church has a Norman S door, pulpit of old bench ends, and wall tablet to Ann Fortescue, d 1815, by Flaxman, showing her sorrowing husband and son.

Buckland in the Moor [31] Set in moorland and sloping steeply down to the plashy brown Dart; from above you look across from hilltop to hilltop, the valleys dropping quickly and mysteriously away. The road S from the old church through Holne Chase down to *Spitchwick Nature Reserve* is particularly beautiful. *St Peter's* church is hemmed by flower-spangled banks. Built of moorstone, the church has a Norman font with palmettes, rosettes and cable pattern, plain 18c pulpit, screen with upper part renewed, painted wainscot with barbaric half figure painted in the broad panels behind, and mediaeval tiles below tower arch. *Buckland Court*, near by, is Georgian.

Buckland Monachorum [23] The church spacious but not very interesting except for a weird bun-shaped font and hammer-beam roof with angels playing musical instruments. Family monuments in the *Drake aisle* include a fulsome specimen to the heroic defender of Gibraltar. Outside a sundial is built into the capital of a pillar, it may have come from the Abbey near by.

The *Lady Modyford School*, endowed 1702, but much older, is a small neat building just by the church; it still keeps the connection by serving as the present-day school canteen. At the S end of the village is a 17c house, probably once an almshouse, with niches around the door.

Buckland Abbey, 1 m S. Sir Francis Drake bought this house in 1581 just after his return from circling the globe in the *Golden Hind*. Still a young man, he was already a legend. Here he remained during the difficult years when the Queen either favoured him too much to let him out of her sight, or

cooled towards him and refused him permission to voyage abroad. Finally in 1595 she let him go and he sailed again for the Spanish Main and died off Puerto Bello after a disastrous voyage. The house was originally a Cistercian Abbey dating from 1278. At the Dissolution it passed to the Grenvilles and so to Sir Richard Grenville (of the *Revenge*), who converted it into a house. Or rather built a house into it, for even today it has the bones of a church. Outside, the great arches are simply bricked up and smaller windows cut into them; upstairs you may meet the points of an arch starting up from the floor, like the jaw bones of a whale, to meet just over your head. The most splendid room is the Great Hall, paved with red and white tiles, with Grenville's frieze in plaster: a knight putting his armour aside so as to enjoy the contemplative life; also fine Jacobean panelling. Upstairs is the *Devon Museum*, interesting, local and not too large; and a naval museum. There is a series of water colours by W. Prynne (1760–1830) of old Plymouth. The house and its exquisitely peaceful garden lie in sunny dip of the hills, utterly quiet except for bird song. Just behind is a great *Tithe Barn*, 180 ft long.

Bickham Roborough. An unpretentious mansion built 1880, looking out towards the Tamar and Cornwall. Its chief charm is the subtle gradation of its park and garden. Outside the gates is rough heath. Thence you pass to rich, tranquil parkland, shaded by great trees and grazed by plump cattle. Beyond is the garden with beds, walks and flowering shrubs. Each stage is most marked, and the whole intensely English.

Milton Combe. An unspoilt village dropped into a steep little ravine ½ m S of Buckland Abbey. A stream runs through the middle and the "Who'd Have Thought It!" Inn stands in the middle of the village looking down the valley. The odd name was apparently the exclamation of another innkeeper when his rival was granted a spirit licence.

Buckland Tout Saints [34*] Narrow lanes leading to this remote village have grass thrusting through the middle like the ridge of a donkey's back. Church stands high and alone with views across the coastal plateau. Late 18c, it was completely restored in the late 19c; still lit by oil lamps hung in pretty Victorian

holders. Some fragments of 16c carving in the reredos; the central panel may be 15c.

Bearscombe, 1 m SSW, modest, grey stone, 16c house in a sheltered valley. Having been altered in the 18c it has, oddly, a double porch: the Georgian doorway standing alongside the original.

Bucks Mills. *See* Woolfardisworthy, nr Bideford.

Budleigh Salterton [30] The most architecturally distinguished houses are not the most typical: it's a town of comfortable Edwardian villas in large well kept gardens. Millais lived here and painted his *Boyhood of Raleigh*. The wide bay has a shallow curve of pebbly beach and on a sunny day the long line of surf makes an exquisite contrast with the blue sea and low red cliffs. Fronting the sea are the gardens of Edwardian villas, unexciting, uncommercial, relaxed. On the hill behind is East Terrace, a row of red brick Georgian. At the end of West Terrace is *The Lawn*, Georgian, overarched by trees and, at the time of writing, peeling and derelict, like some colonial mansion of the Deep South. *Lyndale* in Chapel St is Gothick with a nice lozenge window. *Victoria Place* has pretty 19c cottages. The town is surrounded by beech and pine woods—pleasant for walking.

Bulkworthy [5] Hamlet of old farms. Opposite the church a magnificent tithe barn. The church was built by Sir William Hankford, the Judge who imprisoned Prince Hal; when the Prince became Henry V he appointed Hankford his Chief Justice. Church largely restored 1873, but the font bowl is Norman and there is a 15c squint. Pulpit made up from old panels, some very charming: two birds in a nest holding three eggs etc. Reredos also of assembled bits, surrounding Victorian painting of the Lord's Prayer etc.

Haytown. ½ m W, a semi-circle of pretty, old cottages and chapel with Georgian details including a fine doorway.

Burlescombe [15] A very large parish in a wide, flattish valley. The church has

near **Buckland in the Moor**
above farm
below the Dart

some fine monuments to the Ayshfords, a Perpendicular tomb chest and Jacobean wall tablets in deep relief. The Ayshfords lived in the Manor House of Ayshford, 2 m SW of Burlescombe. Parts of this building, 17c house and a 15c chapel, are now attached to a farm; surrounded by meadows and great trees, they look very pretty from the bridge of the canal which was cut just below them.

Burlescombe churchyard stands high, and from it you can survey the whole valley. SW is the great running hump, or hog's back which marks the quarries of Wistleigh. These are still thriving and have encouraged a lot of modern building around. The canal used to carry the stone away, but now it goes along the narrow country roads in thundering great lorries.

At *Canonsleigh* farm, between Westleigh and Burlescombe, are the fairly extensive ruins of an old Priory, founded by Maud, Countess of Devon in the 12c.

Burrington [6] On a high plateau between the Taw and Torridge with double views to Exmoor and Dartmoor. Close set village of thatched cottages, good looking pub and a little local industry, all snugly grouped round the village oak. Church, rebuilt 15c, has fine woodwork: screen, S door with original Perpendicular tracery, wagon roofs in S aisle. Altar rails *c.* 1700.

Butterleigh [14] A scattered hamlet on a series of gently rounded hilltops between the valleys of the Exe and Culm. The country here is rich and wooded and seems more like parkland. Church much restored from time to time. There is a beautifully plain Norman font, bowl-shaped with traces of diamond patterning; also an 18c poor box.

Cadbury [17] Dominated by an ancient earthwork, *Cada's Burgh*, with sensational views of Dartmoor and Exmoor

and, on a clear day, Somerset. The hamlet is set on a slope below overlooking a small, steep valley. Church has Norman font, some 15c stained glass in a window in E wall of N chancel aisle, and Elizabethan lectern. Fabric restored but old bench ends were made into a reader's desk, and the floor of the N chancel aisle is ancient.

Cadeleigh [14] Village on a ridge with a double view. The inn overlooks a small bowl-shaped valley, narrow and steep: the church, facing the other way, has a wider view. *St Bartholomew* is basically 15c. Handsome monument to Sir Simon Leach and family, erected 1630. Great tomb chest with coffered arch, high as the church roof and surmounted by a forest of angels, obelisks, cherubs and shields, painted in faded green and gilt, the whole jammed up behind the organ. 18c plaster panelling and box pews. The S porch restored 1922 with corbel portraits of King George V and Queen Mary.

Buckland in the Moor:
painting on the back of the screen

Buckland Monachorum font

58

Aysford Manor and the derelict Grand Western Canal (*see* **Burlescombe**)

Cadhay. *See* Ottery St Mary.

Chagford [9] Small, ancient, stannary town on the edge of Dartmoor. Surrounding countryside of deep woodland threaded by plashy, brown streams in contrast with bald, bold Dartmoor above. Chagford has some Victorian building but it blends happily with the older thatched cottages. An example is the *Moorlands Hotel c.* 1841: Italianate with Georgian details, it has an Alpine air and with its slightly bizarre paintwork, makes a welcome exotic.

At the centre is *The Square*, with octagonal Victorian market; W of this is the church with the town's more obviously ancient and wealthy houses;

a continuously thatched row, including the *Three Crowns Inn*, handsome early Tudor and the former house of the Guild of St Catharine. The churchyard, with view S, is set around with pretty cottages. Over-restored church but with the tomb of John Whyddon, d 1575, with lively dancing figures, birds and beasts. In the S chancel floor, a Whyddon daughter, d 1641: "Behold a matron yet a maid". Also in the chancel a painting of the Madonna and child, but deeply suspect as to date. There is a pleasant stroll along the river to Chagford Bridge, granite, 16c.

Challacombe [3] Remote valley below Exmoor. The hamlet and inn are on the Ilfracombe–Simonsbath Road. The

church is buried in the country beside an old barton. Font, possibly 13c. Otherwise nothing of interest to the tourist.

Chardstock [36] A soft, scattered, village with a tough centre of late, 19c work. St Andrews, 1864, repellent. Opposite is *Chardstock Court*, a hard-faced house built on to a pre-Reformation core; other housing in sympathy with these. However there are any number of pretty, thatched Tudor farmhouses in the shallow valley. At *Holy City* there are *Old Orchard* and *Whitehouse*, also *Ridge*, a T-shaped house with a great barn forming the shank of the T.

Charles [3] On a hilltop, above the

59

The Leach monument, **Cadeleigh**

Beside the lych gate a peculiar stile, hinged and lifting.

Cheldon [13*] An unusual little church only superficially restored. The floors, for instance, are large, worn, mediaeval tiles. Some old bench ends; wagon roof with Tudor bosses; plain 18c pulpit and altar rails. Two elaborate painted and gilt rails form a rood screen, not quite a matched pair, one 1737 the other 1743. Two plaster portraits in high relief, two ladies, no names or dates, but the style of hair and dress suggests the same period as the screens and, like them, nearly but not quite identical. Attractive font, blackened in parts, long hexagonal goblet, not quite symmetrical; it could be late 12c.

Cheriton Bishop [28] Part of the village is on the A30 and rather soulless; the old kernel is by the church $\frac{1}{4}$ m N in a tight fold of the hills. Exceptionally interesting church in the matter of furnishings: Norman font of unusual form carved to resemble a sheaf of corn; fragment of carved alabaster in S chancel: group of knights; 15c S door hinged in the centre and with a little carving; screen 1520 across N aisle, the figures in the wainscot preserving their original colouring now soft and faded; coats of arms of Elizabeth I (very rare, the only other examples in the county that come to mind being in Bradley Manor near Newton Abbott and, much obliterated, at Honeychurch); 16c pulpit with restored Renaissance panels; parish constable's staff and handcuffs of 1831.

Cheriton Fitzpaine [13] Substantial, thatched village, Georgian and earlier, built on many levels, tending happily to arrange itself into pictures; almshouses of 1594 with four massy chimneys like buttresses. Like the rest of the village the 15c church has a good exterior, angel corbels in the S porch with ugly, anxious faces.

Upcott Barton, $1\frac{1}{2}$ m N, set in a small, serene valley, as in a basket overflowing with blossom. Late mediaeval mansion altered in Tudor times. According to Dr Hoskins once the scene of intense violence.

Chittlehamholt [6] Name means "Wood of the dwellers in the valley",

river Bray, an area of many quarries. The church has a font of 1727, high goblet shape, fluted round the bowl and with acanthus at the base. A similar font is at King's Nympton, but this is perhaps finer. A small *Iron Age hillfort*, not difficult to spot from the South Molton–Ilfracombe Road approaching from the N.

Charleton [34] Luxuriant countryside within the embrace of the Kingsbridge estuary. This alluring situation has attracted much recent, unsympathetic building. *Frogmore*, a hamlet $1\frac{1}{2}$ m E at the head of the creek, is peaceful, with a low and ancient bridge.

Chawleigh [13] On a remote plateau N of Dartmoor. Church interior high and graceful with slender 15c pillars and rounded arches, with a criss-cross wagon roof and notable rood screen. Outside in the S wall an 18c sundial.

Chagford: the churchyard and The Square

Chulmleigh

that is, the village once belonged to Chittlehampton. Naked church of 1838 by Gould.

Chittlehampton [6] Standing in a shallow, orchardy valley, a long village of unassuming cottages, many of them thatched. In the centre is the Square with a chapel of 1858 and the village pump; at the top is the church with the Square spread before it like an apron. There were formerly houses in front of the church, and this would have been a typical Saxon village settlement (as at Bradworthy). Indeed the church is named after St Hieritha (or Urith), a Celtic girl whom the Saxons murdered with scythes; at the E end of the village there is a well said to mark the spot where she was martyred.

The church tower is famous for its height (115 ft). Beautifully proportioned it tapers gently upwards and is topped by crocketed pinnacles which give it an airy elegance. The interior

was restored 1872, but not harshly. *Shrine of St Urith.* is unusual: small arched recess in the N chancel now containing a sarcophagus with inscription *c.* 1550; the niche formerly contained St Hieritha's image until the suppression of pilgrimages in 1539. Her "portrait" may be seen in a figure in the pulpit nearest the steps, carrying a palm to signify her martyrdom; this pulpit is early 16c. On the floor near by is a 15c brass. In the N chancel an elaborate Elizabethan wall tomb to the Giffard family.

Chivelstone [34] This cliffside parish looks blasted and windswept; hedges stand bent and the few trees grow sideways. The scenery is fine: *Prawle Point* on the S (OE "look-out hill") is a Lloyds' signal station. Church is set well inland among a few cottages and barns; unusual pulpit formed from a single block of oak, bucket-shaped and covered in dense, flat carving.

Christow [28] Scheduled for development, and, since it is only an average village, this is no tragedy. *St James* church has a Norman font, old screen, a few bench ends. Monument to Sir Fleetwood Pellew, d 1861, Admiral of the Blue, his honours set forth on a bellying sail, surrounded by emblems and symbols: Victorian Masonic.

$1\frac{1}{4}$ m S by the roadside is *Old Canonteign House*, enormous Elizabethan mansion in decay. It was abandoned *c.* 1820, when Sir Edward Pellew became Viscount Exmouth and built himself something smarter, in Greek Revival style, sparkling white like a set of dentures.

Chudleigh [29] At the SW approach to the town, beyond a nurseryman's garden, are *Chudleigh Rocks*; a limestone outcropping which used to form the goal of picnic parties from Exeter, being pleasantly romantic and "horrid". The town is unremarkable, though the little streets away from the main road are pleasant enough. Church was ruthlessly restored 1868, only the screens remain, unusually broad in section; a 13c tower still presents a handsome sandstone front to the road. Behind the churchyard is the *Old Grammar School*, 1668, now a private house with Georgian façade. E of the church is *The Old House*, Tudor with two-storey porch on massy pillars.

Chulmleigh [6] On high rising ground above the Little Dart river, mostly unassuming Georgian and earlier. It remains a sleepy little town looking back to more exciting things before the railway drained prosperity away. The church has 51 ft rood screen, wagon roof with angels, 16c helmet by the organ, and over the S porch a piece of Norman carving: crucifixion in the form of a mandala.

Colleton Barton, 1 m W, 1612. Home of the Burys; gatehouse and chapel remain from a mediaeval house.

Churchstow [34] 2 m NW of Kingsbridge and a far older parish; a place so balmy and protected that oranges and lemons have been grown here in the grounds of *Combe Royal*, a Tudor house. Church's fine, high tower is a local landmark. Restored 1848, interior has little except a Norman font with crude blank arcading. *Church House Inn* is said to be 13c.

Leigh, 1 m NE. In a narrow country lane you suddenly see the rough, monolithic masonry of a 15c gate house: double arch, two-storey porch, remains of a staircase. Behind it is the old Domesday manor, now a farm.

Churston Ferrers [35] A new suburban village, an overflow from Paignton, has grown up near the main road. The church lies E in a fold of the hills near the sea, still quiet and unspoiled. S porch has 15c image above door; 18c pulpit. *Churston Court*, early 17c with its own walled garden, is now a hotel.

Clannaborough [16*] Tiny church and handsome barton, *c.* 1800, look across rolling country to Dartmoor. *St Petrock's* is small and criblike, still lit by candles set in graceful wands. Restored 1858–9, but a few ancient tombstones line the floor.

Clawton [8] Heavy clay country. The

Clawton

village lies in a hollow with the church away and above. Norman font, primitive and interesting with scratched cable decoration and below four heads interspersed with formalised flowers; single panel of Elizabethan carving saved from the old pulpit; boss in S porch of two bishops' heads.

Clayhanger [14] Rolling hillocky country. *Nutcombe Manor House* is partly Elizabethan with some plasterwork. Church restored 1879–81, but the nave suffered less than the chancel and still has some old bench ends and lovely incised stones in the floor; Reredos has re-used Jacobean carving; simple Jacobean lectern and altar table; fluted font *c.* 1200.

Clayhidon [15] At the head of the Culm valley. Near by is a wooded escarpment with wide views of the Vale of Taunton; at the very edge an obelisk stands black against the sky: a memorial to the

Duke of Wellington. Church has a 16c pulpit and a Victorian reader's desk, not quite a copy of the pulpit but inspired by it, an interesting pair. In the S wall, low and hidden, is a priest's effigy half engulfed by the rising floor.

Clovelly [4] One of the very few outlets to the sea between Westward Ho! and Bude. The little harbour, at the foot of a steep cliff, provides the only shelter for ships for many miles. In plainest terms Clovelly is quaint and picturesque: the little houses cling to the cliffside, each perching upon the shoulder of the one below. Sleds used for dragging loads are lashed to the side walls lest they careen down the cobbled street. Donkeys, the local horse power, pose for photographs.

But Clovelly has been lucky. If you look carefully you will notice that many of the cottages have had a facelift and now incorporate carving brought from elsewhere, or pretty plaster panels.

Clovelly

Many of the houses have the initials C.H. and a date somewhere between 1914 and 1925. This restoration is the work of Christine Hamlyn, whose family have lived for many generations at *Clovelly Court*, just behind the church. Mrs Hamlyn's taste seems to have been for the folksy (see the motto above the lodge to Clovelly Court), and her wall tablet in the church shows a kneeling lady in vaguely Tudor dress. Her imagination found its natural outlet in beautifying Clovelly and she created there a minor Portmeirion, though less sophisticated and eclectic. She also gave *Mount Pleasant* to the National Trust as a war memorial, so ensuring that this land SW of the village with wonderful views to Bideford and Morte Point should remain unbuilt upon. By her efforts the village today is prettiness personified; all cars and coaches remain at the top and up there are the snack bars, ice-cream stands and souvenir shops. If you want to see

Clovelly you have to climb. When Mrs Hamlyn died, aged eighty, in 1936, she had owned Clovelly for fifty-two vital years, during which the motor car had arrived. Christine Hamlyn was continuing a family tradition. The *Hobby Drive* is a 3m stretch to the E landscaped by Sir James Hamlyn in 1829.

Well above the village is *All Saints'* church. It has a Norman doorway to the S porch with flat zigzag decoration; Norman font; Jacobean pulpit dated 1634 with initials W.C. – said to be the initials of Will Carey of Westward Ho! (Charles Kingsley's father was Rector here). By the pulpit an 18c hour glass on a modern stand; many fine monuments and brasses including General Asquith, d 1939, with his medals hanging in a glass case set in the wall tablet.

Clovelly Dykes. Early Iron Age earthworks stretching for $\frac{1}{4}$ m where the road to Clovelly leaves the main road. Easily visible and accessible.

Clyst Honiton [29] Dull village with much interwar rebuilding. Too near Exeter for comfort. But *Exeter Airport* could be a diversion. Buildings are functional and intimate. The traffic control tower, boxed up with barge boarding, looks like the quarter deck of an 18c man o' war. In the bar, or out in the public enclosure, you are only a few yards from aircraft on the apron. Principal destinations for the scheduled flights are Dublin and the Channel Islands, but there are many light aircraft buzzing about as well. Free parking. Great place for children.

Clyst Hydon [17] Perfectly peaceful village in dullish, undulating country. Church, set back behind cottage gardens, is over restored but still has an exquisite S porch with fan-vaulted roof, and a small angel holding shield above the door arch. Inside little survives except for a small elephant, wearing a crown, on the W pier of the N aisle. By the porch an ancient cross.

Chelves Hayes, N of the church, early 18c, long, low house with unusual plaster moulding to windows: grooving interrupted on each side. Georgian plaster ceilings.

Clyst St George [29] Red earth and red brick, just above where the river Clyst flows into the Exe. Church almost entirely destroyed by an incendiary bomb in 1940. (One of the tiny bombs is shown in the porch.) A few monuments from the old church, including a brass to Julian Osborne, d 1635; severe, kneeling matron in tall hat: "A hundred yeares almost she led her life . . .".

Clyst St Lawrence [29] Set in a shallow bowl the village is alive with echoes: a dog barking receives its own clear answer. Attractive church. Image of the Virgin and child gazes down from the tower on the weather-beaten remains of an elegant 15c cross. Inside is a primitive Norman font; screen, tracery gone, coving garishly repainted in front but the back of the screen is delicate, untouched carving: two arches in different, and later, style from the third; 18c pulpit; Tudor door to tower stair; grotesque heads carved in tower arch.

Clyst St Mary [29] The two elements of the village, church with the *Winslade Estate* and the village proper, were always far apart but are now fundamentally divided by the A30. This is now diverted to a by-pass but it once ran through the village and on over a long, arching bridge, dating from the early 14c. Fronting the main road is a *Lodge* in formal Greek Doric of 1812 with pediment and pillars; it looks like a screen but is actually a cottage. *Winslade Park* behind has been filled in to become a new housing estate, an overflow from Exeter. Beyond is *Winslade House*, c. 1840, heavy block, now a boys' school. The church has some architectural interest in that it was reoriented in 1895 and the altar stands at the W end. Near by *Grindle House* is Georgian.

Cockington. *See* Torquay.

Coffinswell [32] Winding village on a hillside not far from Newton Abbot. There is much modern overspill between the old thatched houses. Church lies away from the road ap-

proached through the farmyard of Court Barton, or by a half-hidden grassy path. Inside is a Norman font: red sandstone with saltire crosses above, palmettes and cable pattern below; early 18c altar rails set in tower wall; collection of parish documents, including list of parish militia for 1715.

Colaton Raleigh [30] Large, scattered village near the river Otter in a countryside of small conical hills shaded by great trees, mostly oak. Buildings mixed; cob and thatch, Edwardian and modern suburban. *Place Court* is a mediaeval manor house surrounded by a handsome barton wall of crumbling red cob topped by a ridge of thatch. Church has a Norman font with cable decoration round the base.

Coldridge [6] Exposed position on a hilltop north of Dartmoor. *St Mary's* is an exquisite church. The first and most lasting impression is of beautiful restrained colour: none of the woodwork is stained or painted, so that all is grey, white and bleached brown; glorious rood screen springing upwards like rhubarb leaves; parclose screen in different style, similar to that at Brushford (but here in better condition); carved bench ends; and a few very old pews, distorted but infinitely solid. Mediaeval tiles with pictures of lions, roses and pelicans in front of the altar and N and S aisles. Norman font.

Colebrooke [28] Hamlet on a hilltop looks across rolling countryside set with nestling farmsteads. An interesting church, *St Andrew's*, with some fine, carved wood in its natural state silvered with age. *Coplestone chapel*, c. 1460, has a screen with unusual swelling tracery, linenfold panelling below; prie-dieu from the chapel now the reader's desk; 17c altar rails; two pulpits, one plain 18c; old bench ends; in the transept two 12c corbels dating from the Norman church; outside by S aisle wall two plain 13c slabs with simple crosses.

Coleford, $\frac{1}{2}$ m N, hamlet of ancient thatched cottages and a 13c pub. *Spencer*, Tudor house, now divided, with two-storey porch. $1\frac{1}{2}$ m N of Colebrooke in the village of Copplestone is a Saxon cross with interlaced carving.

Colyton [ ] First settled by the Saxons about 700 AD, a very attractive village, the streets set on winding slopes and

lined with pretty houses and cottages of the 17c and 18c. Largest is *Colyton Cottage*, 1610. The *Congregational Chapel*, 1814, is a little tucked away but worth looking for. *Great House*, South St, is Elizabethan with chequerboard frontage. The *Vicarage*, 1529, SW of the church is probably the finest house in the village, built by Dr T. Brerewood. The porch has his motif: initials T.B. and a briar, also his motto, *Peditatio totum, meditatio totum*. S of the church is the *Old Church House*. At the time of Henry VIII a group of Colyton men clubbed together and bought up part of the confiscated Manor of Colyton; they called themselves the Chamber of Feoffees and this body has run the town since. The Feoffees founded the Grammar School in 1546 and built the Town Hall.

St Andrew's Church has a lantern crossing tower (not common in Devon) topped by a gay and handsome weather vane; base of the tower is Norman as shown by the massive supporting masonry. There was extensive renewal in the late 19c. The arches of the nave were built then, and the enormous W window which looks heavy and Victorian close up, but beautiful from a distance. With the other large windows in the aisles it gives the air of grace and lightness that is characteristic of this church. In 1933 there was a fire, and more renewal; at this time pieces of a Saxon cross were retrieved from the tower where they had been built in by the Normans.

The most important features of the church are probably the stone screens: Jacobean in the N chancel, Perpendicular in the S chancel. The S chancel also contains a number of Elizabethan monuments to the Pole family. Grandest is that to Sir John and Lady Pole, who lie back to back; Westover monument, painted Elizabethan with kneeling figures, is in the sanctuary, as is the little monument to Margaret Beaufort, Countess of Devon, only 3 ft wide but grandly embellished.

Colyford, on the main coast road has some pretty cottages but no distinctive features.

Combeinteignhead. *See* Haccombe with Combe.

Combe Martin [3] Mostly living off summer visitors now, the town was once known for its silver and lead

Bench ends, **Colebrooke**

mines, and several of the old workings are said to run under the main street. The setting is most beautiful, best seen from the road above on *Knap Down* (a Standing Stone up here). You look down on the long village running down the combe to the sea, rich little market gardens climb the hillside to catch the sun—the combe is particularly sheltered and supplies garden produce for nearby towns. Beyond the gardens you can see shadowy shapes of the old strip system; indeed the gardens themselves are probably remains of these. Apart from the rocky and picturesque bay it's really best to see Combe Martin from a distance, the individual houses are not good. Only the *Pack of Cards* catches the eye, a folly said by the literal minded to have windows and chimneys relating to the number of cards in a pack, but with curious angles and thin sloping roofs.

The church is exceptional: tall graceful tower, with primitive statues in niches, on the W side a man climbs out of his coffin. Screen with painted panels and a modern cornice. The old one was taken down in 1727 and what remained was "sealed and beautified" with plaster; remains of this treatment can be seen on the back of the screen in N aisle. Also in N aisle finely carved wall epitaph with a half figure. Old bench ends, one topped by a dragon, now headless; ancient chest traditionally used for "Peter's Pence", the levy demanded from 8c to 16c for the support of the Papacy.

Combe Raleigh [18] *The Chantry* is a small mediaeval house 1498, probably built for the priest, or chanter, of the church. Although the house is very pretty, nearly all the old windows have been enlarged and modern casements inserted. The church, *St Nicholas*, has an unusual door, massive and probably

as old as the church itself, but hinged and folding in the middle.

Combpyne [36] Secluded, pretty and unspoiled. *Manor Farm* may have been a mediaeval nunnery. The church is charming. Small and chapel-like, it stands on the foundations of Saxon church; the present building dating from 1240, restored a little during the 19c. A rough graffiti-like sketch is scratched in the plaster of the S wall: sailing ship, intricately rigged, with man attending to it. Obviously it was drawn by someone with real knowledge of ships (Combpyne is very near the sea). A similar sketch in plaster was recently uncovered in St Andrew's, Plymouth.

Near by, on the coast, and not far from the great landslip, is *Rousdon*, by Vaughan and George for the Peek (biscuits) family. A farm stood here until 1878, when a heavy Victorian mansion was built: an ornate hotch potch of all the favoured Victorian styles from Italian Renaissance to Louis XIV via Tudor and Flemish. Now a school.

See also Dowlands Landslip (under Axmouth).

Compton Castle. *See* Marldon.

Cookbury [8] Shapeless village overlooking a shallow valley of the Torridge. Church with unique dedication: *St John and the Seven Macabees*. For once the original Norman fabric has been barely touched: N aisle added 1500, S transept 1535. Massy old pews probably 16c; floor of mediaeval tiles; jumbled Jacobean panelling in pulpit and transept pews; altar formed from bits of Perpendicular screen.

Cornwood [24] Large moorland parish thick with prehistoric remains. The village itself is dull, but the church, *St Michael's*, has a Jacobean pulpit delicately carved overall; two wall monuments: in the chancel to Robert Bellmaine, d 1627, and wife; another similar in S chancel chapel to John

Savery, d 1696, tablet showing him at ease in a dressing gown. By the lych gate a carved tomb chest of 1665.

A low cottage opposite the school is said to be the old priest's house, much renovated but the massy, low door arches look convincing. The parish is dotted with exceptionally fine old farmhouses including *Cholwich Town*, 2 m NW according to Hoskins a fine example of a moorland yeoman's house and dating from the 15c. *Blachford*, $\frac{1}{2}$ m NW, now a humble farmhouse but showing signs of great age including a 15c doorway. *Fardel*, $1\frac{1}{2}$ m SE, with details going back to the 14c, a solar, and chapel licensed early in the 15c. *Slade*, 1 m SW, Tudor porch and hall—very fine with sixty carved bosses; Georgian additions.

Cornworthy [34] On a hillside sloping toward a creek of the Dart; large, rather mixed village. W is the massive 14c gatehouse of former Augustinian nunnery. At the other end of the village is *St Peter's* church, originally 1350–75, restored 1788 and again 1820. Still Georgian in feeling: 18c box pews, pan-

elling and window seats, pulpit with sounding board and gilt angel, elaborate candelabra. S porch 16c. Grand monument in chancel to Sir Thomas Harris and wife, d 1610, lying under a carved and painted tester.

Coryton [20] Dull church standing in a pleasant widening of the river Lyd Generous provision for malefactors: three-seater stocks are kept just outside in the churchyard.

Cotleigh [18] The church has wagon roofs in nave and aisle. E of the village two farms front each other across a miniature gorge like embattled fortresses; it looks like mediaeval Germany.

Countisbury [10] Cliff parish. Roman signal station here on *Old Barrow Hill*, the low outer vallum easily visible from the road. Ancient earthwork SW of the village on *Wind Hill*, where a battle was fought with the Danes in 873. Further W is the 1900 lighthouse.

Church, *St John the Evangelist*, has unusual screen, *c.* 1700, classical with

Combe Martin

broken pediment; N aisle pews same date as screen; particularily fine bench end in S chancel wall of swan chained.

Creacombe [13] The name means "crow's valley", and indeed it lies in a rather dull and scraggy part of the county. The church was rebuilt 1857, but the site is infinitely older. A sketch in the vestry shows a Saxon doorway which still existed in 1844. The font is very plain, so plain that, at a guess, it too could be Saxon.

Crediton [16] Ancient market town, mostly Georgian and Victorian, the earlier thatched and timbered houses having, as often in these market towns, been consumed by fire. Most houses in the main street have shop fronts cut into them: e.g. above the ground floor of Mills Bros is a Georgian house with pediment and four pilasters. In Parliament St is *Gothic Cottage*, early 19c with castellated garden screens and complicated fenestration.

The town was an early religious centre after St Boniface (missionary to the Germans and founder of Fulda Monastery) was born here in 680. A minster was established in 739 and a bishopric in 909. But such was the Danish threat that the see was removed to Exeter in 1050. In 1547 the parishioners bought the church for £200 and appointed 12 governors, an arrangement which still stands.

It is a large, spreading church in red sandstone. Present building started 1150, earliest visible remains include the font and the massive base of the crossing tower, both Norman. Lady Chapel, *c*. 1300, was used as the Grammar School 1572–1860. The church was badly decayed by 1413 and much work was done including the raising of a clerestory. Also of this period is the sedilia, backed by an Easter Sepulchre; at the E end of the N aisle is a fine Flemish chest, probably 16c, with an exquisite carving of the Adoration. Behind the font a little door leads to the Governor's room, which used to house an ancient library, now removed to Exeter. Ornate tombs at the E end of the S aisle: Sir John Sully and wife, d 1387; he fought with the Black Prince but is said to have died in his bed aged 105; in the chancel:

The Buller memorial,
Crediton

Sir William Peryam, d 1605. Judge at the trial of Mary Queen of Scots; John and Elizabeth Tuckfield, 1630, two medallions and a seated figure divided by black columns. But the most eye-catching memorial in this, or perhaps any church in the county, is to Sir Redvers Buller, who fought in the South African War and relieved Ladysmith. He was thus a national figure, associated with an event which brought immense joy during the short, but intensely self-conscious climax of the British Empire. His monument does him proud: finely lit by the clerestory it climbs the W wall of the tower, a cliff of red sculpted figures interspersed with mosaic coats of arms. Sir Redvers was born at *Downes*, a Georgian mansion which can be seen 1 m E on the Exeter road.

St Laurence Chapel, built c. 1200 but overrestored 1920 and now a school chapel. *Congregational Chapel*, 1721, but a bit heavy and looking later in date.

Fordton House, $\frac{3}{4}$ m SSE by a pack bridge over the Yeo. You can stand on the bridge and see the lawns gently sloping down to the broad stones of the ancient ford.

Croyde. *See* Georgeham.

Cruwys Morchard [13] Church and Manor House stand close together, the centre of the parish, no other houses near by. The estate has been farmed by the Cruwys family since King John and their house, though not very distinguished, has a comfortable look. Parts of it may go back 500 years or more but the present façade, simple and ivy covered, dates from late 17c.

Holy Cross church has remarkable 18c screen, small but very grand and classical, as if it were a scale model for some furniture in St Paul's; Jacobean altar rails, and homely box pews with place names for the local farmers' families. Those for "boys under 16" and "girls under 14" are placed well in the public eye to quell giggling and ogling; some of the pews have pull-out seats at the side to cope with overflow; pew cover is onion-shaped and surmounted by a dove (probably Georgian, though not the wrought-iron scrollwork above). Outside is an 18c revolving lych gate.

Cullompton [14] Old market town in the fertile Culm valley. The town is strung along a main street, very narrow in parts, the pavement often below the level of the roadway. At the narrowest part of the road is *Walronde*, 1605, in warm red sandstone with two wings and a central recess. A little further on is the *Manor House*, now an hotel, with elaborate shell arch to the doorway; the name is relatively new but parts of the buildings date back to 1603.

Wool trade built these two handsome houses and wool built the church, *St Andrew's*, one of the finest in Devon. A 100 ft church tower in the local red sandstone with decorations in whitish Beer stone, very weathered; the top of the tower pinnacled, crocheted, gargoyled and pierced, with no fewer than three weather vanes. Of the exterior the S, or Lane, aisle is the most showy, built by John Lane, wool merchant, c. 1525, pierced parapet above and buttresses carved with emblems of sheep shearing, tin mining and shipping. Inside the church has a great screen: five bands of heavy carving, richly gilt, each band stepped proud of the one below, the whole appearing more rich and massive in that it springs from slender pillars; above is the original rood beam from which at one time would have hung the rood a representation of the crucifixion. The *Golgotha*, an ancient wood carving of skulls, bones and rocks, which would have originally supported the base of the rood, is preserved in the church. Fan vaulting in the Lane aisle is similar to that at Ottery and marvellously rich; Jacobean gallery supported on squat Ionic pillars; piece of Jacobean carving in the chancel chapel; wagon roof stretching the whole length of the church in lovely faded blue and gilt.

Cruwys Morchard

Culmstock [15] A treasure here: the *Quaker Meeting House* at **Spicelands**, 1½ m W of Culmstock; founded 1650 only about 15 years after the movement itself began, rebuilt 1815. The building has the feeling of plainness and goodness one associates with the Quakers but, building when they did, they achieved elegance as well. The inside with narrow benches and a balcony in bleached pine is very simple but exquisite in proportion and colour. A small burial ground at the rear with low rounded headstones, totally unpretentious and almost anonymous. No status symbols here—Rowntrees, Frys and Cadburys, their names are sufficient memorial. In front is the 17c linhay. It was the duty of the Meeting House Warden to provide provender for the horses of visiting Friends; a field was bought for the purpose and the hay stored in the linhay.

These early chapels of dissent are generally remote because Charles II's Five Mile Act, only allowed the building of chapels 5 m or more from a town centre. Persecution, sometimes martyrdom, was the early dissenter's lot. At Spicelands a family came twice to try and bury a dead child and were stoned away each time, the burial finally taking place at night.

Culmstock church has a 15c cope, once used as an altar cloth and now on display in a glass case. The embroidery, vigorous in design and faded now, must have blazed when new. The church also has a Burne-Jones window, and a yew tree growing out of the top of the church tower.

An old wool mill down by the river, early industrial. At *Prescott* a Baptist chapel 1715, rebuilt 1785, renovated 1892.

Dalwood [18] An otherwise uninteresting village has a little Baptist chapel, one of the oldest in the country, its records going back to 1653. Outside, great buttresses make it look monolithic. These early chapels were often built, or converted from cottages by amateurs and at Dalwood they made quite sure that their work would not fall down. The inside is simple and beautiful: box pews of weathered deal, a gallery at one end, a pulpit at the other. Below the pulpit the boards of the floor

Cullompton

may be removed to show the old baptistry for total immersion. The only "decoration" is a warm, testimonial to Isaac Harm, "an old disciple" who ministered here from 1747 until his death aged 88. The chapel is near Loughwood Farm (where the key is kept) just off the main A35 Axminster–Honiton Road.

Dartington [31] Dartington springs from history, idealism and money. Inspired by the monastic aim of a self-financing rural community that shall spiritually fertilise the countryside it serves, it is centred on Dartington Hall, the 14c palace of the Duke of Exeter. In 1925 this great building, ruined and derelict, was bought by two Americans, Leonard and Dorothy Elmhirst. They established a trust in 1931 and this trust now owns 4,000 acres of land including a model farm and dairy, textile mill, three shops, building, electrical and forestry firms and a sawmill. The trust controls Dartington Hall School, (progressive, co-educational, from nursery school to 18 years) and Dartington College of Arts with full-time courses in music and drama and short residential courses on many subjects. The Arts Centre arranges concerts, theatre shows and exhibitions in S Devon, and, through its subsidiary at the Beaford

Centre, covers N Devon too. The trust also controls an adult education centre.

The Hall was roofless when bought by the Elmhirsts and the great hammer-beam roof was recreated from oaks grown on the estate. This hall covers the W side of a large grassy quadrangle. The E block is probably older, the original small manor house. N is a row of small apartments for retainers and servants; all had exterior staircases but these were replaced during the 18c and 19c. Scattered around the Hall are the houses the trust has built for its helpers over the last 50 years; these reflect an attitude to design which was the best and most characteristic of its period, noticeably the houses built 1933 by Lascaze of New York. W of the Hall is a mediaeval tiltyard: a great spade-like well set below incisive terraces. On the W slope is a magnificent early Henry Moore. The sense of idealism and craft is everywhere carried through to the smallest details: the very gate catches are of hand-wrought iron. The gardens surrounding the Hall merge softly into the park. Nothing is shoddy.

Only the tower remains of the old church N of the Hall. The new church was built 1878–80 by J. L. Pearson, architect of Truro cathedral. The tower has bands of diapering.

Dalwood: The Baptist chapel

Dartmoor: Galloway cattle
(Brentor in the distance)

Dartmoor [21, 24, 28, 31] Moorland,
not mountain, gently undulating. Its individual characteristics are jagged out-
crops of granite tors, often weathered
to fantastic shapes, and much boggy,
peaty land. No natural lakes, but a
growing number of reservoirs, cause of
some controversy but actually less in-
trusive than the large areas of afforesta-
tion; the true moor is noticeably bare
of trees. Dartmoor stretches 21 m N to
S and 15 m E to W, slopes upwards

Haytor Rocks (*see* **Dartmoor**)

from the S, until reaching *High Wilhays*, the highest point on the moor, 2,038 ft, and *Yes Tor*. Here the moor ends and the land drops with startling suddenness to Okehampton.

W edge is relatively barren with little greenery except in *Lydford Gorge* and the *Walkham Valley*. The E edge has many deep wooded valleys, the Teign valley and Buckland-in-the-Moor being outstanding. Most rivers run S. Only two, the Okement and Taw, flow N.

Roads. Two main roads: Tavistock to Ashburton, and Plymouth to

Dartmoor ponies below Great Mis Tor

Dartmouth

Moretonhampstead, quarter the moor, linking Princetown, Two Bridges and Postbridge. (These roads were made by French prisoners, for whom the gaol was built, during the Napoleonic Wars.) There is a notable loop of road running S from Okehampton and rising to only 180 ft below the moor's highest point.

Prehistory. There are numberless individual sites and in such a guide as this we can do little more than refer the reader to the 1 in ordnance maps (Okehampton and Plymouth), or even better the 2½ in series; the *Tourist Information Centre* at Two Bridges displays an annotated set. A compass is useful as even in fine weather the remains are seldom clear from a distance. All but the most dedicated may like to start on the A384 ½ m E of Merivale, where the road starts to ascend steeply. Here S you can see many clearly defined *hut circles*. Beyond, only a few hundred yards from the road, are two *double stone rows* running parallel E to W for 500 yds. Rather larger standing stones

mark each end, and in the middle of the S row is a small stone circle with *burial cist* in the centre. Just S of this row, and about 80 yds E from its centre, is a fine *burial cist*: vertical slabs form a tomb 6 ft long and 3 ft wide. Over it are two capstones. The longest of all the stone-rows is remote and hard to reach; it runs for nearly 2 m S of Green Hill, 7 m N of Ivybridge. One of the finest *stone circles* is at Scorhill ½ m WSW of where the road ends at Berrydown, ¾ m SW of Gidleigh, nearly 100 ft dia. The largest stones are 4 ft high, in a good setting sloping to the upper Teign valley. Grimspound, 3 m W of Manaton, is an important *Bronze Age settlement.*

Ancient *stone crosses* are found all over the moor. A series marks the old pilgrim route from Tavistock Abbey to Buckfast Abbey; *Bennett's Cross* is probably the best known and can be clearly seen S of B3212, 2 m NE of Postbridge.

Mining. From the 12c onwards tin mining was one of the staple industries of the moor; Lydford, Tavistock, Chag-

ford and Ashburton were stannary towns to which the miners had to take their tin to be assayed and stamped; at *Crocken Tor* the stannary "parliament" met, and the laws it made for the miners' benefit had teeth, malefactors being held in the stannary prison at Lydford. There remain many "blowing houses", where the tin was melted; an easy one to see is at Merivale, 4 m E of Tavistock. In the 19c mining for copper became immensely profitable especially in the SW corner of the moor; the skeletal remains of the great Devon Friendship Mine can be seen 1 m N of Mary Tavy, just below A386.

Still active are the *china clay pits* at the Lee Moor between Shaugh Prior and Cornwood: a weird landscape of furrowed, white conical hills—the waste soil from which the china clay has been washed—and wide pits filled with water, a man-made volcanic landscape.

Tors. Innumerable, but many are fairly near the roads. Most accessible is *Haytor Rocks* above Ilsington, set on the moor's edge with fine views both of the moor and E across the Haldon Hills to the Exe estuary and beyond. An even finer view is from *Hound Tor*, $\frac{1}{2}$ m to the NW, and $\frac{1}{4}$ m from the road. In central Dartmoor one of the best all-round views is from *Great Mis Tor*, $1\frac{1}{2}$ m N of A384, just E of Merivale; here the distant view is to Bodmin Moor and Plymouth Sound.

Devonport Leat. Still partly used, the Leat originally provided water for Devonport from the W Dart valley just N of Two Bridges. It takes the form of a miniature canal about 6 ft wide, which gently descends following the contours and can be seen crossing under the two main roads just W of Two Bridges and again where the road S from B3212 descends through woods to the Burrator Reservoir; here the Leat now ends, still providing water for Plymouth. It is fun to follow the Leat on the moor. Take the path (rather boggy) going $\frac{1}{2}$ m N from Two Bridges to Wistman's Wood, a remarkable natural wood of stunted and twisted scrub-oak, then make your way across the infant W Dart and clamber halfway up the moorland slopes opposite. Above you, almost hidden by a bit of bank, is this charming canal of clear water slowly flowing over a gravelly bottom, the side lined with granite slabs with small fish darting to and fro. You can then follow the Leat along a path as it curves round the hillside.

Bridges. Two of the most famous bridges are not strictly on the moor: *Staverton Bridge* over the Dart N of Totnes and *Fingle Bridge* over the Teign near Drewsteignton, the latter a noted beauty spot. High up on the E Dart is the ancient *clapper bridge* at Postbridge. There are bridges on the W Dart at Two Bridges, and a fine bridge at Huccaby 1 m up from Dartmeet. Many little packhorse bridges are scattered over or near the moor.

Postbridge. A rather dull village in a very pretty spot in mid Dartmoor. The 12c or 13c *Clapper Bridge* is its chief claim to fame; the other bridge was built 1728.

Two Bridges. One bridge built in 1780 and the other in 1928, when the road was straightened. A market was held here in Roman times. The National Trust has an information

Dartmouth

centre here with maps and booklets about Dartmoor and ready advice to help you find what you may want on the moor; open during the summer months.

See also Burrator Reservoir (under Sheepstor), Grimspound (under Manaton), Spinster's Rock (under Drewsteignton), Peter Tavy, Princetown.

Dartmouth [35] On each side dark wooded hillsides reach down to the green waters of the Dart; the small town is stacked above itself looking across the lively river. The railway runs along the Kingswear bank and three ferries ply and re-ply. In this sheltered haven fleets for the Crusades gathered in 1147 and 1190 and, thriving on the wine trade with France, the town grew to prosperity in the 14c. A brawling age: a man of the period still stirs the imagination—John Hawley, seven times mayor of Dartmouth, whose great, grand, brass is in St Saviour's church. Chaucer, Inspector of Customs, visited Dartmouth in 1373 and gives a picture of a typical "shipman of Derthmute":

Ful many a draughte of wyn had he
  ydrawe
From Burdeux-ward, whyl that the
  chapman sleep.
Of nyce conscience took he no keep.
If that he faught, and hadde the hyer
  hond,
By water he sente hem hoom to
  every lond.

Dartmouth was threatened by Breton men with as little conscience as Hawley and so the town looked to its defences. *Dartmouth Castle* was built 1481, an immensely strong artillery point, its guns raking the harbour entrance with the additional defence of a great chain stretching across to Gomerock opposite. Forming a group with the castle is *St Petrock's* church, 1641: Norman font; Jacobean pulpit, 1641. There followed *Kingswear Castle*, 1491, and *Bayard's Cove*, *c.* 1537. Later redoubts are *Gallants Bower* and *Mount Ridley*.

Hawley gave large sums to help build St Saviour's church, 1372; it was to be a chapel of ease to St Clement's Townstall, which stands up on the hill by an ancient trackway, but too far from the bustling new town by the river. St

Doddiscombsleigh: detail of stained glass

Saviour's has an exceptional 14c door, iron-bound with two leopards stretching through a leafy tree. Rood screen; stone pulpit decorated with enormous succulent leaves; Hawley's brass in chancel floor; altar table, 1588, supported by grotesque figures; S porch, 1620; W gallery, 1633, with 18c staircase, where are kept the old fire-engine and reredos; corporation pews of 1817, as at Tiverton.

Two houses survive from Hawley's time: *The Cherub*, Higher St, *c.* 1380, and *Agincourt House*, Lower St, 1415; relatively austere, they reflect a time before life became easy and luxurious.

In the late 16c, the Newfoundland cod fishery brought a fresh wave of prosperity and the town has a number of rich buildings of this period. *The Butterwalk*, 1635–40, is set on granite pillars with oriel windows and richly carved half timbering; inside are plaster ceilings with a "Jesse" ceiling in No. 12. The Museum is here and it too has good ceilings and fine panelling in its front room. In Higher St are *The Shambles* and the *Tudor House* (No. 5), 1635, looking top heavy as a ship's stern of the period.

Bayard's Cove, close to the old fortification, is a row of modestly attractive houses of all periods, including the *Old Custom House*, 1739. A stone here records the first departure of the Mayflower (when 300 m off Land's End she was forced back to Plymouth for repairs). N in Mansion House St (rear of W. J. Batterbee), is a *merchant's town house* of 1763 with elaborate plasterwork and gracious 18c staircase. It makes an interesting comparison with the simplicity of Agincourt House and the elaborate self-confidence of the Butterwalk; by the second half of the 18c standards of taste and workmanship had become so refined that the work here looks provincial.

In earlier times Dartmouth consisted of two villages: Hardness and Clifton, divided by the deep Mill Pool. Boats tied up at St Saviour's church wall. Later, when this area was filled in, it formed *The Quay* with the *Castle Hotel*, 1639, classical facelift of 1831; and *York House*, a great dollop of Victorian Elizabethan. Here too is a little public garden with a shed which houses a *Newcomen steam engine*; the great inventor was born in Dartmouth, 1663.

The town is now dominated by Sir Aston Webb's huge *Royal Naval*

College, 1899–1905, yellow and sprawling.

Dawlish [32] The railway runs right along the beach, nearer to the water it could not be, and yet it is not an intrusion but a curiosity. Instead of facing the sea the town looks in upon itself across the chestnut-shaded lawns by *The Strand*, 1822, by Patey. From here the Dawlish Water, a shallow stream, with black swans and small ornamental bridges, traces its course inland, passing the early 19c houses of great charm, such as Barton Terrace and Brunswick Park, until it reaches the churchyard of *St Gregory's*, the old parish church, restored by Patey. Two Flaxman monuments: Lady Pennyman, d 1801, with four mourning daughters, in Roman style; Mrs Hunter, d 1805.

Two houses by Nash: *Stonelands*, 1817, and *Luscombe Castle*, 1800–4, 1 m W of the church, with grounds by Humphrey Repton. Chapel, 1862, by G. G. Scott. In Old Town St, an aged survival: thatched house dated 1539.

Dean Prior [31] A dual carriageway of the Exeter–Plymouth road has been set unpleasantly close to the church. Robert Herrick was vicar here from 1629–49 and again from 1660–74, having been removed in the interim in favour of a Roundhead minister. He wrote a memorial for his friend Sir Edward Giles and wife, d 1637—not his best poem but in his best vein, unsolemn, human and original:

"These two asleep are: I'll but be
  Undrest
And so the Bed: Pray wish us All
  Good Rest."

Norman font in red sandstone, crosses above and unusual formalised dragons below.

Denbury. *See* Torbryan.

Diptford [31] Approaching from Rattery you see the gatehouse to Diptford Court, archaic in style but recent in erection. *Crabadon Court*, 2 m ESE, in a deep valley, is late mediaeval with two-storey porch and beautifully gnarled farm buildings. Church sundial dated 1694. *Gara Bridge*, 2 m S, is a mediaeval packhorse bridge.

Dittisham [35] Stone built, thatched cottages inclining steeply down to the

Bench end detail at **Down St Mary**

aisle three wall tablets by Laurence Whistler to J. H. M. Furse, himself a sculptor, d 1950 aged 90, and his two wives; his first wife d 1887 after only one year of marriage and is commemorated in a roundel with delicate celtic script set in tight circles, and her symbol, a *fleur-de-lys*; the second Mrs Furse d 1963 and is remembered in an exactly similar roundel but with a wild rose. This exquisite memorial, and the story told by the dates, enchant the eye and imagination. Under a beech tree in the churchyard is the grave of the first Mrs Laurence Whistler, Jill Furse, beneath a tombstone designed by her brother-in-law, Rex, and adapted by her husband.

Dowland [6] On a plateau above the Torridge a tiny hamlet consisting of church, church house and barton. The church, now little used, has timber arcading *c.* 1500 and old bench ends, one dated 1546; some 18c panelling re-used for vestry.

Down St Mary [16] Hilltop village in rolling countryside N of Dartmoor. Church S door has a Norman tympanum: man with two weird beasts and palm trees. Church restored 1878–80: Victorian pulpit of brass, coloured glass and wrought iron, very Christmassy. Modern screen in 15c style, the work of Zachariah Bushell and his son William — local men. It makes you appreciate that almost all the great screens (and there are many in this area) were the work of devoted local craftsmen.

Drewsteignton [16] Perched on a ridge above the Teign gorge, a picture book village of plump, thatched cottages. 1 m. SE a narrow, Tudor packhorse bridge spans the Teign at the bottom of the gorge, footpaths lead on down the valley. From the Okehampton–Moretonhampstead road you can see *Castle Drogo* rearing up: granite pile by Lutyens, finished 1930, its romance and arrogance in this day and age are extraordinary. You can catch another glimpse on a side road 1¼ m WSW of Drewsteignton: keep battlements, curtain walls and all.

Spinster's Rock, 2 m W. One of the

Dart; ferry crosses to Churston Ferrers. Countryside dotted with plum orchards, drifting with blossom and wild daffodils in springtime. *St George's* church has a famous pulpit: 15c stone, carved with canopied niches each housing a figure and foliage, all in fine preservation, having somehow survived the Commonwealth. Norman font in red sandstone with same unusual key pattern as at Rattery. Early 15c screen; stained glass windows in N aisle by Pugin, neat, delicate, restrained.

Dodbrooke. *See* Kingsbridge.

Doddiscombsleigh [28] Set among hills above the Teign valley. Church has unique mediaeval stained glass: a set of five large windows in the N aisle. Colours are pale yellow, and white with touches of red, green and blue with sen-

sitive drawing and a whiskery line; the artist has looked at men without romanticising but with much charity. All the windows are fine, the one at the E end is the most complicated, showing the seven sacraments: mass, marriage, confirmation, penance, ordination, baptism, extreme unction. Mediaeval painting can seldom be seen on so large a scale. There are also 16c bench ends and an 18c pulpit.

Dolton [6] Deepest, unvisited Devon. Exceptionally fine stone carving in the church: font formed of two parts of a Saxon cross, the carving clear and well preserved, lower half strap-work, the upper half more free and fantastical. Wall tablet in N chancel to Barbara Lister, d 1696, epitaph enclosed in an elaborate and highly finished frame of cherubs, scrolls, flowers etc, masterly work for so remote a place. In the S

Detail of the font at
Dunkeswell

St Constantine's, **Dunterton**

finest megalithic tombs in Devon: 12 ft stone supported on three others, it stands, like a gigantic milking stool, in a field by a farmhouse.

Dunchideock [28] Magnificent barton set on a hillock forming itself to the contours as a vessel cuts through water. Opposite is the old priest's house, rather over-restored. Church has a narrow interior with rich little screen interrupted by a pillar; this has been masked by panels to resemble image niches. Memorial to General Stringer Lawrence, d 1775, of the Indian Army, who left his fortune of £50,000 to "his lifelong friend" Sir Robert Palk, Governor of Madras. Sir Robert bought a mansion here, *Haldon House*, and built in 1788 *Haldon Belvedere*, a triangular tower, almost a folly, in grateful memory of his friend; it stands on a wooded ridge 1 m S. The Palks owned the land on which Torquay was later to rise and, understandably perhaps, rebuilt Haldon House in 1900.

Dunkeswell [15] The village lies comfortably in a niche below the plateau. Church, rebuilt 1868, has a marvellous Norman font: primitive carving of a warrior king with shield, bishop with crozier, soldier with bow and arrow, elephant.

Dunkeswell Abbey, 2 m N. Hamlet grouped round a tiny green with pump. Romantic group of the ruined Perpendicular Abbey gatehouse standing in the garden of a pretty thatched cottage, itself built from some of the worked stones from the Abbey. Beyond is a ruin, part of the Abbot's house, and on the site of the Abbey church is a chapel built 1842 and rather dull. During the building of this chapel two 13c stone coffins were found in the excavations, one remains in the church, probably Lord William de Brewer, who founded the Abbey 1201. In the chapel is a small display of copies of the Abbey seal, charter and the document of surrender at the Dissolution, the text of this last understandably grovelling and servile.

Dunsford [16] The Teign valley, thickly wooded, slopes steeply down and the village, perched on the N side, commands a view that looks like the Scottish Highlands; it's a pretty village of thatch and cream-washed cob.

The Fulfords are the local great family, having lived at nearby *Great Fulford* for over 800 years. Theirs was the last household in England to keep a jester. The family pew in *St Mary's* church houses a monument to Sir Thomas Fulford, d 1610, one of those zesty Elizabethan tablets compressing much action into small space.

Dunterton [23] Church lies by itself, clear of any village, in a fold of the hills above the Tamar set apart from the surrounding fields by a mere ridge of earth. Beyond it sheep peacefully graze and bleat. In April the churchyard is adrift with delicate wild daffodils and primroses. Polygonal pinnacles to the tower outside; inside, a simple wagon roof and 18c pulpit.

East Allington [34] Village in a valley lying between Fallapit House NW and the church S. *Fallapit* dates from the early 15c but was modernised by William Cubitt, who had made a fortune building Osborne and endless tracts of Victorian London; he bought it from the original owners, the Fortescues. It is now a school. Cubitt also restored the church. There remains an interesting but botched-up screen filled with rectangles of Elizabethan carving with date 1633 in one panel; pulpit later built but in archaic 15c style; brass in S chancel chapel to John Fortescue, d 1595, and wife (spaces for her age and date of death left blank); good Victorian font: small roundels with carvings of the Ark etc in high relief.

East Anstey [13] On an open situation facing south across fields and woods. The parish reaches up into Exmoor.

East Buckland [3] Restored church beside the ghost of an earlier church. The old tower from the previous building stands on the S side. At the base of the tower you can clearly see the line of the old tower arch – very narrow; it must have been a tiny building. On the W side of the old tower is a Norman doorway, bricked up.

East Budleigh [30] A pretty village and Raleigh's birthplace, near Budleigh Salterton. It makes a convenient trip inland for seaside visitors. From the churchyard you can look across the thatched roofs below. Inside the church is a large collection of old bench ends, all good and lively. Raleigh was actually born at *Hayes Barton*, 1 m W, a handsome Tudor house in a sheltered, sunny setting.

East Down [3] Lies in the wooded Yeo valley. *East Down House* is *c.* 1700, altered from an earlier 16c house: grey stone with white pilasters and central pediment, very handsome. The church, *St John Baptist*, restored: capitals carved in the same style as Shirwell, livelier here, but less well preserved; most fun is a jolly hunting scene with men and animals. Remarkable font with Renaissance carved wooden shaft, bowl and foot, *c.* 1700. 16c Spanish lectern, iron with nude, bucolic figures; altar table in S chapel is Jacobean, unvarnished, very attractive.

West Worlington church (*see* **East and West Worlington**)

East and West Ogwell [31] *East Ogwell.* Church and Manor House in almost crushing proximity. Church has a tomb chest of 1633 to mark Reynell family vault below, clumsy carving; rood screen now across chancel; Jacobean screen with small caryatids in tower; 18c altar rails in N chancel chapel; three old bench ends (not good but unusual in this part of the county).

West Ogwell. A perfectly simple little 13c church still with its original plan. Furnishings as attractive as the building: 13c sedilia; Jacobean pulpit; plain 18c altar rails set on a curve; high box pews. One of the most engaging of the smaller Devon churches. It stands on a hill next the large, extremely plain, house of 1790, now a convent. No other buildings near by.

East Portlemouth [34] Facing Salcombe across the estuary with views to Dartmoor, the coastal scenery very grand. Pretty drive along a side creek from Chivelstone; few roads follow these creeks. This creek is tidal, passing *Goodshelter*, a yachting haven. Church has a restored screen showing attempts at rear to burn and destroy. In the churchyard is the grave of Richard Jarves, d aged 77; a rhyme records that his servant girl was accused of poisoning him and burned at the stake.

East Putford [5] High above a valley where the Torridge is still scarcely more than a stream. Church has some old Barnstaple tiles in the S porch, a few old bosses remounted on Victorian beams, and a Norman font; otherwise restored and very plain.

East and West Worlington [13] Unbelievably remote, along narrow twisting roads. Once two parishes and two churches, they were amalgamated in 1885. Both attractive villages, the thatched cottages rather mossy and crumbly, overlooking the steep valley of the Little Dart. The hillsides are thick with oaks, beeches, and hazels. At

Exeter cathedral: west front

the valley bottom is an old ford.

West Worlington church is approached up shallow cobbled steps and under an arch beneath the old church house. Small, unpretentious but attractive, not too drastically restored. Old oak benches, massive and sunken; original wagon roof; bosses in S aisle and S porch.

East Worlington church has Norman arch in the S porch with deep band of zig-zag. Interior of the church given a thorough going over in 1879.

At *Affeton*, 1 m. W of West Worlington, are the restored remains of the 15c gatehouse of Affeton Barton, home of the Stucley family.

Exeter cathedral:
west front detail

Eggesford [6] The village is mainly the railway station; the church stands some distance away in a valley planted with conifers. It has Chichester monuments including one to Lord Chichester, erected 25 years before he died, showing him standing between two wives who had died by then. Fellowes Monument, 1723, is purest classical in veined marble of different shades of grey. This exquisitely severe composition now has an ugly modern safe standing on its base.

Eggesford House, originally Jacobean, rebuilt 1832, Gothick, now a ruin, stands in Romantic decay looking like Nightmare Abbey.

Ermington [27] Saxon plan village on a hillside above the Erm valley. Church is famous for its spire: leaning and twisted like a jester's cap. Inside the church is a 17c screen, late in date and open in design; good brass in the vestry 1583, with three kneeling figures; in S chancel chapel a florid Elizabethan tomb of about 1580; the stone in front, dated 1583, came from a priest's house in the village; 18c Bannerole in the south aisle; by S door a scrap of lettering: "Remember the poor 1680".

Exbourne [9] Intricate village with sloping orchardy gardens lying within the Okement valley. Church's unique feature is its early 14c E window; plain pulpit dated 1665; elsewhere in the church there is carving 1911 by Herbert Read of Exeter including some *Art Nouveau*.

83

Exeter [17, 29] The Romans gave the city its essential character. They not only imposed the forthright central crossing at North St and South St, but, even more important, they built the city wall. In the following centuries the walls gave protection from the Danes and within them the city grew and seethed; although it was sacked in 1003 and the cathedral was destroyed, to be rebuilt sixteen years later. Even so Exeter had walls, and in 1050 a decisive event in its history occurred when the diocese was transferred from undefended Crediton. As the foundation charter says (now in the Cathedral library) ". . . for pirates have been able to plunder the churches of Cornwall and Crediton—it has seemed clear that there is a safer defence against the enemies in the town of Exeter." And so, under Leofric, its first bishop, the great cathedral was built retaining, with its close, the largest area of greensward inside the walls.

Elsewhere during those early centuries there were still gardens within the city; St Nicholas Priory, founded 37 years after the Cathedral, managed to find $6\frac{1}{2}$ acres for its buildings and cloisters. But by the 14c many of the private gardens had gone and the whole pattern of growth in the restricted area inside the walls became a matter of filling and rebuilding. Many of the town churches were enlarged at this time, as they were throughout the country, and their cramped and crooked plans show how they had to swell into the land available. Few of the mediaeval churches of Exeter have a normal plan: a chancel lies at an odd angle to a nave, a pulpit is tucked into a tower, an extra chapel is fitted behind an altar, and so on. These odd arrangements show how dense buildings must have been by the mid 14c.

With the Dissolution the city at once began to nibble into St Nicholas Priory. Houses were built over its garden to within a few feet of its old main entrance; a lane was cut along the S cloister; old burial grounds were built over.

In the city time lies impacted. At No 7 Cathedral Yard is the Devon and Exeter Institution, originally a Tudor gatehouse. The courtyard was covered over in 1814 to form two reading rooms, behind which is an Elizabethan room with plaster ceiling, and behind that the Hall of the Annuellars refectory of 1450. Near by, at the rear of No

16, is a Roman well. The end result, just before the city began to break out of its carapace, can be seen in a model of the city as it was before 1769, when the first of the city gates was demolished. To judge the congestion you should find St Petrock's church, which now stands at the narrowest point of the High St; it was then hemmed in by houses on all sides. The model, about 6 ft by 4 ft, showing every house and alley, can be seen in the Rougemont Museum.

Then suddenly the Georgians broke the spell. It is as if the Age of Reason really did enable men to free themselves from the irrational womb-like security of the old city walls and all that inbred, teeming life. The Georgians built outside the walls; the mediaeval and Tudor city is ringed by their graceful crescents and promenades. There are a few 18c and early 19c buildings within the city proper, but the Georgians delighted to build in planned sequences, as in Pennsylvania Crescent, a graceful phrase of five houses, or in the stately composition of Southernhay, and for this they had to have open spaces, which were simply not available within the old walls.

Then came the fourth decisive event in the shaping of the city: the German "Baedeker" raids of 1942. In May of that year the mediaeval centre of Exeter was obliterated, apart from the Cathedral, which was bombed but reassembled bit by bit. Only a small area N of Fore St now remains to give some flavour of the old city.

The war ended in 1945 but rebuilding has been gradual and very slow. For many years the flattened bomb sites were used as car parks. But now, nearly thirty years later, the city of the mid-twentieth century is taking shape; at the moment of writing it does not seem unduly exciting: there are many office blocks. But a vast new shopping precinct is being built over the bombed area bounded by High St and North St, and using the façade of Fowler's *Market* of 1838.

The Cathedral stands at the point of the Roman city centre, as present excavations on the site of St Mary Major show. Then came Saxon churches, plundered and burnt by the Danes, the last in 1003. In spite of the threat Edward the Confessor transferred the diocese from Crediton to Exeter in 1050. The first bishop was *Leofric*; his effigy is on the S side of the Lady

Chapel, spurious, and made in 1568, but intriguing for that very reason. The first great builder was *Bishop Warelwast*; his magnificent Norman cathedral was as large as today's without the Lady Chapel, but only the two great towers remain, N and S, massive but gracefully decorated with bands of blind arches, orderly as samplers.

A hundred years later *Bishop Branscombe* started to rebuild the Norman cathedral; the Lady Chapel was half complete at his death, and his tomb is there. The third builder was *Grandisson*, bishop from 1327 to 1369. He completed the nave and the imposing façade. This is a great screen fronting (and diminishing) the visitor as he approaches: three tiers of kings, queens, angels and saints guard the entrance and testify to the church's wealth, status and power on earth and in heaven. Grandisson is buried in the midst of this display in a tiny chapel in the thickness of the W wall, just by the main entrance.

Passing through into the church is like entering the belly of a whale: pillars and roofs are grooved and vaulted like the thews and sinews of an anatomical drawing. The Beer stone is of an exquisite soft colour: grey and cream in the nave, pinker over the choir from the reflected colour of the glass.

Exeter Cathedral offers three sublime visual experiences: first the bold view down the nave; second the quire, "the outward expression of an inward ecstasy", as E. M. Forster once defined the aim of religious architecture; the third is to walk around the quire aisles looking at the chantry chapels — exquisite caskets, each one unique.

The Nave—300 ft of rib vaulting, the longest, unbroken stretch of Gothic vaulting in the world. The eye is carried up to a massive, central ridge which then takes it back and forth the length of the building. Ahead stands the great screen and, perched above it like a huge tooth, the organ. At the time of the Commonwealth a wall was built across the cathedral at this point; East Peters was then used by the Independents and West Peters by the Presbyterians. Tucked into the NE corner of the nave is *St Edmund's Chapel*, incorporating fragments of the Norman building; its

Exeter: Stepcote Hill

simple wooden screen is the oldest in the building.

Above your head, right and left, look at the *corbels* which mark the junction of the arches and the shafts of rib vaulting; in each one dense, knobbly carving drops down into the space like grain filling a sack. *The Font* is SW. Princess Henrietta, daughter of Charles I, was born in Exeter in 1644, while the city was under siege by the Roundheads, and christened in the Cathedral – but

not in this font, which is 1687, with cover of the same date. High up on the N side of the nave is the *Minstrel's Gallery* (with angels playing various instruments) used today in carol festivals and such like. Below in the N aisle are two favourite monuments. The first is the large tablet, in marble with bronze reliefs of mounted lancers and palm trees, to the Queen's Royal Lancers, erected 1860 after they had returned from duty in India during the Mutiny;

the list shows that twice as many died "from the effects of climate" as from wounds. The other popular monument is to Matthew Godwin, d 1586 in his eighteenth year, charmingly decorated with viols and trumpet.

Quire Screen (Pulpitum), 1320–4. Panels above the arches are now filled with 17c paintings and surrounded by the same dense carving as the nave corbels. The screen is formed from a series of little booth-like rooms: ribbed,

Exeter: Southernhay

Throne, 1313, of wood, supremely skilful and fantastic with breathlessly tall canopy climbing steeply heavenwards decked with banks of crockets and pinnacles. It was dismantled and stored during the second world war and so escaped destruction during the 1942 raids. The same is said to have been done during the Commonwealth — surely true for it would not have otherwise escaped pillage. *Sedilia*, late 13c; the canopy above is astonishingly rich, a complicated exploration of space, the carving at once knobbly and fine like barley. Below the canopy the backs of the seats are painted to represent hanging cloth, each seat having a tiny carved head above. The statues in the canopy are modern. The quire stalls were restored by Gilbert Scott in 1870 but he retained the *misericordes* beneath: engaging and various, elephant, mermaid, lion, lady centaur etc. *Great East Window*, 1390, incorporating six lights from the earlier window of 1303. In the quire there is also a collection of modern kneelers, each worked with a different device drawn from nature; birds, flowers etc, which give much pleasure to visitors.

Quire Aisles with Chantry Chapels and Lady Chapel. Starting from the NW entrance: *Chapel of St Andrew. Chapel of St George* (*Speke Chantry*); 15c tomb to Sir George Speke with figure in armour. Chapel screen particularly well preserved since it was plastered over during the Commonwealth and remained covered until 1870. *Chapel of St John the Evangelist*, 1413; brass to William Langton. *Lady Chapel*, remarkable series of tombs including Leofric and Branscombe already mentioned. But also Sir John and Lady Doderidge, 17c; Bishop Stafford, d 1419, marble scratched over with countless initials, names and dates many from 1606 and 1616. *Roof bosses*, lively and well lit: cow suckling calf, heads, foliage etc. *Sedilia*, early English and much more restrained than the one in the quire: canopies with stiff leaf foliage above simple, pointed, trefoil arches. N side: 16c *sculpture of Virgin and child with St Anne.* At each side of the entrance to the Lady Chapel are two wooden *book boxes. Chapel of St Gabriel*, painted screen. *Chapel of St Saviour and St Boniface*, carved stone reredos: three panels showing Annunciation, Nativity and bishop at mass, damaged but still fine. *Chapel of*

bossed and cusped, dark within and conveying a sense of mystery and richness.

N Transept. 14c clock; door below it of the same date. *Sylke Chantry* with stone cadaver. *Chapel of St Paul.*

S Transept. A row of organ pipes stacked like javelins. Tomb of Sir John Gilbert, d 1596: canopied, with colouring garishly renewed *Chapel of St John the Baptist*; exquisite stone screen of 1310. Inside is a charming little 15c

throne with gilt canopy, reminiscent of countless mediaeval pictures of the Virgin seated. (A similar throne by the High Altar.) At the entrance to the quire aisle: engaging, and deservedly popular *carving of the Shepherds*, 15c.

Quire. A glade set in the midst of the forest of the cathedral, the stone surround richly detailed, fretted and pierced, drawing the eye forward yet revealing the glitter and mass beyond. Commanding the eye is the *Bishop's*

Exeter: Iron Bridge, North St

St James: pall contrived from three pieces from different pre-Reformation vestments all made between 1450 and 1530.

Chapter House. S of the transept. High and rectangular with gorgeous painted roof, late 15c. Lower walls *c.* 1225.

Cloister set in a snug and sunny corner between Chapter House and S wall of the Cathedral; most of the cloister was destroyed during the Commonwealth and little now remains. On the S side to the E is the *Cloister Room* of 1887 with painted glass of 1706 by William Peckitt of York. Next to this: *Church House*, Georgian, red sandstone

Bishop's Palace. Behind the Chapter House; restored by Butterfield. This houses the *Cathedral Library*, which was started by a legacy from Bishop Leofric in 1072 of 66 books including the *Exeter Book of Anglo-Saxon Poetry*, which is on display: austere and noble mediaeval script; Foundation Charter; display of mediaeval MSS. Collection of early medical and scientific books deposited here by the Royal Devon and Exeter Hospital. Also a copy of the Bible in a Red Indian language, printed Cambridge, Mass., 1663–5.

The Cathedral Yard and the Close. In Palace Gate, SW of the Cathedral and opposite the Cloister, is the *Cathedral Choir School* by Butterfield, *c.* 1860, in his familar style of red brick patterned with blue. Next, the *Deanery*, with 14c Great Hall. A new precinct and way will cover the recently excavated Roman city centre on the site of the demolished church of St Mary Major. Tucked behind are three 16c houses formerly for the use of Cathedral servants. The next section of the close was opened up by bombing and is uninspiring. NW is Cathedral Yard, mostly Georgian and including *Tinley's Café*, 1820; inside at the rear is a section of the old cathedral wall of 1285. Further along the *Royal Clarence Hotel*, opened in 1768; it was simply "The Hotel" until the royal duke stayed here in 1808.

Continuing E you reach the Close proper. First is *St Martin's* Church, consecrated 1065 and enlarged in the 14c; as a result the chancel runs off at a different angle from the nave and the tower projects across the parish boundary. The interior not only crooked but crammed: 17c altar rails, W gallery with painted panels, low box pews. The early Georgian reredos seen on a previous visit has now been painted over and obliterated. Behind St Martin's is Catherine St, with bombed remains of *St Catherine's Almshouses*, *c.* 1450, now made into a garden; also the kitchen fireplace of the *Annuellars' College* (they were monks appointed to sing annual masses for the dead). Lying along SE just behind the houses and shops of the Close is the *Annuellars' Refectory*, also 15c; this may be reached via 5 Cathedral Close. Also behind St Martin's is a *Roman Well*, reached by 16 Cathedral Yard. No. 1 Cathedral Close *Mol's Coffee House*, 1596, where Drake, Hawkins and Frobisher used to gather. Then a row of lovely houses mostly mediaeval and Tudor but often

Exeter: 19th-century warehouses

with Georgian facelifts: No. 7 is the *Devon and Exeter Institution*, originally a Tudor gatehouse. The open courtyard was covered over in 1814 to form two exquisite little reading rooms. Behind them is an Elizabethan room with plaster ceiling. No. 8, *Law Library*, mediaeval hall with hammer-beam roof. No. 10, *Residence of the Bishop of Crediton*, early 17c. No. 15, *Chancelleris*, 1740. Then comes the *New Cut* of 1814 opening up the Close to Southernhay and overarched by a delicate iron footbridge. Beyond this the Close meets the wall of the Bishop's Palace garden.

Roman Exeter. The Romans gave the city its name: *Isca Dumnoniorum*, its basic plan, the axis of Fore St/High St with North St/South St, and its walls. These great banks of stone and rubble can be seen in various parts of the city, perhaps most easily just N of Southernhay. Parts of the *Underground Passages* (see under *Mediaeval*) may also be Roman: former water (or perhaps sewage) channels. In the seventeen centuries since the Romans there has been

so much rebuilding that little Roman work survives elsewhere in the city, but there is a Roman well at 16 Cathedral Yard and two mosaics: one in the Rougemont Museum, the other inside the Magistrates' Court, Waterbeer St.

Mediaeval. Completing their conquest the Normans had to force Exeter's surrender in 1086 and then built *Rougemont Castle* to remind the city who was who. Only the red sandstone *Gatehouse* has survived on a knob of land N of the city. After this there was no more trouble from the Danes, the Norman quickly became anglicised and the city settled down to ever growing prosperity.

The building of the Cathedral had confirmed the city's importance and it became the main centre of trade for the SW; its harbour could easily handle the small sea-going vessels of the day. Then, in 1290, the Countess of Devon, in a fit of pique, built a weir (*Countess Wear*) below the city and the river began to silt up; but such was the tide of prosperity that even this could not kill

the city's trade, and Topsham began to be developed as Exeter's outlet to the sea. The walls were now crammed to bursting; there is a relief map of the city in the Rougemont Museum, actually made in the 18c, but it gives a good idea of the crowded mediaeval town.

Underground Passages: these are actually freshwater conduits built during the Middle Ages but parts may be Roman. The passages are relatively high and narrow with a gentle incline of 6 ins in 100 ft so that water would run slow and deep. They were enlarged and elaborated throughout the 13c and 14c and form a network under the old city. The crumbling remains of old entrances and outlets can be seen all round the edges of the town. Those houses fortunate enough to stand directly above them had holes cut into the cellar floor through which a bucket could be let down to draw up the water. The conduits were continuously used until the 18c, when piped water began to be laid.

You can visit these passages, and it is

a fascinating experience; the entrance is in Princesshay. Only eight people can go at a time, and they are only open at certain times, so it is best to check beforehand at the notice board by the entrance and then go a bit early. The air about you is still and cool, with soft, dry gravel beneath your feet. You pass in single file, sometimes stooping. They are coffin shaped, the walls of glistening, naked rock broadest at your shoulder, narrow straightly above your head. The guide marks the distance by referring to the bustling city above ("Just below Boots . . . under the kiosk at East Gate . . .") but down here the air is heavy and still.

Some Mediaeval Buildings. St Katherine's Priory, Polsloe, 1 m NE just N of the railway. Founded 1150–5. So hidden behind suburban houses that even those living near by do not know it is there. The shell of an exquisite building, now the City Architect's store, with the 13c great oak screen half hidden by drain pipes. *St Nicholas Priory*, in the Mint; founded 1087. Tucked away is one of the few surviving bits of mediaeval Exeter, probably the most interesting building in the city apart from the Cathedral. What you see today is the only complete example in the country of a 15c guest house of a Benedictine monastery. Part of the interest is to trace the layout of the original priory, which was cut about and built over after the Dissolution. What is now the Mint runs along the S side of the old cloister; the line of the cloister is preserved in the School of Printing opposite; the original great entrance to the Priory was on the other, N, side of the building so that the guests arriving went directly into their own quarters without disturbing the monks. Apart from the guests' and priests' rooms, each with its garderobe, there is a great kitchen with two fireplaces, one for roasting, one for boiling. The whole is built over an 11c cellar. After the Dissolution the building became a private house and there is a plaster ceiling from this time and traces of wall painting *c.* 1580. On the N side near the original entrance is a *Saxon Cross*.

Just opposite St Mary Steps at the bottom of West St: a fine 14c *timber frame house* with two overhangs, which was moved to its present site due to the demands of road widening. *Bowhill*, 1429, $\frac{3}{4}$ m W on A30, once an outlying manor house, now on the main road

and transformed into a craft shop and restaurant, so that many of the old features are cherished; unfortunately the great hall is ruinous with merely a tin roof clapped on above the hammer-beams—an exquisite hall falling apart for lack of funds. *Chapel of Wynard's Almshouses*, 1436. The almshouses themselves are picturesque, set around a cobbled court with pump. Above Hepworths at the main crossing of North St and South St, a late mediaeval *sculpture of St Peter. Tucker's Hall*, 1471, Fore St, the great hall of the guild of tuckers and weavers, later divided horizontally. The upper room has a 15c hammer-beam roof and panelling of 1638. The front façade is restored; you can get a glimpse of the old mediaeval red sandstone through a lavatory window at the rear.

Some of the Mediaeval Churches. St Pancras, in the middle of the new shops N of Waterbeer St. Said to be the earliest and built on a Saxon foundation. The area was badly bombed and the little church, once cramped, is now at the centre of the shopping precinct. Very simple interior: 12c font; pulpit 1600; bulging angels and caryatids support the reading desk; a little late 18c panelling in W wall. *St Mary Arches*, Mary Arches St off Fore St. Two arcades of Norman arches; 16c tomb chest to Thomas Andrew, thrice Mayor of Exeter; 17c communion rails. *St Mary Steps*, West St. (Nice that these two churches of St Mary have become vulgarly identified with their principal features.) By a steep and quaint lane of irregular mediaeval steps rising from the old city gate (now gone). The main road into the town passed in front up West St, and a little chamber in the S wall of the church was originally a room above the old West Gate. Norman font decorated with palmettes. Outside an early 17c clock: *Mathew the Miller and his Sons* strike the hours with articulated precision; in spite of the homely name they look like Saracens. *St Petrock*, High St, once even narrower than it is now when St Petrock's was hidden by houses fronting the High St. You can see the situation in the model in the Rougemont Museum. Still secretive and generally locked. A restoration of 1881 reoriented the church to face N, the original chancel, still there, faces E. *St Olaf*, Fore St; for lack of space the pulpit is crammed into the tower arch, which itself juts into the

chancel. Behind the pulpit a scrap of mutilated 14c sculpture said to represent the scourging. *St Stephen*, High St. Again using all possible space a little street runs through a low arch under the chapel at the E end of the church. Built on Norman foundations with 13c arch dividing church and E chapel. Inside the whole effect is very "Alice through the Looking-Glass". Otherwise a pretty Gothick restoration.

16c and 17c. The Shipping Canal was cut in 1564 and this was the decisive event of the period. Countess Wear 1290 had threatened, not throttled, the city, which found alternative outlets to the sea. The canal more or less restored Exeter as a port. It was begun on a tide of prosperity which it markedly helped to swell; the outward and visible symbol of this prosperity is the *Guildhall*, which was enlarged and completed in 1594, a real status showpiece of a rich mercantile city. Even here the city fathers were compelled by the demand for space to cram all their splendours onto a tiny site. The result is an extraordinary bulging fantasy, an overhanging mass. Like an elephant stranded in the High St, the four great, granite pillars patiently endure the swish of traffic. The porch leads to a low, massive, inner door and thence into the Hall (roof 1466). It houses a collection of pictures, including Princess Henrietta, daughter of Charles I, born here during the Civil Wars, and the City Insignia.

By 1500 all available land had been built and rebuilt over and there are relatively few buildings of this period within the city. One of the finer outlying manor houses is *Cowick Barton*, 1540, 1 m SW, modest but handsome, built on an E plan. It is now a pub with piped muzak etc., but at least you can go in and have a drink and look around. In 1621 the *Gardens of Northernhay* were laid out just below the city walls, one of the first municipal gardens in the country. In 1681, a further sign of the growing importance of Exeter as a port, the *Customs House* was built, a marriage of sturdiness and grace; two storeys and five bays, hipped roof, blank arches framing the ground floor windows; inside are two fine plaster ceilings.

Georgian and Early Victorian. A burst of civic building began in the 1740s, foreshadowing the later private developments. The *Assize Courts*, Palladian in yellowish stone, were sited within the stronghold of Rougemont Castle. In 1743 the *Royal Devon and Exeter Hospital* began to rise at the E end of what is now Southernhay; the hospital may then have been regarded as a place to be avoided, and there was a lapse of 60 years before the Georgians turned again to this desirable location, so close to the Cathedral and city centre. In 1790, on a site outside the city walls (New North Rd), the *Prison* was begun. This occupies an important site opposite Northernhay Gardens, and commands the eye with its triple gateway; the outer parts are 1853 by Hayward. *Topsham Barracks*, neat, and almost Prussian they are so concise and military, were erected 1804. Between 1805 and 1825 the graceful Georgian compositions began to rise in earnest. *Southernhay* in 1805, *Barnfield Crescent* c. 1805. *Dix's Field* c. 1808; all are restrained, almost austere in style. In 1814 the number of people living outside the city on this side was so great that a new entrance was made in the walls at the E end of the Close for the convenience of those approaching from Southernhay. In 1810 came the *Imperial Hotel*, just near what is now St David's Station. *Rougemont House*, now a museum, is also of this period. *Victorian and Later.* One building, still Georgian in feeling, in grand Greek Doric, is Queen St *Market*, 1838, by Dymond and Charles Fowler. Neglected and decaying for many years the façade is now aptly integrated into the new shopping centre; it recalls mediaeval shopkeepers boothing themselves in between the pillars of Diocletian's palace at Split.

But a more obviously recognisable popular image of the Victorian style: Romantic, Mediaeval and Italianate, as opposed to the Georgian Classical and Greek, is probably most clearly seen in Butterfield's *Cathedral Choir School* of 1860 (see notes on Cathedral Close). But the *Royal Albert Memorial Museum*, Queen St, 1865, by Hayward is robust and uninhibited in red and beige stone. Very different from his earlier designs for the Prison, it has bold, deep set Early English windows and inside some ravishing Victorian decoration, including wrought-iron pillars and balusters. The Museum houses a good mixed collection and an Art Gallery; this is the parent museum to Rougemont House and St Nicholas Priory.

In 1899 came St David's, Hele Rd, by Caroë, something of a break with the

past; it's a distinct example of its period which was in strong reaction to the mediaevalism of Pugin and the Victorians. The style, while much influenced by *Art Nouveau*, takes its inspiration from the Celtic and Druidical; there is a marked feeling of Stonehenge. It was a period when artists were fascinated by the contrasts of dark and light, space and mass, and St David's has the same feeling as a stage design by Adolphe Appia or Gordon Craig.

Recent years have seen the great post-war expansion in further education. The *University of Exeter* lies in a campus N of the city, its generous use of space gives it a more American than British air. It has, in the *Northcott Theatre*, one of the best theatre buildings in the country: a steeply raked auditorium, intimate actor–audience relationship and comfortable bars and foyers which make theatre going rather more of a pleasure than it is in London.

Maritime Museum: newest, and one of the greatest, pleasures in Exeter; housed in beautiful Victorian warehouses down by the Quay. Rich collection of boats of all periods and from all over the world, some actually afloat on the water, many may be explored from top to bottom; everything from a Danish tug to a Fijian proa and a State Barge (from the film of *A Man For All Seasons*). One of the most romantic and imaginative museums in the country, a great place, and not just for small boys.

Exminster [29] Extended village along the Exe estuary, a dormitory to Exeter. Church has an unusual plaster ceiling of 1683: 15 panels representing apostles, evangelists etc.; discreet 17c altar rails; pulpit c. 1700. *Peamore House* nestles in a fold of hills on the main road from Exeter to Plymouth; original Tudor gables but with a Georgian façade below.

Exmouth [29] A long wide swath of sandy beach fronts this large seaside town; behind are packed rows of small houses. When Exmouth was first developed as a resort it was popular and working class, the nobs having been attracted to Torquay which was reached by the railway thirteen years earlier. All the same, there is a lot of older detail to be seen among the Victorian work. The pride of Exmouth, architecturally, is *The Beacon*, a row of pretty, well kept Georgian houses look-

ing across the wide sweep of the bay. Here lived two decorous and genteel ladies each of whom had been deserted by her husband: at No 6 was Lady Nelson in neat red brick Georgian, at No 5, larger and Italianate, was Lady Byron. Down below, nestling in the gardens of the huge Imperial Hotel is a one-storey building in Classical Revival, c. 1820.

The parish church is enormous, although it is officially a mere chapel of ease attached to Littleham (q.v.). Heavily restored just before the first world war. Hung in a very bad light is a picture of the old chapel which stood 250 yds N on Chapel Hill. Originally erected 1412 and pulled down in 1799; the picture was painted in the 18c and shows an arcadian scene of Exmouth 200 years ago: the old chapel and a few thatched cottages set amongst rolling meads.

A la Ronde off Summer Lane N of Exmouth. A little fantasy house built 1798 by the Misses Jane and Mary Parminter. Travelling abroad for the younger sister's health they saw San Vitale, Ravenna, and were inspired to build their house. Not quite circular, but sixteen sided, its tiny rooms radiate from an octagon which is lit from above by a lantern. Around this lantern is a gallery entirely decorated with shells; from its windows there are wide views of the estuary and across to Powderham Castle. The rooms below are crammed with pictures and objects which the sisters collected or made themselves: miniatures, doll's mittens, seaweed pictures, little objects made from shells etc. One room is decorated in Pompeiian style but the whole worked in *feathers*. The place is entirely feminine in the sense of being Romantic, unacademic and entranced by the trivial. An infectious pleasure.

Point in View a little further up the road, the masculine counterpart to A la Ronde. A chapel and four almshouses built 1811. One-storey building with low, lead spire and four squat chimneys. Very severe, it reminds you of coastguard cottages, and is attractive in the same way. Near by is *The Manse*, the minister's house, built 15 years later, with diamond-paned Gothick windows.

Farringdon [17] Gently sloping valleys of the Clyst and Exe dotted with elms and oaks, roads full of potholes and churchyard overgrown. Church

91

restored 1871 with *Art Nouveau* designs painted directly on to bare brickwork. Norman font, the carving freshened up somewhat.

Farway [18] At the head of a remote valley which runs down to Colyton. Above is a ridgeway with an ancient track or *faer weg* (way for travelling) which gives the village its name. Church has a neat bust to Humphrey Hutchins 1628; also the Prideaux monument where two figures lie one above the other as in a sleeping compartment. After his second marriage Granville Barker, one of the great figures in the revival of English drama at the beginning of this century, retired to *Netherton Hall* near by. His aim, or rather his American wife's aim, was that he should become a country gentleman — to the rage and sorrow of G. B. Shaw, who felt Barker should be getting on with Saving the English Theatre. ½ m SE *Farway Countryside Park* Nature trails. Fine view over the Coly valley. Animals, domestic and otherwise, some hand tame.

Feniton [18] An interesting church, *St Andrew*, with carved cadaver, much emaciated, lying by the altar; gilt screen; doorway to the S aisle has been progressively lowered through the years: first a Norman arch, then Tudor, and finally a little 13c arch removed from some other part of the building and built in here. N and W of the church cottage gardens full of vegetables slope up to the backs of houses. S of the church is *Feniton Court*, late Georgian. John Coleridge Taylor was born here, became first Bishop of Melanesia and was killed by natives in 1871; judging by the display of literature and maps in the porch the church likes to keep up the connection.

Filleigh [6] Dominated by *Castle Hill*, an enormous mansion, home of the Fortescues, built 1684, basically Palladian but much altered and enlarged after successive fires. You cannot help seeing the house from the South Molton to Barnstaple road: great blocks of masonry surmounted by cupolas and pediments, linked by arches and curtain walls, are disposed in regular piles amidst the rolling countryside. The Castle Park was designed by William Kent, and the landscape appears sublimely smooth, green, well cared for.

Church is a whole-hearted Norman Victorian restoration: lush, massive font and pulpit, painted roof gay and Christmassy, chancel heavily tiled and mosaiced in a style nearing *Art Nouveau*. Monuments include two brass plates to Richard Fortescue, both 1570, same pose in both but his beard short in one tablet and long in the other.

Fremington [2] Harrowing example of ribbon development. Large army camp and the army now occupies *Fremlington Hall*, built 1881 but an early example of neo-Georgian. Church restored but a few things remain: carved Norman water stoop by S porch; fragment of mediaeval wall painting on S wall; 15c pulpit unearthed during the restoration, but itself heavily restored; Royal coat of arms of Queen Anne.

Frithelstock [5] Lying in hilly, wooded country overlooking a side valley of the river Torridge, 18c houses grouped around the green. Just behind the church are the remains of an Augustinian Priory founded 1220 by Robert de Beauchamp with monks from Hartland; the ruined W end of the Priory church still stands with a noble three light window. *Cloister Hall Farm* is the made-over Prior's house. Right up against ruins is the W wall of the church, *St Mary and St Gregory*; old bench ends and fronts in choir, plain roughly hewn pews; Jacobean pulpit; plaster Royal coat of arms, 1677, as at Milton Dameral.

George Nympton [6] Quiet, unspoiled, on the river Mole. The lane from here to Kings Nympton by the river bridge is very pretty. Church tower rebuilt 1673 with high, rounded arch, beam across the arch carved, and with faded paint. 16c font with 18c cover. Roof bosses N aisle and chancel. Above the harmonium an angel with trumpet such as used to be set above the sounding boards of 18c pulpits (as at Molland and North Molton). Kerslake memorial, 1769, is a small, classical affair with cherub leaning on a minute sarcophagus.

Georgeham [2] On a plateau behind Putsborough Sands at the S end of one of the best beaches in Devon. Georgeham is a village of thatched cottages, pretty and unimportant. *St George's*,

the parish church, shows the continuous face-lifting our village churches have undergone. First mentioned 13c, complete Georgian restoration 1762 when it was turned into a classical building — windows altered, W gallery and screen inserted. A hundred years later the Victorians, no doubt irritated that the Georgians had destroyed a perfectly good mediaeval church, tried to restore it to its earlier style. Windows changed again, Georgian features thrown out — except the classical screen; and this time the old, original bench ends were destroyed. Some good monuments weathered the changes, all in the S chancel chapel: 13c Sir Mauger St Aubyn, knight in armour lying with legs crossed below the knee (i.e. he went on the First Crusade) in a low, arched recess. Newcourt family, late 17c, jolly heads in roundels. John Harris 1775, classical piece. Also a *c.* 13c sculpture of Crucifixion in N chancel wall. In the churchyard Sergeant John Hill's tombstone proudly describes him as "A Waterloo man"; he had served in the Peninsula too and died 1861 aged 77. *Croyde* village down by the sea, half olde worlde, half bungalows. *Baggy Point*, jutting out into the sea between two fine stretches of beach, is National Trust.

Germansweek [8] On a hillside above the Wolf, a tributary of the Tamar. These distant villages, poor and unvisited, sometimes spring a surprise: we found a village shop much as it must have been in 1910, its scales and other equipment such as you see now, at a price, in smart London antique shops.

Gidleigh [9] One of the loveliest parishes in Devon with steep hillsides plunging down to lively brown streams, higher up the perfect stillness broken only by natural sounds. Gidleigh church has an unusually low screen restored, painted wainscot; mediaeval stained glass E window in S aisle; ancient sarcophagus by N door. Just by is *Gidleigh Castle*, a small Norman keep, its main room vaulted by three arches, built by Baldwin de Brionne, Norman Lord of Okehampton. Surrounded by low ruins out of which a garden has been made, said to have been the Saxon Manor of Gytha, mother of Harold. The name derives from *Gydda's Lea*.

Gittisham [18] The village must have

Point in View, **Exmouth**

looked much the same 200–300 years ago. There is very little new, or even 19c, building, and the cottages cob, flint and thatch, are unselfconscious and even scruffy. Village green with church and handsome thatched house with "R.H. 1600" above the door. Church, *St Michael*, is small, low and leaning; box pews; monuments aptly reflecting the values of those who made them: Henry Beaumont, d 1591, and his wife, kneeling, in relief and painted: stocky, ugly, lively. Sir Thomas Putt d 1686 only a hundred years later but totally different: classical with marble urns and garlands, a real status symbol. *Combe Barton*, an Elizabethan house, now an hotel, in rich parkland. *Prehistoric remains*: Outside the Hen and Hounds inn at the crossing of the main roads from Honiton to Sidmouth and Ottery to Colyton, is the *Rolling Stone*. Legend says human sacrifice was celebrated upon it; when the moon is full the stone rolls down to the river Sid to be washed free of blood. Just across the road, in

the Lyme Regis direction are large Bronze Age barrows, easy to pick out, near the roadside.

Goodleigh [3] On a hillside approached by extremely steep roads. A little thatch, some suburban clutter (overflow from Barnstaple). Church has a Royal coat of arms of George III, 1788. *Chelfham viaduct*, 1 m. NE, relic of the old Lynton/Barnstaple line, a graceful survival. Below it an old mill now part of a school.

Great Torrington [5] Deliciously sleepy market town poised at the edge of a ravine above the river Torridge with a sheer drop of several hundred feet from the gardens and terraces of Castle Hill. The castle site is now a bowling green, and this whole area, facing S, pleasantly and intelligently laid out, is a place to stroll and sit enjoying the view and the thrilling chasm. From Castle Hill there is a way back through the Pannier Market, 1842,

with pediment and cupola, now used as the County Library; the old market building survives with a row of booths, very picturesque. At the W end of the (later) market place a passage leads through to the churchyard. The church was blown up in 1645 with two hundred royalist prisoners inside; the present building dates from 1651 but like Charles church, Plymouth, is wholly Gothic in character despite its date. Not very interesting except for the late 16c pulpit carved and gilt above with alternate heads of cherubs and griffons, plain arched panels below separated by gilt Corinthian pilasters. The houses of the town are generally unassuming Georgian, but *Palmer House*, New St, 1752, is exquisite in red brick with Ionic pilasters and a neat and elegant little curtain wall at each end surmounted by an urn; built by John Palmer who married Miss Reynolds, Sir Joshua's sister. Reynolds and Dr Johnstone both stayed here. Further up New St is the *Baptist chapel* of 1828 set discreetly back

Near Great Torrington

down a little alley closed by wrought-iron gates. *No 28 South St* has a hooded porch adorned with trophies. The *Dartington Glass Factory* is in School Lane, and may be visited.

W of the town is *Rothern Bridge*, 15c, now forming a lay-by to the main road. *Town Mills* by the New Bridge, was built by Lord Rolle *c.* 1846: false tower, castellated walls which rise above a normal roof, pseudo painted windows; a piece of whimsy.

Beam House is 1½ m N of Great Torrington. Where the drive now crosses the river an aqueduct used to carry the canal which then ran along the river's W bank to its sea lock and basin 1¾ m above Bideford Bridge. In 1871 Lord Rolle closed the canal and sold it to the railway. An economical move on both sides, for canals were doomed and railways needed dead level.

Haccombe with Combe [32] *Combe-in-Teignhead*. In a pretty combe leading, as the name implies, down to the Teign estuary. *Bourchier Almshouses*, 1620, woodwork still Tudor in style, with doorways painfully small and low. Church has a Norman font; exceptionally fine old bench ends in S transept; tomb chest to Alice Hockmore, d 1613, coarse, vigorous village work.

Haccombe, 1 m SSW. Set in rolling parkland with great stretches of smooth grazing and few hedges; plain and heavy Georgian house with a small chapel alongside, said to be still on the

94

original groundplan but heavily restored. However it houses a collection of mediaeval monuments including three early 14c effigies some with traces of original colour and also a small alabaster figure *c.* 1400; many 15c and 16c brasses, not the finest of work but very attractive; early 14c stained glass a good deal more coherent than the usual fragments and including a *pieta*; many mediaeval tiles of uncommon pattern; curious outstretched arms set in the walls, were they sconces?

Halberton [14] The Great Western Canal, now disused, meanders around the countryside as it follows the contour; some parts of it are dry, some weed-filled like lily ponds and very pretty. The canal is crossed by small stone bridges and you can walk along much of it; a good place for picnics. In the church a mediaeval pulpit explores space with exquisite complexity: small rooms, as it were, are carved in high relief each furnished with elaborate little arches and railings. The whole

pulpit has a most sensitive line, rising delicately toward the front. A duck pond in the depths of the village is said by Hoskins in his *Devon* to be fed by warm springs, and thus never to freeze even in the coldest winter. *Priory House* is pre-Tudor. *Rock House*, to the E, is heavy, rustic Georgian.

Halwell [34] Hamlet nestling in a small valley. 14c church much restored; Victorian box pews. *Stanborough Iron Age fort*, 1 m S of the village, with wide,

flattish views to Dartmoor and Start Point.

Halwill [8] Three railway lines used to meet at Halwill Junction and now the place seems untidy and decayed as if, not unnaturally, it had lost heart. The *Winsford Hospital*, 1900, by Voysey, now a geriatric unit, is a fine example of its period: low and squatting with sloping buttresses rising to huge gables, any dullness relieved by small blocks of dark stone set random around small panel windows, all very druidical.

Harberton [31] Modest village, orchardy cottage gardens climb up the hillside. At the top is the church, embattled with two-storey 14c porch. Inside a 14c sedilia carved with narrow ribs dissolving upwards into basketwork pattern. Great 15c rood screen

painted and gilt, the wainscot was covered in Victorian times (some of the original panels are in N aisle); magnificent 15c stone pulpit as at Dittisham but with 17c figures in niches. There is a 13c gravestone from Harberton in Totnes Museum: a simple cross barely a yard high.

Harbertonford. 1½ m S. Stone-built village on main Totnes to Kingsbridge road. The ford is just by the bridge S of the road leading down to the Dart; very pretty.

Harford [24] On the edge of Dartmoor studded with many handsome and ancient farmhouses attended by massive, mossy outbuildings. Church has a tomb chest of 1566 in the chancel with brass on top representing Thomas Williams, Speaker of the House of Commons. On S wall coloured brass wall tablet to John Prideaux and family set up in 1639 by his fourth son, a courtier and great divine.

Harpford [30] Nestling in a wooded dell with large thatched cottages and small Georgian houses neatly slicked

up with fresh white paint. The village as a whole not so much unspoiled as prosperously preserved. The Rev. Augustus M. Toplady, author of *The Rock of Ages*, was incumbent here from 1776–8. The cleft rock is in a wood just by the churchyard.

Hartland [4] The stretch of coast running S from Hartland Point is one of the grandest in Britain. It is not linked by any one cliff path and must be approached point by point; a 1 in map is advisable for the smaller roads and tracks. *Hartland Point* itself, with its much visited lighthouse, is spectacular, but so stupendous is this coast that other points are even more magnificent, *Shipload Bay* for instance, on the N facing coast near to the lighthouse road. S, *Damehole Point* looks N to the lighthouse and S to beyond Welcombe. There is a fine contrast between jagged reefs running out to sea and gentle grassy slopes inland. It is approached past a pebbly cove by the path from the lighthouse car park down through Blagdon Farm, or from Blegberry.

Hartland Quay, at the end of the road

◁ Hartland Quay and –
(*below*) Welcombe Mouth
(*see* **Hartland**)

Hartland

beyond Stoke, is a fine viewpoint with fascinating contortions of strata; easy to reach but the cliff paths are poor though well marked. 1 m S is *Speke's Mill Mouth*, approached from Trellick on the road from Stoke marked Welcombe. *St Catherine's Tor*, a finely shaped rock, dominates the bay N. 2 m further S this road comes near the cliff edge but the coast is here rather too straight for it to be seen at its best. Further S again the road reaches the sea at *Welcombe Mouth*, a good beach and recalling Bude in the parallel bands of rock running seawards; a good path leads to the high cliffs N.

The small market town is Georgian and earlier; many pretty, old shopfronts; opposite *St John's Chapel* are a few larger houses. St John's is a chapel of ease to the parish church; it stands on the site of the old Town Hall on a N/S axis; built 1837 (porch 1839). The parish church, *St Nectan*, is set on the bleak upland toward Hartland Quay. 14c, it rivals Ottery St Mary as the loveliest church in Devon, but is quite different in feeling. The highest tower in the county, 128 ft, which may be climbed from an entrance in the SW; an original statue of St Nectan is set in the tower. Interior high and spacious, filled with pale, once rich, colour, applied to the painted wagon roofs: blue, white and gold in the aisle, soft terracotta, green and gold in the N chancel chapel; richly carved Norman font; magnificent rood screen, stretching right across the church 15 ft high, 45 ft long, 6 ft wide at the top. Above the N porch is the Pope's chamber, once the priest's room and now a small, informal museum; panels of the old Jacobean pulpit are kept here, also several early monuments and brasses. In the S chancel chapel bits of a 14c wall monument. Outside amongst the few houses E of the church is the old church house: two primitive image niches and traces of early windows.

Hatherleigh [9] Hillside village looking now as it must have done a hundred years ago. In the centre the newest buildings are the Town Hall, 1840, and the National School, 1838 (in 15c style). Otherwise there are pleasant houses of all periods dating back to 15c, including the thatched *George Hotel*, 1450, and *White Hart House* of the same period. Church set high looking across Dartmoor. Two fonts: Saxon and

Holcombe Rogus: the Bluett pew

Norman, the latter with 18c cover; old Barnstaple tiles set round font; ceiled wagon roofs with *ceilure*; pulpit and reader's desk made up from bits of the old screen; old bench ends; pew by S door made up from Jacobean panelling, the window above has three roundels of Flemish glass of 1653. A rich and interesting church.

Just outside the town W at *Stoningcross* is an ancient wayside cross marking the way for travellers and pilgrims to the Hatherleigh holdings of Tavistock Abbey, which had a foundation here in 974.

Obelisk, 1 m W, to Lt J. H. Thomson, d 1859 at Balaclava, looking across a great dish of rough pasture to Dartmoor.

Hawkchurch [36] Hillside village on the Dorset border with cottages of flint —a material more commonly used in Dorset than Devon. The church, although much rebuilt still has Norman and 13c work, the carving particularly attractive. N chancel arch: strapwork and heads above, dragons below, other arches: man plays bagpipes, ram plays fiddle, goat plays flute, also an angel feeding swans. *Wylde Court*, Elizabethan 1593. S of the village the country rises steeply giving good views of the vale of Axminster. At the top is *Lambert's Castle*, an Iron Age hill fort. The stroll to the top is not too taxing (the easiest approach is from the S, or Dorset, side) and on a clear day you can see E along the coast to Portland Bill, W as far as Start Point and N inland to the line of the Mendips. It is an unusual view: the site is so high and far inland that the line of the cliffs ripples up and down below you like a frill of seaweed.

Heanton Punchardon [2*] Perched on a hill with sweeping view over the estuary to where the rivers Taw and Torridge meet. Pride of the church is a richly carved Perpendicular tomb in N chancel to Richard Coffin d 1523. Fine but not so fine as a similar tomb chest at Bishop's Nympton. R.A.F. Chivenor is near and many overseas airmen are buried in the churchyard. There is also the grave of Edward Capern, "The Postman Poet", whose little postman's handbell hangs in a niche in the tombstone.

Hele. *See* Ilfracombe.

Hemyock [15] Unlovely village but good things in it. W of the church is the old castle, its gatehouse and fortifications now used as farm buildings, ivy clad and romantic. Church gate is 1813, Gothick. Town pump, 1902, cast iron like dripping wax and economically celebrating the reign of Victoria, the coronation of Edward and the peace in South Africa.

Whitehall, 1 m NW. Unassuming L-shaped house, much altered but once the home of the Brewers and probably containing parts of a 13c building; Lord William de Brewer founded Dunkeswell Abbey near by in 1202. Upstairs is some brilliantly coloured Jacobean plasterwork.

Hennock [28] Meaning "High oak" and exactly so above the Teign. Ancient village dating from Saxon times it passed to the Norman lord of Okehampton and then, in the 13c, to Torre Abbey. Parts of the Vicarage date from this time. Another ancient house is *Longlands*, now a farm: early Tudor in stone and half timbering, with two-storey porch and screens passage.

St Mary the Virgin is granite, 15c. Carved ceiling above the rood: suns and stars in original colouring of blue and gold. Beneath is the 15c screen, simply and truthfully restored, cornice now gone, painted wainscot well preserved having been covered by box pews; Norman font c. 1170 with crude leaf carving. In the S porch delicate

boss of madonna and child by Harry Hems of Exeter. At the lych gate an exhortation to children to respect the churchyard, precisely Victorian in style and sentiment.

High Bickington [6] On a plateau above the Taw. Churchyard has an avenue of yew alternating with beech, the two greens making felicitous contrast. Inside, the first impression is of glimmering, polished carving: this is the largest collection of old bench ends in Devon, 70 of them. S door has a Norman arch with bands of decoration in fair preservation; Norman font deeply carved with formalised flowers, wheels, strapwork, surrounded on two sides by an 18c balustrade, probably the old altar rail.

High Bray [3] On a spur above the Bray valley with double view. A quarry to the S. Church has a Norman font decorated with zigzags and palmettes; one of the capitals has an engaging carving with heads and twined rope. Parts of the rood screen removed to tower arch.

Highampton [8] Dull village set high above the Torridge. The church, about ½ m away, has grand views in all directions from a churchyard deep in drifts of meadowsweet. Norman S door with carved capitals; inside is a Norman font with tall, gawky piers of 1834. *Burdon Manor*, ¾ m SW, now a farm and much decayed, dated 1569 but, apart from two mullioned windows, details are Georgian.

Hittisleigh [16] Church on a hilltop with barton and farm cottages; the village, such as it is, on the next hill. Simple church still lit by oil lamps; nave 1250–1300; N aisle 15c; Norman font; original ceiled wagon roof; box pew in N aisle with inscription dated 1619.

Hockworthy [14] Hillside village of substantial stone cottages. Church, *St Simon and St Jude*, rebuilt 1865 by Davies, has a bold, clear interior with subtle use of coloured marble; plain Norman font; simply carved Jacobean chest.

Holbeton [27] Steep village street of stone-built thatched cottages, the road beyond leading a mile or so on to the

head of a creek. There is no direct outlet to the sea and so, with little pressure to develop, the village remains quiet and unspoiled. The church has remarkable carvings, 15c and Victorian. Rood and parclose screens, c. 1535, were tactfully restored by Sedding; he carved the sedilia in the same style as the screens, using the same motifs. You may see how he subjugated his own style to that of the mediaeval craftsmen by comparing the choir and the bench ends in the nave which have luxuriant, natural forms similar to Sedding's work at Salcombe. The door, possibly by a different hand in a more craft style with hounds, fox, rabbit and pheasant. Font, c. 1160, with lions and palms, abstract pattern and two sides blank arcaded. In N chancel chapel the Hele family monument has four tiers of kneeling figures like the dress circle at the last judgement.

The *Dartmoor Union* is the old workhouse turned pub. *Flete House*, 1¼ m NE, rolling pile in Victorian Tudor, twin turreted tower, numberless windows mullioned and transomed. Built about 1878 by Norman Shaw for an Australian millionaire: archetypal palace for the *nouveau riche*.

Holcombe Burnell [28*] Countryside of deep, fertile valleys with views of Dartmoor. Church and charming Tudor barton stand side by side, the village (rather poor) lying at some distance. Church has remains of a Norman arch above the S door. Inside are painted panels from the lower half of the old screen; in the N chancel monument to Sir Robert Dennis: 16c tomb chest beneath an ogee arch, effigy missing, also used as an Easter Sepulchre; on ledge of a window in N aisle small headless St Peter in alabaster, delicately carved; Victorian box pews.

Holcombe Rogus [14] *Holcombe Court* presents a superb Tudor façade. There has been a house here since the Conqueror but the present mansion was built c. 1530 by the Bluetts, who lived here, generation after generation, until gambling debts forced a sale in 1858. The next owners altered the interior but not the front. This presents a three-storey tower with arms of the Bluetts. The mass is balanced by the Great Hall with vast transomed windows and by a huge dovecote. The hall is Victorian inside but there is much Elizabethan carving and plasterwork. Perhaps the most unusual room is the 65 ft, 16c Long Gallery running across the top of the house: the low plaster ceiling coves down like the top of a railway carriage to meet the panelling below. The house is set in a wooded landscaped garden with a chain of ornamental ponds.

Near the house, but on the other side of a high wall, is *All Saints* church. Approached up a quiet street, the vicarage on one side and, on the other, the old priest's house, said to be 16c but looking older. The church stands just beyond and draws your eye with the rich and delicate S porch of 1343, fan vaulted within. Interior is very fine: magnificent Jacobean carving in the screen of a large pew in the N aisle, plain panelling below, balusters above topped with medallions showing scenes from Genesis and Exodus. This panelling formerly enclosed the Bluett chapel (N chancel) and was placed here during the restoration of 1875–89. The woodwork used in the N (Bluett) and S chancel chapels is from St Peter's Tiverton, according to Pevsner; the E side of the Bluett chapel has been eked out with a little carving from another old screen. Fine 15c wagon roof in N aisle. Elaborate Jacobean monuments in the Bluett chapel.

Hollacombe [8] Remote, scattered hamlet near Holsworthy. *St Petrock's* church: unbuttressed, 14c with saddleback roof; plain Norman S door with rosette carving to lintel.

Holne [31] Parish below Dartmoor, tranquil and remote, the stone-built village looks down a valley and is unspoiled. Church has a good screen with primitive wainscot paintings, the whole little renovated; pulpit, contemporary with screen, has early 16c coats of arms. Charles Kingsley was born in the vicarage in 1832. Two fine 15c bridges: Holne (Old) Bridge, 2 m ENE, and Holne New Bridge, 1 m NNE.

Holsworthy [7] Clay country. Near by the old railway viaduct strides across the countryside, a more compelling memorial to the Victorians than anything in the town. Holsworthy has had fairs and markets since the 12c but nothing before mid 19c appears to have survived. Church has a small panel of Norman carving in the S porch: a lamb carries the cross and fails beneath the load; also the top of a Norman column.

Inside is a fine, much travelled, organ in carved 17c case; first built for All Saints, Chelsea, during the reign of Charles I, it was sold to Bideford in 1723. Bideford was restored in 1865 and the organ came to rest here.

Blagdon Moor Wharf, 1 m NE of Holsworthy, terminating point of a branch of the Bude Canal cut in the 1870s by James Green. Instead of locks a cheaper system of inclined planes was used: four-ton tub-boats fitted with wheels were hauled up, water-filled barrels acting as counterweights. The old wharf is silted up now but the line of the canal is marked by willows and rushes and there are a few of the old buildings.

Honeychurch. *See* Sampford Courtenay.

Honiton [18] A long handsome street of small town Georgian, remarkably all of a piece owing to a large fire in 1765. Coming at the rise of the age of coaching (Honiton was an important stop on the London–Exeter run), the fire provided the impetus for extensive rebuilding. The only important house from an earlier period is *Marwood*, 1619, at the E end of the town, built by a local physician, John Marwood; Charles I is said to have stayed here on his way to Exeter.

St Paul's church is interesting, built 1837–8 by Fowler. The old parish church, *St Michael*, meant a stiff climb up the hill. The original specification for St Paul's required that it "be built in a plain, substantial manner with as little ornament as can be applied without rendering the building conspicuous by its plainness". The result is an Early Victorian church with Norman decoration. An old print in the vestry shows the church as it appeared at its opening, with the original "Norman" pulpit standing high on a single, twisted column in the middle of the chancel and obstructing the view of the altar — reflecting the importance of sermons in those days. It has been replaced now by the less romantic Victorian brown, in a more conventional position.

Just beside St Paul's are *All Hallows Grammar School*, 1770, and *Chapel*, probably the oldest building in the town and now a museum. There is a small exhibition of lace making with examples of Honiton lace, including a wedding veil which cost £84 in the 1860s. Honiton lace is light and deli-

cate, like Brussels lace, and was probably introduced by the Huguenots in the 16c.

At the extreme E end of the town is a pretty tree-lined approach with 19c toll gate and the *Copper Castle*, early 19c castellated. At the extreme W is *St Margaret's Hospital*, thatched early 19c Gothick almshouses in fairly ruinous condition; the St Margaret's Charity dates from 1374 and is still active.

Up on the hill S is *St Michael's*, the old parish church. Inside completely gutted by fire in 1911 and the rebuilding was pretty successful: spacious, there are no pews, and with natural coloured wood, it feels like some high pleasant barn. Thomas Marwood, father of him who built the house, is remembered here by a beautifully incised stone. He was physician to Queen Elizabeth and in 1592 he cured the Earl of Essex when the case had been given up as hopeless.

Hope, Inner and Outer. *See* South Huish.

Horrabridge [23] At first sight a large and unpleasing village on the A386 between Tavistock and Plymouth. But just off the main road is an enclave of old cottages, some hung with coloured slates in jolly, geometric patterns. Their gardens run down to the river, which is here crossed by an ancient bridge with crude pointed arches and recesses for foot travellers. Near by is *Sortridge House*, early Elizabethan.

Horwood [5*] On the end of a ridge overlooking the Taw and Torridge Estuary. Attractive village, with *St Michael's* a most interesting church. Early 16c bench ends in the N aisle and some older, child-sized benches. Lady recumbent in the N chancel chapel, a delicate and individual face, she wears a horned headdress and her children shelter beneath her cloak – probably Elizabeth Pollard, 1377–1430. Odd piscina with drain, unearthed in the 1889 restoration, as was the small figure, originally from the reredos, which now stands in a niche above the S porch; Jacobean altar rails in N chancel chapel; pulpit, 1635, elegantly carved; fragments from the top of the screen plastered into the S wall. 1 m W is *East Leigh Manor*, Gothick windows and pillared portico. St Michael's well was said to cure "sore eyes and eruptions".

Huish [6] Surrounded by rich park-land of the Heanton Satchville estate. Church rebuilt 1873 by G. E. Street and a striking example of his style. Structural work: pillars, arches etc. is bold but with subtle nuances; decoration is confined to furnishings: altar rails, font, all rich and faintly Moorish. Hammer-beam roof in nave, chancel ornate with thorn-like carving.

Huntsham [14] The village post office is housed in a quaint lodge-like structure with steep pitched roofs and diamond leaded panes. *Huntsham Court,* "Tudor" pile of 1869 by Ferrey, built on the site of an earlier house. Within its park lies the church: bits of old screen in the reredos; pulpit formed from three fine, old bench ends.

Huntshaw [5*] Undisturbed and tranquil hamlet amidst the conifer-clad uplands of the Forestry Commission. In 1439 all who helped in rebuilding Huntshaw church were granted indulgences and most of the fabric is of this date except the chancel, which is 12c. Wagon roof with carved ribs and bosses; richly carved piers with rope-twined figures; three image niches in capitals of N aisle; Thomas Saltren monument is a medallion surmounted by elaborate gilt plasterwork.

Huxham [17*] A tiny parish above Exeter. The church (rebuilt 1871) adjoins a large farm and seems almost part of it. Norman font (restored) with fluting below and formalised flowerets round the rim; a delicately carved screen saved from an earlier church.

Iddesleigh [6] At the point where the Torridge begins to cut into a gorge before Torrington, shallow views S to Dartmoor with spreading hills like some majestic reclining figure. Church W door has a fragment of 15c carving. Some good things inside: late 13c effigy of cross-legged knight in N chancel chapel, in fair preservation, a tough face; remains of 15c screen across N chancel; Perp. font with Jacobean cover; pulpit also Jacobean, later and more restrained in style; in N chancel, tablet to wife and daughter of Walter Veale, both d 1681, naïve carving of

Horwood: detail of the Pollard monument

101

mother and child standing between pillars topped with pineapples.

Ide [17] Pronounced Ede. Near Exeter but keeping its individuality. At the bottom of the village street *The College*, small enclave of 17c cottages, a ford across the Alphin river and the thatched *Huntsman's Inn.* Further up *Tudor Cottage* is bogus but fun and incorporates some ancient gargoyles. Small 13c bridge.

Ideford [32] Fine, thatched village. Church tower, pinnacled but unbuttressed, has gargoyle on S side. Above a small S chancel door is a Norman tympanum: serpent, palmette and bird, variously described as cock or pelican (perhaps a swan?). Original wagon roof with "Gloria" across nave: single arch of richly carved and painted panels.

Ilfracombe [2] There is an archetypal seaside town plan and Ilfracombe might be its model. Nucleus is an ancient fishing village. By Norman times Ilfracombe had a church $\frac{1}{2}$ m S of the harbour and this marked the limit of the town's natural growth: until the early 19c it remained essentially a single curved street, church at one end and small harbour at the other. Then came the early Victorian craze for sea bathing, the follow-up to the fashion that created Brighton. This early development may be seen in Bath Place with the *Tunnel Baths*, 1836 (Greek Doric entrance), and the terraces up on the hill: Adelaide, Montpelier, Hillsborough. This early development fizzled out, not being supported by efficient transport and paid holidays.

In 1874 came the railway, the harbour was greatly enlarged at the same time, and there followed extremely rapid development in the last quarter of the 19c. The main street was still the same long, narrow curve but the houses were replaced with tall Victorian buildings. The town spread, inland and up towards the railhead on a level spur above. Finally came an entertainment nucleus, the Pavilion and Winter Garden, set among lawns and formal beds.

At the mouth of Ilfracombe harbour is a conical rock topped by *St Nicholas' Chapel*, landmark for sailors and once their votive chapel. From here you can see the plan: in front is the old harbour and Georgian *Manor House*, much cut

about now; right the *Royal Britannia Hotel*, early Victorian, you can have a drink on its broad terrace and watch the boats. Above that the town proper: terraces of boarding houses, identical yellow brick, with gables, pinnacles and simple bargeboarding picked out in colour (there does seem to be *extra* decoration to seaside houses, is it a kind of liberation?) each with its own individual sign: "Napoli", "Strafford", "The Glen"; wave upon wave they ride across the dips and hillocks of this rocky coast. Away S, at what was the far end of the old town, is the parish church.

Holy Trinity. Parts are Norman. Gorgeous roof: wagon braces terminate in carved wooden figures with gilt crowns and shields, these in turn resting on gargoyles; by the chancel a "Glory", the roof lavishly painted and decorated; Elizabethan pulpit; ancient sarcophagus, mounted in N wall.

Lee. $2\frac{1}{2}$ m W. Rocky bay veined with marble. The broad combe has a large hotel smack in the middle. Up a pleasant footpath is *Chapel Cottage*, 1840, and a farm, reputedly 14c, where you can have tea in a fuchsia-drenched garden. Church of *St Matthew*, very odd; built 1837, full of black, Jacobean, carved oak, including musician's gallery, pulpit, panelling and front pews.

Chambercombe Manor. 1 m SE. 15c house; domestic, twisted, sunken and romantic. Furnished with period furniture; private oratory with some early stained glass; secret room; kitchen with enormous 800-year-old cider press. Standing in a pretty sheltered combe with its own water garden, tea arbour.

Ilsington [31] At the edge of Dartmoor with *Haytor Rocks*, a significant landmark from many points E of the moor, lying within the parish. The village perches on a steep valley side with woods below; John Ford (1586–1639), dramatist, was born here. *St Michael's Cottages*, the 16c church house subdivided, mark the entrance to the churchyard. Porch above the lych gate was once used as a schoolroom and fell down in 1639 when the gate below was banged too hard. Church's most dramatic feature is just in front of the chancel where the wagon roofs of nave and transepts meet at the fourth bay of the nave with a timber bridge to carry the lateral thrust. Churchyard was en-

larged N during the 19c to include parts of the derelict Manor House, of which traces can still be seen.

Instow [2] Small resort looking across the Taw estuary to Appledore on the opposite bank. Pretty early 19c villas down by the shore. The old village lies well away up the hill: a few farmhouses and a good view. Church has two carved capitals recording that Richard Waterman and his wife Emma built the aisle in 1547; mediaeval Barnstaple tiles in chancel; Sibthorpe memorial in painted slate to the great botanist, d 1797.

Inwardleigh [9] Hilltop village in rolling country N of Dartmoor. Church has a re-cut Norman font. Ancient sarcophagus lid by the S door.

Ipplepen [31] Name derived from Celtic means "upland enclosure". Dismal village with an interesting church. Fine. Ashburton-type tower: aisle and porch embattled like a castle. Ancient S door with huge, 1 lb 11 oz, key; part of a Norman tympanum above a N door; pulpit 1430–50 richly carved and gilt; screen *c.* 1450 reached by an elegant 18c stair. Altar rails dated 1724; 18c candelabra in tower arch. Small carved wooden figure in messenger's attitude high on a pillar by organ.

Ivybridge [27] Tiny village until the mid 19c when the combination of china clay deposits, water and the railway caused the building of large paper mill. The present factory of 1862 is not at all unhandsome with imposing round-headed windows. The wizened heart of the old town is just below the mill with a narrow bridge over the brown and splashy Erme. Beside it is the *London Hotel*, early Victorian but progressively enlarged to cope with growing custom. Main road now runs further down over a new bridge. The town proper, although quite small and perched on the edge of Dartmoor, seems like a bit of the Midlands: dull and sooty.

Jacobstowe [9] Lower half of church tower is Norman with semi-circular W door enlivened with a little Perp. carving. Interior totally restored, with fireplace, the chimney being dressed up

as a buttress. Near by is the *Old Rectory*, given new façade *c.* 1840, Gothick details including a glass porch. *Broomfield*, ½m W, vast neo-Tudor of 1870 by Devey; the lodges, economical in finish, can be seen by the road. *Lower Cadham*, 1 m. N, exquisite Tudor house on the E-plan, two-storey porch; the farm goes back to Domesday.

Kelly [20] The house is Georgian added on to an earlier Tudor building. Near by stands an early 18c granary, cool in style with a wheel window above an ornate portico, it looks like some 18c Swedish castle; now in a state of romantic decay: from inside comes the cackle of chickens. The villagers used regularly to perform plays in the granary and in the church is a memorial to Mary Elfreda Kelly, founder of the Village Drama Society.

Kenn [29] Countryside of red earth, red roads, red sandstone and red cattle. Two distinct villages: one Kennford just off the A38 and the other, more peaceful, just S of the church. This has a Norman table top font and early 16c screen with painted wainscot; below the tower arch are early 16c paintings in panels, which probably lined the sanctuary until the restoration of 1858. The church guide contains an interesting contemporary account of this restoration. Old bench ends and ancient pews in nave; mediaeval stained glass in vestry.

Haldon House, c. 1900, 3 m WNW. More interesting for its history than present appearance. Earlier house built late 18c by Sir Robert Palk. In 1788 Palk built *Haldon Belvedere* as a memorial to his friend and fellow Anglo-Indian, Stringer Lawrence, who had left him a fortune; this is a triangular Gothick keep on the edge of a wooded escarpment; a landmark for miles.

Kennerleigh [13] Remote and hidden village of a few thatched cottages. Church much restored but with bits of the cornice of the old screen re-used in a vestry partition in the NW corner; N aisle has ceiled wagon roof.

Kentisbeare [14] Surrounded by pretty, hummocky hills. The church stands on one of them, which gives it a pleas-

ant outlook. Inside a good screen, but a more unusual W gallery dated 1632 with painted panels and meandering verse. In the S chancel chapel is some Elizabethan panelling stuck over with simple coats of arms and bits of baluster, from Bradfield House; also a painted door to the rood screen. Two 16c tomb chests; 18c pulpit and reader's desk. In the churchyard a crooked yew said to be 1,300 years old.

Priesthall. Just by the church gate a mediaeval priest's house with three rough screens similar to those at St Katharine's Priory, Exeter, but here better preserved, probably 13c. An unglazed 14c window. Good example of an unpretentious dwelling of the period.

Blackborough. On an extraordinary situation: a high promontory 2 m ENE, the once magnificent view now obscured by overgrown trees. Built by the Earl of Egremont in 1838, the church is lean, but not austere, neo-Gothic, now getting a bit crumbly. A cheap church with something of the feel of an 18c nonconformist chapel.

Kentisbury [3] No village, the parish is made up of a few farms and houses often ½ m or more apart. The church stands by an old barton dated 1674, making a pretty group. *St Thomas* remained completely unaltered until 1875 and then met the usual fate. One reads of altar rails disappearing into a farmhouse to mend the banisters, roof bosses thrown away. However, if you didn't so mourn the old church you might say the restoration wasn't a bad example of Victoriana: pulpit in coloured plaster, simple wooden screen to the N chapel, roof painted in *Art Nouveau.* S porch has some original 15c roof bosses, and a sundial dated 1762. A good walk along the disused railway track opening up to marvellous views.

Kenton [29] Main road village in a dip of the hills not far from the Exe estuary. Voluptuous countryside: in mid July great dark trees ride against golden fields of ripening oats and barley.

The church is architecturally all of a piece, built late 14c and not much altered since. Charming exterior of local red sandstone encrusted with decoration in Beer stone: image niches, fleurons, gargoyles, pinnacles, castellations, a delicate riot. The S porch corbel

heads of lady in horned headdress and bearded man are said to be portraits of Henry IV and Joan of Navarre. Tactful restoration inside, mostly by Herbert Read. Pulpit is 15c, wooden, painted, the style full blown and elaborate (restored parts are left unpainted); it is there thanks to Baring Gould who discovered the discarded pieces in 1866. Screen with remarkable painted panels of 1455, a series of apostles et al, clumsy but very attractive; above is the 10 ft rood (by Read), the great weight carried on slender pillars like a grove of trees. Door leading off chancel to Lady Chapel made from old bench ends.

Starcross. A watering place that never quite made it, on the marshy W bank of the Exe, half forgotten and curiously attractive.

Oxton. 2 m W. Manor house 1781–2 with Greek Doric porch in a setting of tropical luxuriance. Small lake, with Victorian ironwork bridge. The area around is dotted with prosperous thatched farmhouses.

Killerton. *See* Broad Clyst.

Kilmington [36] Sprawling agricultural village. *Coryton Park*, 1756, brick, stone dressed and handsome. *St Giles* church ruthlessly rebuilt in 1862 except for the tower, monuments rehung since the older church including a lady, d 1756, "who in her last moments desired her bones might not be removed from hence".

King's Nympton [6] A sacred place since immemorial time. *Nymet* derives from the old name of the river Yeo and means "holy" or possibly "river at a holy place or grove". The local pub is called "The Grove".

Important and beautiful church, *St James.* Only superficially restored, it still has its Georgian furnishings and a late mediaeval screen with Renaissance carving. The structure is basically 15c; a tiny primitive door in the N chancel has a sanctuary ring, suggesting it may have been moved from elsewhere. It is certainly earlier than its Tudor frame; wagon roofs and bosses; two bands of highly decorated gilt above the rood screen form a *ceilure*; the rest of the wagon roof above the chancel was removed during the last century and replaced by painted and gilt stars, clouds, crucifix and texts: "Glory, Honour, Wisdom & Power", a visual

Hallelujah Chorus; Jacobean panelling in S chancel chapel; 18c box pews, pulpit and altar rails. 18c reredos: Ionic pilasters picked out in gilt with texts. 18c font, as at Charles, which is dated 1727, the one here is rather more dumpy. The best of the King's Nympton plate is on loan to the Victoria and Albert Museum, but it has a second best set dated 1756, given by the squire to mark the innoculation (sic) against smallpox of himself, his family and 80 villagers.

Kingsbridge [34] Set at the head of an estuary. You can stroll along the waterside watching yachts; roomy Victorian villas to the E. The town has many 18c houses, some slate hung in local style with varied patterns and colours. The old nucleus of the town starts midway up Fore St with the early Victorian Town Hall fronted by triple arched doors and surmounted by an unusual ball clock of 1875 on a curved neck, slate hung like an armadillo. Just beyond is *The Shambles*: market arcade supported on stout granite pillars of 1585, the upper part renewed in 1796. Behind is *St Edmund's* church, dedicated 1414 but the font is 13c and probably came from the earlier chapel. S porch is 15c; fragments of 15c rood screen used in pulpit; fine parclose screen; E pier in S aisle has a primitive carving of St Martin dividing his cloak; in the same aisle is the Drury monument by Flaxman *c.* 1817: grey marble with fluid composition of female figures. Pair of 18c churchwarden's staves. On the outer S chancel wall is a tablet to "Robert, commonly called Bone, Phillip" d 1793:

"Here I lie at the churchyard door
Here I lie because I'm poor.
The further in the more you'll pay
Here I lie as warm as they."

Further on up Fore St is the old *Grammar School*, founded 1670; there is a monument to its first master in the S transept of the church. In Wallingford Rd is the Tudor gatehouse to *Well House*; the surviving mansion behind is Georgian. On the hill E is *Dodbrooke* with St Thomas church. It has a 15c wall painting much redone, wagon roofs with bosses and a Norman font, but none of this is of great interest.

King's Nympton

Kingskerswell [32] Large village sliced through by main road and main line railway. The new village, overflow from Newton Abbot, is characterless; the old centre round the church has many pretty and distinguished houses. Church has three 14c effigies, knight, man and woman all Dirhams, the local family. Wainscotting of screen now serves as choir stalls; large panels of 18c carving: putti and winds, in S transept; a little mediaeval stained glass in S aisle; ancient, unusually small S door. Churchyard has been enlarged and now includes a few stumpy walls, all that remains of the Dirhams' mediaeval manor house.

Kingsteignton [32] Large urbanised village NE of Newton Abbot. A stream runs through the churchyard dipping underground by the W door and then emerging to power a mill wheel. From the S porch you can view the Newton Abbot marshalling yards. Inside of doorway has delicate pattern of spiralling cords; S door densely carved with leaves and fruit—the same carving down but painted wainscot now forms choir stalls.

Kingston [27] Dull village not far from south Devon coast. Church has a reader's seat made from an ancient pew.

Kingswear [35] Lying on the estuary opposite Dartmouth. It rises up a steep slope with very little level ground; the churchyard is cut deep into the hillside. The *Redoubt Hotel* crowns the summit where once there was a Civil War strong point. *Kingswear Castle* at the mouth of the estuary was built 1491–1502 as part of the Dartmouth defences. Linked to Dartmouth by car ferry.

Lamerton [23] The village strings out along three roads in a triangle; at its apex there is a pleasant grouping where an avenue of trees leads to the church, the vicarage and a priest's house, this last rebuilt from 15c materials. The old church was destroyed by fire in 1877—"such was the fury of the flames that the bells melted without falling". Two interesting monuments were saved: that to the Tremaynes was erected 1588, re-erected 1707 and has a potted history in verse of three generations. Fortescue monument 1650: busts of man and wife in an arched niche stockily holding hands. *Collacombe Manor*: Handsome Tudor manor house off the main road between Tavistock and Launceston; dating from late 15c, imposing central section added 1574: Tudor influenced by Italy, porch with pediment, the pattern echoed by the garden gateway and a huge hall window; they make the house beautiful and proud.

Landcross [5] Smallest parish in Devon, in a bowl-shaped valley of the Torridge; the village is scattered amongst orchards. Little church, perched above like a hen on its nest, has a charming interior, quite small, with a number of things picturesque and romantic rather than precious or unique. Old tiles, old bench ends, pieces of Elizabethan and Jacobean panelling, very confused and cut about, set on each side of the altar; oddments of linenfold panelling; pulpit with early Renaissance panels.

Landkey [3] Strung along a shallow valley. The church has two exquisite effigies of a knight and lady, the work of a gifted artist: lady lies with her hips swayed to the right, her dress gathered toward that point then falling gracefully back to her feet, a posture feminine, provocative and familiar from countless manuscripts; the knight is turned to one side, his legs crossed, a difficult pose which the sculptor has

Dovecote, **Lewtrenchard**

Wortham Manor, **Lifton**

organised with great ease, E end of the N aisle. Contrast this with the more conventional, stiffer 14c effigy of a lady in the S transept (Acland chapel).

Acland Barton, 1 m N. Home of the Aclands dating from 12c but altered 1591 and later; much early Tudor work. The house itself refaced during Victorian times but the chapel wing at right angles to it retains its mediaeval character.

Langtree [5] Plain cob village with high, wide outlook. Large church with fine late 17c pulpit: cherubs, garlands, fruit covered with a thick coat of shiny brown varnish; two Victorian chairs with 16c Flemish reliefs set in the backs; Royal coat of arms: G2R, surmounted by cherubs and obelisks.

Lapford [13] On a hill above the Yeo valley. A strong local industry making canned milk pudding has brought much new building; local shops loyally stock the product. The church has

remarkable woodcarving: beautiful screen almost complete and little restored; magnificent wagon roof with a *ceilure*; many old bench ends.

Bury Barton, $\frac{3}{4}$ m S. Claimed to be a private chapel licensed 1434 but now indistinguishable from any ancient thatched farm building save for a damaged and blocked 15c E window.

Lee. *See* Ilfracombe.

Lewtrenchard [20] Tudor house, now an hotel, home of the Gould family for 400 years. Especially the Rev. Sabine Baring Gould, author of *"Onward Christian Soldiers"* and fierce champion of the preservation of old churches, but not in the strict sense. Thus for his own house and church he plundered abroad from local Tudor houses, e.g. *Orchard*, which he picked to pieces, even to the date above the door. It would thus be unwise to assume as original any single thing one sees in the house. It now reflects the late Victorian

taste for intense richness in small spaces; a taste possibly inspired by the small private rooms in Italian Renaissance palaces, such as the apartments of Catherine d'Este at Mantua. There is also a ballroom, added by Baring Gould, who had eight daughters to marry off, with lavish plasterwork in the Flemish style. The house contains a collection of Gould family portraits from 1615 onwards.

The church opposite was restored by Baring Gould's grandfather in 1835 and re-restored by Gould himself at the end of the century. He had salvaged some remnants of the original screen when a boy, and had it rebuilt from these fragments. I find his restoration fun, but this is not a purist view. There are some good *original* bench ends.

A little E is the *Dower House*, a pretty, minor Tudor house with a farm and a few cottages grouped around a menhir.

Lifton [20] You approach the village

109

from the E under an old, ivy covered railway arch that looks like some 18c hermitage; thence the extremely busy A30 bisects the village. The church, *St Mary*, sits in command above the town; it has a Norman font decorated with intertwined arches with a pattern of flowers above and heads at the four corners.

Wortham Manor is 1½ m N. In ten years all may be changed but today the manor's charm is that of a distinguished early Tudor house in romantic decay. A splendid N porch gives directly on to a muddy farmyard where healthy hens scratch and strut. On the S side sheep graze by the stone-flagged path which leads to the main doorway of carved stone. The house is L-shaped with a polygonal stone turret at the rear, the whole surrounded by gardens which have long since reverted to the rough.

Little Torrington [5] Standing on a flat-topped hill overlooking the bends of the river Torridge opposite Great Torrington; but the hedges are high and you cannot see the fine views as you drive past. *St Giles* church has been restored: Royal coat of arms: VR in tiles in S porch; font fowl Norman standing on a 15c base. Jacobean cover; organ screen has narrow panels of 15c (?) carving said to have come from the old pulpit; brass on S chancel window ledge to Jone Phesant, d 1635, "esteemed for her grave and matron-like conversation".

At *Taddington* a 17c bridge by an 18c toll house. Also a tiny chantry chapel, complete with miniature tower, formerly chapel to the leper hospital.

Littleham (Nr Bideford). [5] Rolling country with views W. *St Swithin's* church has lush Victorian tomb to General Hope Crealock C.B., C.M.G., lying splendidly bearded atop his tomb chest; in contrast a tender 15c painting of bishop with crozier in the N transept, tactfully restored: ancient muniment chest hewn from a single tree trunk; Renaissance bench ends. On the S edge of the parish is the pretty Yeo valley, a tributary of the Torridge; an old toll cottage here with Gothick windows.

Littleham (Nr Exmouth). [29] An old parish which still includes Exmouth, but the village of Littleham is mostly an ugly hotch potch of recent building.

Of the church, *St Margaret with St Andrew*, the chancel chapel is 14c; monument to Lady Horatio Nelson on the E wall: she lived at Exmouth and is buried in the churchyard. Slate tablet to Henry Stafford, d 1746, with a jolly man o'war, flags flying, picked out in paint. Outside right of the S door four feet from the ground a Saxon scratch dial.

Littlehempston. [31] At the ford which was one of the main river crossings to Dartington, 14c palace of the Dukes of Exeter, stands the *Old Manor*, an exquisite small mediaeval house built *c.* 1400 and continuously occupied since, wonderfully preserved with late 15c fresco in the hall. (Not open to the public.) The main railway line thunders past the village proper. Church has three much battered 14c effigies.

Loddiswell [34] Rambling, stone-built village, the well lying just below. Church has a Norman font with band of saltires above and ram's horns pattern below; Breeches Bible, printed Geneva 1568.

Loxbeare [14] On the B3221 from Tiverton to South Molton above a steep valley. A very small church with Norman arch to S door, zigzag moulding. Interior restored but some Jacobean woodwork retained; Jacobean altar rails and some fragments built into the choir stalls; pulpit with sounding board. According to Hoskins the tower retains a set of mediaeval bells dating from Henry VI's time, and still in their original cage.

Loxhore [3] The villages are much dispersed round here: sometimes ½ m or more between one clump of houses and the next. But the farmhouses are very fine with ancient stone barns and granaries. 15c wooden arcading in the church: two piers carry a straight entablature, the whole held together by wooden dowels. Font cover 16c with original colouring. Unusual tablet in E wall of N aisle to Mary Weber, d 1671: an elegaic verse in incised metal.

Luffincott [7] On the crest of a hill above the Tamar. No village, the church stands almost within a farmyard: an unassuming building with Georgian sash windows in the N aisle and a broad low tower rebuilt 1791; the barton is also Georgian.

Lundy [-] The name derives from the Norse for "puffin". It was certainly a Viking stronghold, a base for raiding the N Devon coast, and many pirates since, English, French and even Turkish, have found the island convenient for smuggling depot and useful for other dishonest purposes. 11 m from Clovelly, 25 m from Bideford, barren, rocky, Lundy was a godsend and temptation to many colourful characters. One of the earliest was Sir William de Marisco, outlaw and freebooter; the castle, built by Henry III, hopefully to subdue the island, was named after the Mariscos. Others followed, including Thomas Benson M.P. who leased the island around 1750, profiting from his investment so outrageously that he had to flee to Portugal to escape hanging. Since 1969 Lundy has belonged to the National Trust.

Lundy today is almost totally unspoiled, in winter the *Lundy Gannet*, the island's own fishing boat, makes the trip to Bideford two or three times a week, serving the population of about 25 people. During the summer there are frequent trips from the north Devon coast bringing holidaymakers to spend a day on the island. During the trip you get good views of the Devon coast and, on a clear day, Pembrokeshire. The arrival is pleasantly primitive: the vessel stands off while two tenders ferry passengers to the rickety landing stage. (Not for babies in prams!)

The village, with hotel (no licensing hours here), general stores and souvenir shop where the Lundy puffin stamps may be bought, are at the S end of the island near the landing stage. Here too are the ruins of *Marisco Castle*, and the *Old Lighthouse*, built 1819. N is a long, grassy plateau with dry stone walling, cattle and ponies. During the nesting season you can see thousands of seabirds along the cliffs: puffin, guillemot, razorbill and kittiwake. The *Devil's Lime Kiln* is a 300 ft deep chasm in the SW.

Luppitt [15] Small, dispersed village lying along a valley leading into the Blackdown hills and dominated by Beacon hill. Church, set just below the top of a steep slope, has gargoyles on the N side. Exceptionally fine Norman font, deeply and vigorously carved with centaur, horses, fighting men etc. Another piece of Norman carving in S chancel. Spectacular wagon roof with

Lundy: the landing

massive semi-circular beams arching across the chancel, forming a great cross. Alabaster head, 15c, on display in N aisle. Part of a brass palimpsest, mid-15c.

Lustleigh [28] Much visited moorland village with well preserved charm and plenty of tourist shops. It has its fair share of interesting old buildings, including the *Parsonage* (hall with 15c timber roof) and the *Old Vestry* E of church and once used as the school. *St John's* has three 13c effigies: two knights and a lady. Door sill to S porch has Celtic lettering; screen freely and richly carved; weird heads above arches, wainscot with small sculptures instead of the more usual paintings; plain 1300 sedilia and piscina; pulpit and bench ends have lively and attractive carving by Herbert Read, late 19c.

Lydford [20] Once one of the most important and largest towns in Devon and site of a Saxon mint. Hard to believe now although it is still part of a huge parish taking in nearly half of Dartmoor, about 50,000 acres in all.

All that remains of past greatness is the Castle built 1195 to house offenders against the stannary (tin) laws. The Stannary Parliament was savage and independent and its "justice" notorious:

"Oft have I heard of Lydford law.
How in the morning they hang and
*   draw*
And sit in judgement after."

St Petrock's church is 15c with additions. Some Renaissance glass in the chancel, all jumbled up but showing faces of a gaiety and grace, utterly different from mournful Victorian glass. In the churchyard a charming stone to George Routleigh watchmaker with a sense of humour who was;

".........Wound up
In hopes of being taken in hand
by his Master.

And of being thoroughly cleaned
and repaired
And set a-going
In the world to come".

Lydford Gorge is a chasm cut deep through the rock by the river Lyd. The sides of the Gorge are thickly lined with oak, beech and sycamore and carpeted with flowers, ferns and grasses, deliciously peaceful and sweet scented. The river cascades through the dark rock with a number of falls, notably the *White Lady* fall of 100 ft. The gorge is now owned by the National Trust, who maintain a path passing through some of the loveliest woodland scenery in Devon.

Lympstone [29] Seaweed smells drift through the town from the estuary nearby. Lying further away from Exeter than Topsham, it has escaped that kind of facelifting, but there are a number of Georgian houses. In the back streets near the river the cottages often open

Luppitt:
the font

directly on to little courts and, un-disturbed by traffic, there is a rich street life: children play, dogs yawn and sleep, neighbours chat, a man goes from door to door selling eggs or fish putting them straight into a held out dish. At the river side, where the house foundations rise directly from the estuary mud, is a local landmark: an Italianate clock, mem-orial to Mrs Peters erected by her hus-band to mark her kindness to the poor.

The church, 1869, is disappointing, but there is a fine vestment cupboard with the date 1594 scratched on it; rich carving represents the Trinity and Pas-sion as well as animals, huntsmen, flowers etc.

Lynton and Lynmouth [3, 10] Lynton above, the new town created at the rail-head on the cliffs; Lynmouth below, old fishing village peaceful and pretty now but, like Aberfan, one of those places touched by fate.

Two valleys meet here. On the night of 15th–16th August 1952 the pressure of the water was so great that the

Luppitt church roof

river burst its banks as it escaped down to the sea. Power and light were the first things to go. The most fearful memory of the living was the terrifying roar of the waters amid absolute black-ness. Thirty-one people were drowned and many houses destroyed in the holocaust.

Lynton became popular during the Napoleonic wars when the Continent was closed to the English just as they were beginning to appreciate wild, rom-antic scenery. Shelley stayed here in 1812 with Harriet his first wife and wrote to William Godwin: "This place is beautiful... Mountains certainly of not less perpendicular elevation than 1000 feet are broken abruptly into val-lies (sic) of indescribable fertility and grandeur. —The climate is so mild that myrtles of immense size twine up our cottage & roses blow in the open air in winter. —In addition to these is the sea, which dashes against a rocky and caverned shore, presenting an ever changing view."

Many of the pretty little houses date from this period. The *Rising Sun* hotel is older, reputedly 14c. On the front is

the "*Rhenish Tower*" built during the last century to house sea salt and re-built after the 1952 floods.

A steep little cliff railway runs up to Lynton. It is fun to ride in, but the views are masked by trees. Lynton was abruptly created by the arrival of the railway in 1898, a branch from Barnstaple, now closed. It must have been a charming line; you meet its small halts and stations dotted along the contour of the land SW through Parracombe and Blackmore Gate. Lynmouth *Town Hall* 1898–1900 is a jolly edifice, "15c" stonework, "Tudor" half timbering, and "Flemish" barge boarding. The Congregational church, 1904, opposite is similar in style.

St Mary's church stands high on the cliff overlooking beetling cliffs and headlands. Between 1868 and 1905 it was rebuilt three times, and now has a Romanesque chancel and *Art Nouveau* glass in pale colours, the font has *Art Nouveau* carving, the font cover is Elizabethan.

The Lyn and Exmoor Museum — small folk museum with a collection of early water colours and engravings of old Lynmouth, and some material on the old railway.

Watersmeet. Well trodden beauty spot where the E Lyn meets the Combe Park, thickly wooded gorge traversed with paths and waterfalls, a pretty little Victorian Gothick tea house at the bottom. Walks to Lynmouth and Rockford.

Lympstone: Mrs Peters' clock

1 m W, by the sea, is the *Valley of the Rocks*, treeless and bare with rocky outcroppings, extraordinarily different from the coast only a few miles away.

Lee Abbey, 1½ m W of Lynton: abbey only in name and fancy. Built about 1850 in a mixture of styles, some totally fantastic but including Mediaeval Monastic and Tudor. The latest style is an entrance so brutally contemporary that it is as if, to parody Sidney Smith, the Queen Elizabeth Hall had come to the seaside and pupped. Toll lodges 1892 in a Carpathian setting of woods, water and rocks, extravagantly carved barge boarding and heavily leaded windows: Rupert of Hentzau may ride past at any moment. Incidentally the toll is worth it; this *corniche* must be one of the most spectacular in the kingdom. The road follows the contours and keeps near the edge of the sea with glimpses of sheltered coves and wooded gorges. Much of the coast is owned by the National Trust and may only be reached on foot.

Malborough [34] Magnificent coastline from Bolt Head to Bolt Tail, most of it owned by the National Trust. Fine wide view from the N side of the church. *All Saint's* itself is rather dull but the 13c S porch has interesting bosses; altar cloth in N chancel chapel made from two 15c copes; Breeches Bible.

Mamhead [29] Overlooking the Exe estuary and the coast to Sidmouth, an old estate dating back to the 15c, the house rebuilt 1828 by Salvin in Tudor style on the site of the mediaeval castle. Park landscaped by Capability Brown, 1779, and, though neglected and overgrown, still revealing the purposes of the design. *St Thomas* church stands 500 yds from the house on a ledge above the view, its low tower dwarfed by an ancient yew. Inside the maltreated remains of a 15c screen.

Manaton [29] Moorland village of ancient stone cottages set around a wedge-shaped green. *Church House* stands E of church. *St Winifred's* screen has figures set above each other in door jambs as at North Bovey, paintings in wainscot.

Across the valley from the village is *Bowerman's Nose* a life-like, rocky outcrop. The area is dotted with beauty spots—some known, others you find for yourself. One of the former is *Becka Falls*, 1 m SE; even in April the worn river banks tell of years of visitors. But there are countless blissful places, often where the old pack bridges cross the river.

Grimspound. 3 m W. One of the largest and most easily appreciated

Watersmeet
(*see* **Lynton and Lynmouth**)

Bronze Age villages on Dartmoor. An outer stone circle 150 yds diameter and now 2–3 yds in thickness by 2 ft high (it was probably once 10 ft by 5 ft 6 in) encloses about 24 hut circles, some with complete entrances including jambs and lintels. Outside the pound the old fields are still marked by stone walls. 1 m further N some clearly defined hut circles can be seen from the road.

Mariansleigh [13] Remote and unvisited. Fire gutted the church in 1932 and uncovered two 13c pillars in S aisle. Church room by the wayside has a small mediaeval carving of jolly monks.

Marldon [32] Hillside village with fine stone houses but also much suburban infilling from nearby Paignton. Church has two unusual monuments: tomb chests under arches open N and S to chancel and side chapels to Otho Gilbert, d 1492, and his wife, one housing a half life-size effigy; screen once ran between them and must have made an interesting composition. 15c piscina moved to S chancel chapel when it was built by the Gilberts c. 1520. Breeches Bible, 1580. *Church House*, ancient but given the Gothick treatment early last century like the house at right angles to it.

Compton Castle, 1 m N. One of the finest fortified manor houses in the country. The main portcullis entrance rears up, connected to E and W towers by great walls top heavy with corbelling, castellations and machicolations. This stupendous façade was built c. 1500, a few years after Dartmouth Castle and presumably also because of the French threat. The walls protect the earlier house, c. 1420, including the tunnel vaulted chapel and SW tower. By 1750 the mediaeval Great Hall was in ruins, and fifty years later the Gilberts sold Compton. Within living memory Commander W. R. Gilbert, R.N., bought back the house and devoted himself to restoring it; in 1955 he reconstructed the Great Hall.

Martinhoe [3] A cliff parish with especially good views: tumbling rocks and trees frame foregrounds to the wide sea beyond. *Woody Bay* is National Trust, like much of this coast, and cannot be reached by car; there is an idyllic, though steep, walk through the combe to the bay, close-arched trees overhead with total stillness all around.

Sixty years ago an attempt was made to turn Woody Bay into a resort like Ilfracombe or Lynmouth: a pier was built, the place was to be served by the then thriving Bristol Steamer Service, but the scheme collapsed and Woody Bay remains unspoiled.

Martinhoe proper is an unexciting hamlet. "11th century" says the notice outside the church, but it was thoroughly restored 1866–7. Elaborate Victorian font.

Marwood [3] The church is set amid a maze of small roads but once found it is very rewarding. Pride is the screen, generally dated 1520, the front richly carved between the ribs of the coving, the back plain with tracery between the ribs like delicate fish bones. Some fine bench ends and old pews, massive, worn and sunken. Saxon font, the square bowl standing on the floor near the present Victorian font. Saxon base under 17c pulpit, helping to support it. Mediaeval floor tiles near pulpit. Jacobean chest. Sundial 1762 outside above S porch shows comparative times at Jerusalem, Vienna, Berlin, Paris, Teneriffe etc. – but not Rome.

Westcott Barton, 1 m NW is a good example of an old Devon barton, originally 17c.

Marystow [20] 14c church has a commanding position on a hilltop. Inside is a Norman font: square with heads at corners, intersecting arches, a little decoration. Also Sir Thomas Wyse's monument: he lies with his wife under a coffered arch, at their heads effigies of children: two older ones kneel, a three-year-old sits plumply in her chair, two babies lie bonneted in their cribs, lace-edged collars and sheets falling tidily around them.

Sydenham. Jacobean manor house built by Sir Thomas Wyse, now a private school for girls. The best view is from the little bridge across the Lyd. The stable block is 18c.

Mary Tavy [23] Mixed village, the old part down by the church is pretty, the new buildings along the main road are not. The church, *St Mary*, is restored, but the original bosses are in the porch. For a short time this was an intensely prosperous area with forty odd mines: tin, copper, arsenic, lead and iron. To carry the traffic the Tavistock Canal was cut in 1803. But by the beginning of this century most of these workings had

closed down and now there are many empty and ruined stone cottages around Mary Tavy. The old workings of the great *Devon and Friendship Mine* may be seen from the main road, and a fine sight they are, gaunt and romantic.

Meavy [24] Lies in a fold of the moors with its church (traces of Norman), the village oak, said to be as old as the church and looking it, and the Royal Oak Inn. It is said that nine people once dined in the oak; it must have been a tight squeeze and a thin supper. Adjoining the church is a Tudor house which belonged to the Drakes. Altogether a pretty, timeless place if you close your eyes to a few suburban houses.

Nearby is *Shaugh Bridge*, where the Meavy joins the Plym in a flurry of brown water, froth and wet boulders. The gorge is clothed with ancient oaks. Fifty years ago B. R. Haydon, among others, came to sketch here; now it is owned by the National Trust. An obvious picnic spot.

Meeth [6] Main road village on rising ground N of the Okement dominated by a thatched 14c inn. Church path of pebbles laid edgewise in patterns and dated 1818. There are a number of such paths in the district made by French prisoners of war. (Did they still languish on four years after the end of hostilities?) *St Michael's* church still has a Norman nave with N window; later additions are Victorian. Norman font with 17c cover. Plain 17c pulpit as at Exbourne (there dated 1665). Royal coat of arms, 1704, primitive and grandiose.

Membury [36] The village is on a hillside with sloping gardens, high walls and banks. A stream runs through the village in a retaining channel – an early form of water supply and drainage. There was a skirmish here between Roundheads and Cavaliers in 1645 and a soldier died, "killed by the church" says the Parish Record; a cannon ball rests on the ledge of his monument. Most of the church is 15c but a Norman pillar has recently been uncovered just below the tower, very short with fluted capital. Yarty chapel with Fry monuments, including one to Frances Fry, d 1758 aged 16, with charming sentimental verse. 13c figure of reclining woman in S transept similar to one at Axminster.

Endsleigh Cottage, **Milton Abbot**

Thomas Wakeley, who founded *The Lancet* 1824 was born in the parish. *Membury Court* and *Waterhouse Farm* are 16c, *Yarty* a little later.

The village takes its name from an *Iron Age hill fort*, ½ m E, easily reached from the road. Up there are good views in all directions and drifting up to you the sweet notes of Membury church clock striking the quarters.

Beckford Bridge, 1 m SW. A miniature pack horse bridge, the oldest in E Devon.

Merton [5] Main road village above the Torridge looking S to Dartmoor. Walter de Merton, founder of the Oxford college, was born here. Church restored and uninteresting except for a Norman font with Jacobean cover.

Meshaw [13] On the main South Molton–Tiverton road. Church is 1838 at its most austere and dull, rebuilt 1879 – a chilling combination. Tower

1690 with tablet recording building by Elizabeth Courtenay, whose husband has a memorial inside the church. Attractive Royal coat of arms 1838 with plaintive lion.

Milton Abbot [23] Fairly ordinary village above the Tamar, it once belonged to Tavistock Abbey, hence the name, and then to the Russells. The estate was considerably developed in the early 19c (when the Bedfords were beginning to make money from their mining interests). A number of attractive Gothick buildings remain from that period, particularly at *Milton Green*, ½ m SE of Milton Abbot on the A384 Tavistock to Launceston road. There is a Tudor building here and in 1829 the 7th Duke built a larger house on to it to form a Poor School and Schoolmaster's House. This was a free school for the children of labourers on the estate, but the master was allowed to take in boarders (most probably the sons of army

officers serving abroad) to supplement his income. The old buildings are very attractive, fronted by a lawn, thick with daffodils in the spring, and shaded by great trees.

Endsleigh. The house stands in a dramatic situation high above a rich curve of the Tamar and looking to the bosomy, thickly wooded hills beyond. Endsleigh Cottage was built in 1810 for the Dowager Duchess of Bedford by Sir John Wyatville; the garden (20 acres) by Repton. Owned now by a fishing syndicate and run as a private hotel.

To call Endsleigh a cottage seems to have been a bit of aristocratic showing off: to anyone else it must appear a sizeable mansion. Its aim is purely to please; thus it is determinedly rustic, romantic and ornate with decorated barge boarding and balconies upheld by barky tree trunks. Here and there arbours nestle against the house, each of a different style and character, and artfully arranged so that one at least will always be in the sun and out of the wind. A broad, grassy terrace, rose arched and with yew walks, leads to ivy covered "ruins" and a charming little shell grotto. This is crusted outside with chunks of marble and flint, the dark and moist interior being inlaid with shells and conches of every size and nature; ferny rocks surround a little pool in the floor. It is the sort of place to give point to a stroll and keep the guests amused. Curiously, although it seeks to entertain, the total effect of the house is a little heavy. It leads the mind on to late Victorian Gothick and to the high seriousness of Victorian ecclesiastical architecture. The N side, where one arrives is a nice example of the domestic, or back side, of Victorian building: a cliff of small windows, drain pipes and dormer arches. It has a character of its own, and perhaps makes the front of the house seem the more strained.

Milton Combe. *See* Buckland Monachorum.

Milton Dameral [5] Dullish upland country. Showy, substantial noncon-formist chapel of 1891, replacing an earlier, humbler version, looks across to the church, whose tower was rebuilt 1892 (any connection in the sequence of events?). Ancient and lovely church door with hinge like a great spider. Inside are old Barnstaple tiles and a plaster Royal coat of arms, 1664.

Modbury [27] Modestly prosperous and well kept little town swinging down hill and up again. At the centre Broad St, Church St, and Brownstone St meet and here are the 16c *Exeter Inn* and the 18c *White Hart Hotel* and *Assembly Rooms*. Brownstone St has the more distinguished houses: at the top is *Traine House* with a long colonnade of double columns like an early Victorian

opera house. Opposite is a conduit dated 1708, a generous composition supported by curtain walls and sur-mounted by balls and pinnacles; another more modest conduit but of the same period in Broad St. Lower down Brownstone St is the *Literary and Scientific Institute*, 1840, with over-massive classical details. Further down on the right is *Chain House*, exquisite Queen Anne in grey stone with portico and dormer windows.

St George's church stands high at the W end of the town. Tomb recesses *c.* 1300 in the S transept the figures very crude and one a mere stump; fine Tudor wall tablet high on E pier of the nave. Outside in the N wall is a 16c door with high band of carving like a square Tudor headdress.

Molland [13] A mediaeval church with unrestored Georgian furnishings, worth going a long way to see. The

Molland

Damage Barton (*see* **Morthoe**)

Georgian work was in itself a restoration of an earlier mediaeval church, and the pillars were cut about to accommodate the box pews; but let that pass: Molland is exquisite. In addition to the pews there is a three-decker pulpit with sounding board and above it an angel with trumpet. Solid tympanum with Royal coat of arms, commandments etc. Below it is a restrained Georgian screen with rounded arch above the gate. Of the mediaeval church there remain fragments of a tomb chest —a double heart stone, according to Hoskins, holding the hearts of one of the Courtenays and his wife. Niche with small figure in last pillar but one towards the E: Norman font. Bishop's chair is Jacobean black and knobbly, all pegs and skittles.

Monk Okehampton [9] Lying in the rather featureless valley of the Okemont. Church, restored 1855 by Harper Arnold, has some delicate Victorian stonework and an E window shown at the 1851 Exhibition.

Monkleigh [5] Above the broad Taw Valley. Old ivy clad lime kilns down by the river resemble some ancient keep. *Annery* is late Georgian fronted with Ionic pillars, one room containing garland framed reliefs of *c.* 1740. More humble *Annery Cottage* at nearby Saltrens has thatched colonnade and Gothick windows. *St George's* church has an unusual Norman font: fluted and gathered in below the goblet and then frilling out again. The *Annery Chapel* is of chief interest: tomb chest to Sir William Hankford, who built Bulkworthy church and was Chief Justice to King Henry V; very fine 16c parclose screen; N chancel wall 16c, bitsy brass wall tablet; wall monument to William Gaye, d 1631: solemn man and wife. This is a church for memorial rhymes, almost every tablet has one. Two slate plates with pictures, 1627 and 1646.

Monkton [18] A little would-be Pre-Raphaelite church, but not quite whole hearted enough. Stained glass by William Morris (except the S sanctuary window). The texts and rather crudely stencilled wall decorations are at least Morris inspired.

Morchard Bishop [13] Large village with a double view, S to Dartmoor and Haytor Rocks and N to Exmoor. Church has an 18c reredos with Corinthian pilasters, 17c altar rails, and reconstructed screen with Renaissance carving between ribs. In the S aisle effigy to John and Margaret Eyston, d 1505, lively carving; he is dressed as a wealthy burgher.

Morebath [14] Set among hills near Exmoor. Church has a Victorian font formed of a magnificent black marble veined pink and grey. Original wagon roof in N aisle.

Moreleigh [34] Long village strung along the side of a hill and looking toward the distant Salcombe estuary. Church said to have been built in the early 14c by Sir Peter Fishacre who had murdered the Rector of Woodleigh in a quarrel. It is now an early 17c restoration with plastered ceiling and grand pulpit with sounding board, overwhelming in so small a church; Norman font, bowl of red sandstone with twining pattern; part of lower half of screen made into reader's desk. W of the church is *Place Barton*, the old manor house, now derelict.

Moretonhampstead [28] Busy little town standing across the main A382 and marking the gateway to Dartmoor. *Almshouses* 1637 with colonnade of

Newton Abbot: street vistas

squat granite pillars, similar to Barnstaple. There are a few 17c and 18c houses round The Square. *Fordar House* with its wisteria-covered neighbour at the end of Ford St are Georgian. Otherwise the town, though pleasant, is unremarkable. Behind the churchyard is *The Sentry*, a piece of common land with a varied view of hills and wooded valleys. St Andrew's church is over-restored; S porch houses tombstones of French officers, prisoners during the Napoleonic wars, who died here while on parole from Princetown.

Morthoe [2] As well as church and inn there is a farmyard at the centre of the village. *Woolacombe Sands* close by: a fine broad swath of clear, clean sand 2 m long with rocky pools and inlets at each end. *Morte Point*, a finger of grass-covered rock stretching out to sea, criss-crossed by footpaths, looking out to Lundy. This coast was an appalling hazard until the lighthouse was lit at *Bull Point* in 1879. Morthoe church has three plain Norman doorways; 13c tower; handsome free-standing tomb chest to Sir William de Tracey, Vicar of

Morthoe, d 1322; and many fine bench ends. Much of the building material is Morte slate the pieces of stone so thin and fine that they give the finished work a very unusual look. The arch to the Norman doorway N of the tower instead of being fashioned with blocks of masonry has narrow, irregular pieces of shale fanning out like a sunburst.

Damage Barton. 1 m. ENE, date stone 1656, fine example of an old Devon barton where the farmhouse (Tudor) and its small, walled garden faces into the farmyard with beautiful old farm buildings. The characteristic shale is used horizontally with great effect in the pillars of the byre—round, like stacks of coins.

Morwellham. *See* Tavistock.

Musbury [36] Small houses of many periods with a good deal of suburban in-filling. The church, *St Michael*, has a large, rather brutal monument to several generations of Drakes, the first d 1588 and the last 1643.

Ashe House. 1 m N. 15c house, 14c tiltyard.

Nether Exe [17*] In the broad alluvial plains of the lower Exe valley: a little, lost, locked chapel, hardly visible for grass growing shoulder high. Reputed to contain a Norman font. Nearby the ruins of an old barton.

Newton and Noss [27] Lying along a side creek of the river Yealm: Newton Ferrers on the N bank, Noss Mayo on the S bank. The steep hillsides sloping down to the water have much modern building but the harsh outlines and colours are softened by thick ilex woods. The creek is prettily lined with old fishermen's cottages and hundreds of yachts bobble about at their moorings, the air rings with the slap of rigging. *St Peter's* church, Revelstoke, by St Aubyn, has a whole-hearted *Art Nouveau* chancel all greenery-yallery.

Puslinch House, 2 m NE of Newton Ferrers. Built 1720 but Queen Anne in style, faded red brick with stone dressings and hipped roof: a square solid house set in lush, yet orderly gardens. The Yonges, who built the house and still own it, came of a line of naval surgeons.

120

Old Noss church, 1½ m SE of Noss village; reached by public footpath to Stoke Point. Abandoned *c.* 1870 and now a ruin, with sweeping views from Bigbury Bay to Bolt Tail.

Newton Abbot [31] A railway town since 1846 and this has determined its character and may seal its fate. S of the main road are rows of small workers' houses. Each street is of a piece yet slightly different from the next, rising one above the other up a ladder-steep hill, their roofs and doorways making charming patterns such as in Beaumont Rd, but there are many more. The professional classes lived over in Devon Square and Courtenay Park in Italianate Cubitt-like villas. The town itself is old, but few early buildings survived the onrush of railway development. *St Leonard's* church tower, 14c, serves the purpose of town cross, the body of the church having been demolished 1836. The other survivals in the town seem out of place: *Manor House*, 1534, with Georgian façade; *Globe Hotel*, 1840, porch with Tuscan columns; *The Hospital*, East St, using parts of

the old workhouse including the impressive entrance, an early work by Gilbert Scott, similar to Tavistock and Bideford. The *Mackrell Almshouses*, 1874, archaic in style and fantastically buttressed, fronted by clipped goblet yews.

There are two churches both on hills away from the town with fine spreading views (they were originally separate parishes). *All Saints'* Highweek has the better position but is almost featureless inside. *St Mary's* Wolborough has a Norman font in red sandstone, cable pattern above palmettes; rood and parclose screens continuing across shallow transepts to form chantry-like chapels, the screens painted and gilt with painted figures on the wainscot, 15c brass eagle lectern, and characteristically 17c monuments to Reynell family. In contrast there is an elegant little 1780 tablet to Mary Frere: grey triangle with delicate ribbon and garlands.

A curiosity is *St Luke's* church, Milber, 1¼ m ESE, built just after the second world war. The design is said by Keble Martin, author of *The Concise*

British Flora in Colour, to have come to him in a dream in 1931. A basilica-like shape distorted to form a broad arrow whose point is the altar. Unhappily the finish and detailing are poor.

Forde House, 1610, built by Sir Richard Reynell, easily seen from the main Torquay road, 1 m E. Flattish E plan. Five light mullioned and transomed windows with semi-circular gables, Dutch feeling. Inside some good plaster ceilings.

Bradley Manor, ½ m WSW. Secluded in a valley, small Gothick manor house. Kernel is the great hall 1419 with plain collar beam roof and arms of Elizabeth I (almost colourless and painted with a whiskery line, most sympathetic to the pale oak beams). Jacobean screen brought here from Ashburton. At the NE end another screen 1530–40 with Renaissance carving, this leads on to the ante chapel. Chapel itself was added 1428. Front added 1495 with charming asymmetrical windows and gables. Owned by the National Trust but still lived in.

Newton Poppleford [30] Long, main

road village of cob and thatch, pleasant but undistinguished. Victorian church of little charm.

Newton St Cyres [28] Village bisected by the main Exeter–Crediton road. The old village street S climbs uphill crossing a ford to a pump at the top, pretty as a calendar, with cottage gardens like baskets spilling over with flowers. Cast iron bridge spans high across the main A377 linking Manor House 1909, with the churchyard. Large church, *St Cyriac and St Julitta*. S porch has boss of sow suckling piglets. This not uncommon boss illustrates an old myth that when there was uncertainty where a particular church should be built a sow was turned free: where she farrowed the church should stand. *Northcote* monument: John Northcote d 1632. He stands easy with sword and baton, one foot upon a skull; two wives, each with her terse verse: "My fruite was small/One sonne was all/That not at all" says one, and the other: "My Jacob had by me/As many sonnes as hee/Daughters twice three". Monument raised by a son who kneels below with wife and children. In the chancel: Sherland Shore, also d 1632, coloured tablet of an intimate little scene: youth leans over a table of books. Early 18c pulpit with sounding board.

Newton St Petrock [5] Rolling dullish country. The church has a Norman font, primitive and irregularly shaped, a tithe map of 1841, many 16c bench ends, and a pulpit, 19c but with old panels.

Newton Tracey [5] On a hillside overlooking a valley. Church, in spite of thorough restoration, still has several 13c windows and an interesting font with decoration of prickly foliage and cable pattern, dated 13c by Pevsner.

Northam [5] The village stands on the top of a low, shelving cliff that rises on a spit in the estuary of the Taw and Torridge. W the rivers have deposited silt to form a marshy plain, on which is Westward Ho! At the mouth of the estuary is Appledore. The three form one parish.
Northam itself is rather dull; a few good Georgian houses high on Orchard Hill; a crowded churchyard full of mariners' graves. The church stands high with wide views over the estuary, its tall tower a landmark for ships. Interior large and restored, but one pier in the N aisle has "This yele was made Anno 1593" carved on it; 13c wagon roof with carved angels; old bass viol, now stringless, once part of the church band.
Westward Ho! Interesting and visually awful. After Kingsley's (to me, unreadable) novel was published in 1855 a company was formed to develop the site as a speculation. It was a promising scheme, as the railway had reached nearby Bideford in 1854 and the site was good with a fine long stretch of sandy beach, one of the best in N Devon and the last before the Cornish border. The Victorian houses, villas and family mansions on four or five floors occupy the best sites just where the cliffs begin to rise. In 1874 the United Services College was opened here. Kipling was one of its first pupils. The level ground in front made excellent playing fields. The school is here no more and now the 20c has spawned its worst on the cricket pitches and football fields: gimcrack, garish and spotty. Just behind the beach is a ridge, or bar, of large, flat, veined stones, and behind that is Northam Burrows on which lies the famous Westward Ho! golf course, grazed by sheep and horses and sublimely open to the sky.
See also Appledore.

North Bovey [28] One of the best preserved of moorland villages, set around a roomy green furnished with pump, ancient cross and commemorative oaks. *Stone Cross* cottage is dated 1736 but many others are as old or older; village hall modern but tactfully thatched. *St John's* church restored 1874 at a cost of £700 so it was not too thorough; many old bench ends; screen door surround has small figures carved above each other as at Manaton; organ loft restored but incorporating small early 18c paintings on wood. *Manor House Hotel*, ½ m NW. Edwardian pile in Jacobean style built 1907 as the seat of Viscount Hambleden.

North Huish [34] Hilltop hamlet overlooking a small side valley of rough pasture. The church looks neglected but this adds to its charm; lower half of the tower may be Norman, spire added later. Inside is a wagon roof with carved bosses and font dated 1662; rich little screen in the S chapel.

1½ m N is *Avonwick*, packhorse bridge crossing a frothy trout stream and overarched by rich, leafy trees; path along the stream, good place for picnics. Nearby, 1 m N of North Huish, is *Black Hall*, with Georgian façade, not easily seen from the road. Victorian lodge, lozenge shaped, with false windows: the diamond leading and mullions picked out in faded paint to balance the real ones.

Northleigh [30] *St Giles* church has some good carving: two 15c screens, bench ends and a Jacobean pulpit. Next the church is a pretty little Victorian Gothick house probably the old school house.

Northlew [8] Village on the Saxon plan: a large irregular square facing inward. It has the feeling of a piazza and invites you to leave the pathways and walk about freely, with glimpses of Dartmoor between the houses. Church is full of exceptionally fine wood carving: old bench ends of 1537, wagon roof in N aisle of the same period luxuriantly carved; screen heavily restored by Read of Exeter who replaced the rood loft. Norman font with decoration of saltires and blank arcading. The old preaching cross, restored, by the church gate.

North Molton [10] Large, rather bleak village on the edge of Exmoor. A couple of handsome houses near the church, neither easy to see: *Court House* 16c and *Court Hall* Georgian. Church restored 1885 but a number of things were left alone, including a tiny Georgian box pew tucked away behind the screen in S chancel chapel. Rood screen has a plain top where you would expect to see a coved cornice. Pulpit Perpendicular like the screen, but the figures in the niches replaced with Victorian work; above it is an 18c angel with trumpet. Jacobean panelling in chancel, Italian in feeling, surmounted by pyramids and spiked balls. S chancel chapel has Bampfylde memorial 1626: man, wife and numberless children in coloured alabaster, cosily railed off—probably during early 19c. W end of nave: solid, workmanlike clock made

above Westward Ho!
(*see* **Northam**)

below **Northam**

Bamfylde monument, **North Molton**

in Barnstaple in 1564, when it cost
£6.13.4. —expensive for those times,
but an economy in the end for it was
used in the tower until 1934.

North Tawton [9] Once a lively little
market town, now declined. In the
Square is *Broad Hall* with 15c carved
frame and mullions; opposite is the
Town Hall, 1849, extremely plain with
blank pediments. *St Peter's* church has
some old bench ends in the nave and
re-used in the reredos.
   The Barton 1 m S on the B3215. Fine
Elizabethan manor house now a guest
house. Two-storey porch with scratch
date 1599; inside a handsome panelled
room with rich carving, fine plaster
ceilings.
   Ruined chapel 2½ m E at *Broad-*

Northlew

nymet. Simple 13c building empty,
desolate, romantic.

Noss Mayo. *See* Newton and Noss.

Nymet Rowland [6] Hamlet in hilly
country between the deep valleys of the
Taw and Yeo. Church has a Norman
font with flat cable decoration on the
shaft, the bowl scratched with a few
motifs by an amateur. S door is also
Norman with a little carving on the
imposts of the arch, finished on the W
side in the same way and probably by
the same hand as the font. There is also
some unusual timber work including a
wooden arcade and extremely primitive bench ends, as at Honeychurch.
Original wagon roof in N aisle.

Oakford [14] Church is 1838 at its most
austere, very light interior due to triple
lancet windows. *Stockridge House*
nearby is late Georgian. You can see its

lodge gate cottages E of the village:
thatched Gothic with pretty windows.
Oakford Bridge ¾ m NE: enchanting
riverside hamlet with old mill athwart
the river.

Offwell [30] Fascinating small church
notable for its carving. Splendid Jacobean panel hanging on the N transept
wall; pulpit and reader's desk about
1700. The desk shows the Lord's
Supper in relief surrounded by
mermaid-like angels, their convoluted
wings and tails stream out to form an
almost *art nouveau* frame. More
worldly carving on the pier capitals.
The Coplestones were parsons here for
generations, one was also Provost of
Oriel and raised the rumpus that got
Shelley expelled from Oxford. The

pp 126/127 **Ottery St Mary**

125

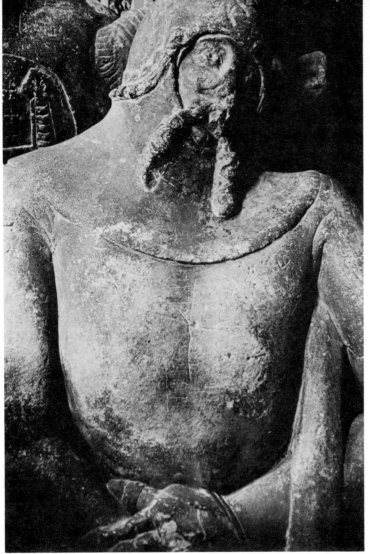

Ottery St Mary: Sir Otto de Grandisson's effigy

verted to its present use *c* 1850. Opposite, the Georgian *White Hart Hotel*. Fore St is otherwise rather tedious unless you notice. *The Arcade*, 1900, tucked behind an entrance of stained glass and wrought iron.

N of the town near where the East and West Okements meet is *Oaklands*, 1830, classical Greek at its most austere; the lodge in extreme contrast: fantastical and fairylike Gothick.

Otterton [30] A straggling village of thatched cottages which ought to look prettier than it does. Perhaps the washed cob walls have not weathered well. *St Michael*, rebuilt 1871, has blue marble columns and a roof of carved pine, diagonally worked, that looks like some Austrian *Gasthaus*. Victorian carving: corbels and capitals are ornamented with heads that look like *fake* local portraits. Outside, the Elizabethan Manor House has been cut about to make cottages. Down below the church, on the main road, is a row of cottages with assorted, fanciful, Georgian doorways including one with polygonal pinnacles.

Near by is *Ladram*, a lovely bay with rock stacks rising from the water. It has been carefully developed so that the caravans, camping site, car park, shops and café are hidden from the bay itself.

Ottery St Mary [30] One of the finest parish churches in Devon, full of grace, richness and historical interest. The manor of Ottery was given to the Cathedral of Rouen by Edward the Confessor; after some difficulty Bishop Grandisson bought it back in 1334 and rebuilt the church extensively. He set it under a body of four governors, to whom eight assistants were added 200 years later; this is still the arrangement today.

The kernel of the church—chancel, crossing and transepts is 13c and pre-Grandisson, the nave and Lady Chapel were built by him, and the "Dorset" aisle is early 16c. By 1841 the church, described as having a "degraded and neglected appearance", was restored by Butterfield, to whom we chiefly owe its present exquisite appearance. And yet he did not impose himself. His most obvious contributions are the elaborate font and the S chapel that houses the tomb of Lady Coleridge, 1879, in Butterfield's charac-

Coplestones also built the ugly great Old Rectory, 1845, S of the church. S is *Barton House* 17c and most attractive. *Offwell House*, 1830, also Coplestone built, is approached by gates at the end of the village.

Okehampton [9] Prosperous market town which fails to reveal its attractions if you merely drive through. There was a Saxon settlement on the hill $\frac{1}{2}$ m W of the town where the church stands. The old church burned in 1842. The present one is by Hayward of Exeter with windows by William Morris. Surviving from the earlier church is a stone sarcophagus lid in the S porch and an un-

usual church path with small flat stones variously dated throughout the 17c.

When the Normans arrived, with their sure eye for a stronghold, they chose another site to the S on steeply rising ground protected on one side by the West Okement. Here they built the keep which became the kernel of Okehampton Castle, greatly enlarged *c.* 1370. Extensive, easily identifiable ruins: a story-book castle.

In the 15c a Chapel of Ease was built which now forms the focal point of the town. Half way down Fore St, the main market street, is the *Town Hall*, a handsome, comfortable town house of 1685 built by John Northmore and con-

Cadhay (*see* **Ottery St Mary**)

teristic style of inlaid marbles. The main features of the church may be catalogued as follows. In chancel: reredos, 1342 (restored Blore, 1833), sedilia of the same date, opposite the sedilia the tomb of John Haydon of Cadhay, d 1587. Screens 1350, among earliest wooden in the county. Roof bosses (also in nave), there are photographs of the bosses in the S transept where they can be examined in detail. At crossing: pulpit 1772. In S transept: mediaeval clock probably 600 years old and still (visibly) working. In Lady Chapel: stone screen, restored Woodyer 1842, with corbel of Bishop Grandisson below. Gilded wooden eagle lectern, one of the few mediaeval wooden lecterns remaining in the county (another at Salcombe Regis). Misericordes. In St Stephen's Chapel (S chancel chapel), Tudor brasses. In ambulatory: original

mediaeval encaustic tiles, the best surviving shows a knight in armour on horseback. Nave effigies: to Sir Otto de Grandisson, d 1358, and his wife Lady Beatrix. Carved capitals including elephant and owl. "Dorset" Aisle: added 1520 by Cicely, Marchioness of Dorset: frothy fan vaulting rears up above your head like a breaking wave (Lane aisle at Cullompton is similar).

Samuel Taylor Coleridge was born in Ottery 1772, the youngest of thirteen children. His father, the Rev. John Taylor Coleridge, was described as "an absent man", a scholar who liked to read to the countryfolk in Hebrew, saying he was bringing them "the very language of the Holy Ghost". There is a tablet to the poet on the S wall of the churchyard (too wicked for inside?).

Ottery is charming even apart from the church. One or two distinguished

houses in Paternoster Row, also *Colby House*, Broad St, and S by the river an 18c serge factory.

Tipton St Johns nearby has a thatched farm house, probably even older than its two-storey Tudor porch.

Cadhay. 1 m NW. Exquisite Tudor house. Nucleus is a mediaeval hall *c* 1420, the fishponds on the S side are of this date. In 1545 the house was built on to the hall by John Haydon, one of the original governors of St Mary's, Ottery, appointed by Henry VIII at the Dissolution; Haydon was very likely able to get stone for his house from the destroyed abbey. The E side, the oldest unchanged frontage, was built then with polygonal stair turret. Less than 100 years later the S side was added. The building of this side created the Court of Sovereigns, which remains one of the features of the house, with chequered stonework and small statues of Henry VIII and his three children. Considerable alterations were made to the N side in 1760, and the house now has some good Georgian plasterwork. At this time the great mediaeval hall was divided laterally into two storeys. The house declined in the 19c and was cut up into two farmhouses; the great hammer beams of what must have been a magnificent roof were removed from the hall, presumably to make more headroom. Even so this roof, which purists may call mutilated, remains very beautiful.

The house was rescued in 1910 by W. C. Dampier-Wetton and his architect Barminster Fletcher, who restored it either to its Tudor or to its Georgian state, whichever seemed more appropriate. In 1925 it passed to the Powletts, whose arms may be found in the original fabric of the Tudor house.

Venn Ottery. 3 m SSW. You approach the church, *St Gregory*, through a tunnel of holly trees. Unhappily one of those churches that makes your heart sink: all that remains after drastic restoration are a few old bench ends and the old tower. A slab in the porch floor commemorates Mary Taylor who died 1708 aged 134 years.

Paignton [32] The railway came in 1859, when the population was 3,000; it is 25,000 today. There is a kernel of the old village, a few pleasant streets round the church, and down by the harbour some fishing cottages. Around these ancient centres come the later Victorian villas and shops, some with pretty iron arcades supported on barley sugar poles. Then acres of boarding houses, and finally post-war suburbia. Paignton is visually depressing, but it has two very fine things to offer (apart from the sea): the one is the Church, and the other its Municipal Offices. The latter are in *Oldway* and were built by Paris Singer, son of Sewing Machines. He, and his architect, G. S. Bridgman, designed it with a touch of Versailles, a bit of Buckingham Palace and a lot of the Paris Opera House a rollicking extravaganza in hundreds of thousands of tons of pale pink stone which shows that Hollywood did not invent the style bearing its name. Singer, with some humour, called it "The Wigwam". It cost him £200,000 in 1874 and Paignton U.D.C. got it for £42,000 in 1945. Seeing this incredible structure you cannot

wait to get inside—and not just to jeer —its self-confidence is breathtaking. What you do see is fantastic: a great staircase in gilt, marble and glass by Turkish bath out of Cleopatra, a ballroom 'modelled on the Austrian baroque ... and that is all you do see. There are a hundred rooms in this exciting house; are they all needed for municipal offices?

St John's church stands on a Saxon foundation and incorporates some Norman work. N door 14c with dog door cut in base; pulpit 15c as at Dittisham, Harberton and Dartmouth, but here damaged during the Civil War; in the S aisle is a recess with a cadaver. But the gem is the *Kirkham Chantry*, late 15c, entered by a deep stone screen, with two tomb chests within the thickness, roofs vaulted with pendants, the whole richly carved in high relief, dramatic and sparkling. Inside is a Jacobean altar.

Just S of the church is the *Coverdale Tower*, all that remains of the palace of the Bishop of Exeter.

Blagdon Manor, 2 m W. Home of the Kirkhams. Date stone 1567. Jacobean doorway. Now a guest house.

Pancrasweek [7] On a high, windy plateau of rough farmland. The Bude canal winds its way along the contours. Originally cut to carry sea sand as fertiliser for the hill farms, it only just managed to stay solvent until the railway came. The Alfardisworthy branch was kept to carry Bude's water supply; it runs shallow now and its banks make a pleasant picnic ground.

At *Lana* is a Methodist chapel of 1838, attached to a farm, in neat, comely Georgian with roundheaded windows echoed by an arched porch on slender pillars. *St Pancras* church, high on a hill, has wagon roofs in the chancel: richly carved ribs terminate in angels with outspread wings; Jacobean pulpit.

Parkham [5] On a hill top, the combes below leading N to the sea; a plain village with many sentry box doorways. The church S door is Norman, with a bird slightly off centre, its beak lying over the arch as if it were a bed spread. Norman font: fluted bowl, cable pattern below (same style as Frithelstock), the carving still sharp and clear; Norman holy water stoop on floor near font, and nearby some old Barnstaple

tiles; octagonal capitals carved as at Woolfardisworthy; 18c altar rails and pulpit, the latter on a Victorian base.

Parracombe [3] Attractive stone village in a steep, narrow valley, all the cottages seem to be climbing up or down hill. The name is a corruption of Petrock's Combe. *St Petrock's* is the old church on the hill which was saved from demolition in 1878 by a protest led by John Ruskin. A new church was built in a more convenient situation, and old St Petrock's was left more or less on its own devices. It has thus remained unaltered for over 150 years and is one of the very few examples of a simple, unpretentious, Georgian church in a not particularly rich village. What immediately strikes you is its affinity to non-conformist chapels of the same period (e.g. Loughwood); there are the same plain white walls hung with a few texts, plain box pews, and a complete lack of pretension or drama. The particular features of St Petrock's are the tympanum filled with plain wood panels painted with the Lord's Prayer, Royal coat of arms etc, three-decker desk for clerk and reader, and painted sounding board above the pultip. Parracombe has a small, easily reached earthwork called *Holwell Castle* lying almost within the village, best seen from the N side of the new church.

Blackmoor Gate. 2 m SW. No village but almost the centre of NW Devon, where a number of roads converge. Huge cattle markets are held here. An old station of the Lynton and Barnstaple line is now converted into an hotel and café.

Payhembury [18] The village centre very neat with church, pub and thatched cottages grouped round the green. *St Mary's* church has a 17c wooden porch gate. E end of the church very rich with screen, chancel ceiling gorgeously painted and gilt; angel corbels and 18c pulpit with sounding board.

Hembury Fort, 2 m NE. Stone Age hill fort; easiest approach is from the Payhembury side. Some of the most exhilarating views in the county.

Peters Marland [5] *St Peter's* church rebuilt late 1860; dull church in dull country. Woollaton near by is prettier, lying snugly in a blossomy fold of the hills.

Peter Tavy [24] Romantic Dartmoor village lying just below *Tavy Cleave*. Church has a tall and graceful spire. Interior disappointingly restored: a little of the old screen, with painted panels, hangs at the W end, and a screen below the tower is made up of old bench ends. *Peter Tavy Inn* is 17c and one of several good inns around here (the *Elephant's Nest* is another), an agreeable place to sit and have a drink while you look at the view.

Two streams meet at *Hillbridge*, where there is an old stone bridge, and a mine leat hives off towards Mary Tavy. In fields around graze Galloway cattle, shaggy picturesque beasts brought here from Scotland about the turn of the century.

Willsworthy is a 16c farmstead. First recorded as a Saxon holding, it later became a chapel. There are numerous prehistoric sites in the area.

Petrockstow [5] Hillside village of mossy thatched cottages, not prosperous but picturesque. Church has a Norman font within an especially fine Jacobean cover. Norman holy water stoop in S chancel; Rolle brass of 1591; tablet beneath tower to Catherine Mallet, d 1810, the vicar's wife:

"She was! –
But words are wanting to say what,
Think what a wife should be!
    – And she was that."

Pilton [3] Once a more important town than Barnstaple, now a suburb. Pilton St is the main street of a market town that has lost its bustle, but many of the prosperous Georgian, and earlier, houses remain. *Bellair* and *Broadgate House*, partly late 18c with a *standing stone* on a grassy verge near by. *Fairfield* is early Victorian. *St Mary's* church is fronted by "mediaeval" almshouses of 1849, fake but pretty. The church itself is large, originally part of a priory; you can see the roof line of the old monastic buildings on the exterior N wall. Inside are a dark, rich screen, massive Tudor altar rails stretching right across the church, font cover also Tudor, with behind it a curious throne-like canopy (Pevsner suggests from a previous screen, in any case painted

Paignton:
the Municipal Offices

Renaissance work). Pulpit probably 15c with outstretched arm holding an hour glass and a late 17c sounding board. An enormous tomb by the altar, 1569 – great, big family piece with kneeling figures almost life size. Sir Robert Chichester, d 1569, large tablet, grand but not gaudy with lots of strapwork.

Pinhoe [17] The village, which has grown up around the main Exeter road, is unattractive. But the church and Queen Anne vicarage stand high with sweeping views across Topsham to the mouth of the Exe. Church has a very simple Norman font and a 15c screen and pulpit. By the S door a poor box with a figure on top 18 in high and full of vitality: bearded and bottle nosed, carrying a staff, holding a book inscribed "Ye poor man of Pinhoe".

Plymouth [26] Plymouth is superb. There are two ways of seeing the city for the first time. The old way is to approach from behind the Hoe: you walk up from Lockyer St, or one of those other small streets giving on to the Hoe. Ahead of you is a slight rise, as you go forward the view suddenly opens: the wide Sound busy with small, bustling boats, wooded hills and islands on either side, Drake's Island and the Breakwater ahead; to the E the river Plym (here called the Cattewater), and to the W is river Tamar (the Hamoaze). The view is so unexpected that you may gasp with pleasure and surprise. The new way to see Plymouth is to take the lift up to the top of the Civic Centre (13 storeys in 18 seconds). It is windy up there but, as well as the balcony around, there's a glass walled restaurant. The whole of Plymouth, living and moving, is spread below you. At your feet the new city, rebuilt on the cross section of Armada Way and Royal Parade, from the ruins of Charles Church in the E to Union Street in the W. Beyond are the cranes and dockyards of *Devonport*. A little nearer SW is *Stonehouse* and the roofs and turrets of the Royal William Yard. E is Sutton Pool, full of yachts and fishing boats, the heart of *Old Plymouth*. N is the great mass of suburban Plymouth, S the Hoe, Sound and Breakwater.

Pilton

The Hoe. Plymouth Hoe, like the Monarchy, is at once domestic and sublime. It enshrines an aura of myth, having witnessed events which are now part of the national consciousness, almost of the national character. Drake playing bowls while the Armada approached, Sir Francis Chichester returning to Plymouth after sailing round the world alone at the age of 70 – such personalities embody an ideal with which we identify. And so Plymouth Hoe has become, in its way, a national shrine.

The great open space looks something between a parade ground, a museum and a promenade. One end is dominated by the *Citadel* which is still occupied by the army, at the other end is the Esplanade – a row of italianate Edwardian houses. In between, adjoining the vast promenade, are furnishings – objects of utility, decoration, history and myth – tea gardens, flower beds, a telescope, an aquarium, a public lavatory (demurely Victorian and surrounded by neat, pretty flowerbeds), a copy of the Boehm statue of Sir Francis Drake, a bowling green, a war memorial, and the beautiful old Smeaton's Lighthouse, 1759, which used to stand on the Eddystone rock. With a sense of the fitness of things, when its long day was done (it lasted 123 years), it was dismantled and brought here.

The Sound. This beautiful opening to the sea is formed by the junction of the rivers Plym and Tamar with wooded headlands shouldering down into the water on both sides. Within it is Drake's Island, or St Nicholas' Island, formerly a state prison and now a youth adventure centre. The great feature of the sound is the *Breakwater*. Started in 1812 but not finished until 1844, the Breakwater made Plymouth a safe harbour during the prevailing southwesterlies – something it had never been. This meant that vast navies could be built and assembled at Plymouth and so it ensures the town's prosperity as long as naval power remains important.

The Breakwater is 1 m long. Three and a half million tons of limestone blocks were ferried out in barges, dumped between buoys marking the line and left for the sea to pound into a solid mass. Shelving more gently on the seaward side, thus breaking the force of the waves, it was finally completed with

squared and dovetailed blocks. A lighthouse stands at one end and a fort in the middle. The Breakwater is the kind of monolithic structure which our forbears undertook with such cheerful confidence and brought to a successful conclusion with scarcely more technical resources than the ancient Egyptians, but without their pool of slave labour.

To the W of the Sound is the headland of *Mt Edgecumbe*. Though strictly speaking in Cornwall, the grounds of Mt Edgecumbe House, a Gothic Mansion, are open to the public twice a week, and from the Battery there you have another view of Plymouth and the Sound. Crossing to Mt Edgecumbe on the Cremyll ferry from Admiral's Hard, Stonehouse, makes a pleasant excursion.

E of the Sound is Mount Batten with the flying school, where T. E. Lawrence hid himself as Aircraftman Shaw.

The Citadel. At the highest point of the Hoe, dominating both the town and the sea approaches, stands the Citadel, a great fortress built in 1666 by Charles II on the site of earlier strongholds; one of the very few 17c fortresses left in England. The King said he built it to guard the town against the French, but Plymouth had a tradition of puritanism (it was no coincidence that the Pilgrim Fathers sailed from here) and had been for Parliament during the Civil Wars, so the Citadel, with gun ports looking over the town, also served to guard the King from enemies within. However, by a twist of fortune, in 1688 the then Governor of the Citadel declared for William of Orange against James II; and so the whole of the SW was lost to the Stuarts.

Charles's military engineer, Bernard de Gomme, designed the Citadel on the French pattern – but a little before it was brought to perfection. The chief fault was that instead of providing a bank of earth into which attacking cannon balls could harmlessly sink he carried the stonework right up to the parapet and then had the guns pointing through stone embrasures. Had it ever faced a siege the defenders of the Citadel would probably have been driven out by flying fragments. "De Gomme hath builded very sililly" Pepys wrote. (Sellman: *Illustrations of Devon History*.)

The fortress is approached by a magnificent baroque portal of 1670. Within

Plymouth
above The Hoe

opposite Devonport Dock

to the left is a little 18c structure with
Doric pillars. Here you may apply to
visit and permission is granted without
fuss. Inside the buildings are grouped
around a parade ground which is furnished with old cannon and an
inadequate statue of George II as a
Roman warrior. All paintwork is army
red. Across the parade ground is the
royal chapel of St Katharine-upon-the-
Hoe, 1668, standing upon the foundations of far earlier chapels. Not
particularly distinguished.

Old Plymouth with the Barbican and
St Andrew's Church. Until Tudor times
the town lay between Sutton Pool and
St Andrew's church, behind the Hoe
and protected from the prevailing SW
winds. Even after the ravages of time
and bombing something remains of
Tudor Plymouth and most of it is con-
centrated in this area.

Plymouth
left Detail of baroque
entrance to Citadel

opposite View Seaward from
the Civic Centre

Catherine of Aragon landed at Sutton Pool in 1501 and this may be the origin of the name Cattewater, here given to the river Plym as it opens into the Sound. Drake sailed into Sutton Pool in 1573 having raided Panama. At the time he returned everyone was at morning service in St Andrew's (strange now to think that the church would have held them all and they would all have been there). "At what time the news of our Captain's return brought to his family did so speedily pass over the church and surpasse their minds with delight and desire to see him that few or none remained with the preacher."

The Pilgrim Fathers left Sutton Pool in 1620, "having been kindly entertained and courteously used by divers friends there dwelling". Their departure is recorded by the *Mayflower Stone*, on the west of the harbour.

The Parade was the city centre of old Plymouth, its cobbles set to the edge of the quay and surrounded by ancient and beautiful warehouses. *No. 18 Old Custom House*, now a betting shop, fine Tudor frontage into which a fake Tudor window has at some time been inserted. Opposite is the *New Custom House* (Laing 1810) with rusticated colonnade. A little further N in the NW corner of Sutton Wharf is the *Cooperage*, 1800, a fanciful artisan's pride, with castellations, barrels in niches and a great portcullis door.

The best remaining Tudor houses are probably found in Southside St, New St, and round the Barbican. No. 51 Southside St, a good three-storeyed Jacobean house, also the remains of the *Dominican Friary* with its old *refectory room* are built into Coates Distillery. The *Elizabethan House* in New St is furnished by the V. & A. Museum and open to the public. Looe St, Nos 33 & 36, Tudor houses with oriel windows. Notte St, two Tudor houses. William Cookworthy, a Plymouth chemist, had his original shop in Notte St; in about 1750 he discovered an English substitute for Chinese kaolin paste, porcelain paste of exceptional hardness and whiteness and hitherto a jealously guarded secret. Cookworthy founded the Plymouth, later the Bristol, Pottery.

St Andrew St, No. 33 Tudor.

St Andrews, the parish church, was almost totally destroyed by bombing, only the shell remaining. Above the N door still hangs a simple wooden board with the word "Resurgam" — "I will rise again", which was hung there when the church was destroyed. The church was indeed rebuilt to its old plan and is unhappily not very interesting, save for the bold idea of commissioning John Piper to design some new stained glass; in an otherwise dull building the colour and freedom of the windows makes a terrific effect.

The destruction of the church displaced some facing on the ledge of the 1st window to the W of the S door revealing a bit of Elizabethan graffiti scratched in the plaster when it was still wet, roughly showing two or three sailing ships, a globe and a line thrown around it; it could represent Drake's voyage round the world. In the S aisle is a head of *Zachary Mudge* 18c vicar, eccentric and friend of Sir Joshua Reynolds and Doctor Johnson.

Behind St Andrew's is the *Prysten*

Sutton Pool, Old Plymouth (*see* **Plymouth**)

Royal William Victualling Yard, **Plymouth**

House, built by Plympton Priory in the late 15c. It escaped damage in the raids but has been restored perhaps a little too thoroughly.

Foulston's Plymouth, Stonehouse and Devonport Civic Centre. At the end of the 18c the French wars brought great prosperity to the town and a rush of building filled the space between old Plymouth and *Dock* (now Devonport) which became Stonehouse. The architecture in this area is very much the work of one man, who had great opportunity and a strong individual style. John Foulston was a Londoner, who entered a competition set by Plymouth Corporation in 1811 for what we today might call a social centre: a theatre, hotel and assembly rooms to be built as one structure. Foulston won this competition and for the next 30 years his hand and eye dominated Plymouth.

Foulston's manner is stocky, robust, classical, his pillars are squat, his buildings never soar, there are no Regency *fol de rols*; but they are always well proportioned, strong, plain, good mannered. A style well suited to a no-nonsense seafaring citizenry. From *Lockyer St* his work stretches W street after street. Much is bombed but *Athenaeum St* and

The Crescent are fairly well preserved. In Stonehouse his work may be seen in *Emma Place, Caroline Place* and *Adelaide Place.* In Stoke Damarel he has allowed himself to be more frivolous in *Albemarle Villas* and *St Nicholas Terrace.*

Foulston kept himself well in hand in domestic architecture but he became weirdly exuberant when he set to work on the *Devonport Civic Centre,* Ker St. This was erected to celebrate Devonport's incorporation in 1824, and still today there is a faint whiff of a *nouveau riche* manufacturing town showing what it could do on its big day. At the head of Ker St is the *Town Hall* in Foulston's squattest classical Doric surmounted by a seated lady holding scales; just behind the town hall, a little off-centre, is a symbol of virility – the Devonport Column, a huge affair which it was originally intended should carry a statue of George IV, but public subscriptions didn't materialise. At its base is a beautifully weathered iron plate with "Devonport 1824" incised upon it. In front of the column was the *Mount Zion Chapel*, a building in Moorish style now unhappily gone. Next is the *Library* (now the Oddfellows' Hall) in head-over-heels Egyp-

tian. Ker St is an architectural Madame Tussaud's. The sad thing is that now Devonport is part of Plymouth its Civic Centre is mouldering away.

Other features in Stonehouse include *Durnford St*, a domestic street of about 1775, each house individual, all charming. At one end is *the Royal Marine Barracks*, Palladian, 1781; at the other end *Nazareth House*, formerly the Earl of Mount Edgecumbe's summer villa. Its vast Italianate windows overlooking the sea suggest some Edwardian sanatorium set to catch the Alpine sun.

Nearby at the mouth of the Hamoaze (R Tamar) is the *Royal William Victualling Yard*, built by Sir John Rennie 1826–35. Superb, severe naval architecture thrusting out into the water (six of its 14 acres were recovered from the sea). Chief façade to the N: two noble blocks, limestone ashlar faced with granite, flank a third which is set back and crowned with a cupola. The public is not allowed inside but this most grand water frontage can be seen from Admiral's Hard, or passing before you on the Cremyll ferry, or more distantly, fróm Mount Wise. The great gate of the yard is near the S end of Durnford St, massively decorated with bulls' heads and the tools of those butchers, bakers,

Plymouth: The Duke of Cornwall Hotel

and coopers who plied their trades within. The whole is surmounted by a statue of the monarch in question.

Devonport and the Shipyards. A vast new navy was demanded by the French wars of the 17c and one of the dockyards where the ships were built was established at Plymouth; not at Sutton Pool, which would have been too cramped, but W on the banks of the Tamar. Founded in 1691 a township grew up round the shipyards tersely known as *Dock*. Dock was incorporated in 1824 (see notes on Foulston's Civic Centre, Ker St) and given the name Devonport. By 1914 the three towns, Plymouth, Stonehouse and Devonport, had grown into each other and logically, if not emotionally, they became one town: Plymouth.

Devonport has still its own unmistakable character. A working, masculine town dominated by the 20 ft walls of the naval dockyards. Above these walls are glimpsed towers, pinnacles, cranes and chimneys: they look virile and provocative above those secretive palisades. The architecture is severe and practical, being built by engineers and naval architects, but far from graceless. Below the great walls, like some mediaeval village sheltering beneath the

castle, run rows of 19c working men's streets, some very beautiful. The streets seethe with a self-contained and self-confident life; the people have an air of security and independence, due perhaps to the docks having guaranteed work to skilled labour for generations.

The Navy allows visits to some yards, not to others. But you can get an unusual view of the Hamoaze, and the navy ships at anchor there, from Wolseley Rd, a little road just below the Royal Albert railway bridge. Above you too is the new *Tamar Toll Bridge*, and near by the old Edwardian pay kiosks of the ferry which the great new bridge has replaced.

Overlooking the Hamoaze is a pretty early 19c enclave with balconies and Venetian windows fronted by wide green lawns clipped with naval precision. These are *Mount Wise House*, *Government House* and *Admiralty House*. Just in front of them, where the hill slopes steeply down to the water, is the *Scott Memorial*, to the Antarctic explorer.

If you should pass down Citadel Rd, (in Plymouth, strictly speaking) spare a glance for the *Duke of Cornwall Hotel*; its nicest feature is its turret modelled on Smeaton's lighthouse and some-

times bedecked with flags. In Union St is an Edwardian pleasure palace: the *Great Western Hotel and New Theatre*, faced with tiles of ginger and yellow, some cast with sailing ships; two great friezes, one of the Armada defeated. The whole gabled, turreted and surmounted by statues of Drake and Hawkins.

Churches. There are more than two hundred churches in Plymouth, not all of them of equal interest. Foulston's *St Catharine's*, Lockyer St, much damaged by bombing, was pulled down. Behind the Museum and Art Gallery is *St Luke's*, Tavistock Rd 1828, a plain, pleasing exterior, now a public library. *St Andrew's*, Paradise Rd, Stoke Damarel, an old village church dating from 15c but enlarged during 18c when the first suburban development of Plymouth got under way. The area is full of pretty Regency villas, many of them by Foulston or Foulston inspired. Surrounded by modern suburbia is *St Budiana*, Victoria Rd, St Budeaux, one of the more recent villages to be swallowed up by Plymouth. The village church is beautifully sited on a hilltop, from which you now view a sea of red and grey roofs. Not an exceptionally interesting church but Sir Francis Drake w. married here in 1569 when the church was only six years old; his wife is buried here. The two relevant pages of the parish register are displayed in a photocopy. There is also a monument to Sir William Gorges, the first "Proprietor & Governor" of the state of Maine, U.S.A. *St Aubyn*, St Aubyn St, Devonport, 1771 bleak Georgian.

New Plymouth. If you enter Plymouth from the N you pass through an area of Victorian villas with big shady gardens like so many rectories, then the houses become smaller, more tightly packed and then—nothing prepares you for it: the new city centre.

On the night of 21 March 1941 Plymouth suffered a bombing raid which wiped out the centre of the town. The devastation was appalling, but immediately afterwards the city commissioned Sir Patrick Abercrombie to draw up plans for a bold and free reconstruction.

The area lies in a bowl behind the Hoe, and so from various points you can see right across it. The main axes are

Saltram House: the Kitchen (*see* **Plympton St Mary**)

the wide avenues of Armada Way and Royal Parade, with lawns and flower beds running down the centre. At the E end of Royal Parade are the bombed ruins of *Charles Church* (1640–58 but Gothic in style) which remain as a memorial of the bombing. S is *St Andrew's Church*, set back from the traffic by lawns. Next comes the *Guildhall*, originally 1870–74 by Norman Hine, but badly bombed and rebuilt. The exterior Victorian frieze remains; it reminds you of Russian propaganda art and has the same didactic purpose of providing an ideal: the models are good looking, youthfully mature, well nourished and arranged in attitudes suggesting grace and high purpose. The interior, which is quite new, is in an unpleasing style of Odeon baroque; the coloured glass windows, depicting scenes from Plymouth history, have much in common with the exterior frieze. Opposite the Guildhall is the new *Civic Centre* (1962, Jellicoe, Ballantyne & Coleridge) with the roof-top balcony and restaurant already mentioned. Linking the Civic Centre, Guildhall and St Andrews is a series of traffic free walks, flower beds, lawns and fountains which give a sense of space and peace and yet the traffic and excitement of the shopping centre

are only a few yards away. The administrative, cultural and religious centre of the town has not been hived off into some remote sanitary zone (as is happening with the South Bank in London) but feeds and nourishes the town it serves.

Plympton St Mary [27] A small religious community founded here in the 9c became an Augustine priory in 1121 and grew in size second only to Tavistock. The priory owned Sutton Prior, nucleus of Plymouth. The church now stands in the large flat priory land, but nothing remains of the old priory except a few fragments S. St Mary's was the priory chapel but it has far outstripped the parish church in size and appointments. Such was the strength and wealth of the priory that it attracted all the important local families. Even after the dissolution of the priory in 1539 the habit persisted and the big men were still buried there, so ensuring a continuing attention in the matter of care and adornment.

S porch is two storeyed enriched with statued niches, castellations and pinnacles, lierne vaulting inside. Early 14c sedilia and piscina. In the N chancel chapel an ancient and beautiful chair

carved with an intricate pattern of figures, animals and palm trees, the style suggesting 13c. In the same chapel is a monument to Richard Strode, d 1464, tomb chest with carving exceptionally fresh and well preserved, unlike that to William Courtenay in the chancel. Wall tablet to Viscount Boringdon, who died a lingering and unpleasant death aged eleven.

Saltram. 1 m SW. Grandest house in England W of Bath. An old estate acquired by the Parker family early in the 18c (original Tudor kitchen is now the tea room), which they rapidly rebuilt and enlarged. In 1768 Robert Adam was commissioned to design a saloon and dining room: with their elegant proportions and great refinement of detail these rooms are now the show pieces of the house, but so extremely grand and chillingly formal that George III, who stayed here with his family, never used the saloon. Upstairs is much Georgian plasterwork and a bedroom in intricate Chinese Chippendale. An interesting collection of pictures hung in the old style: those in the morning room are probably in their original places and resemble 18c pictures of an artist's studio: "papering the walls", Sir Joshua Reynolds, born at Plympton near by, became a friend of John Parker, first Lord Boringdon, and painted most of his family, these pictures are still in the house. Fascinating Georgian, (and Victorian) kitchen with *batterie de cuisine* and much old gear; the arrangements for distributing hot water are surprisingly ingenious. The air is here so temperate that oranges were ripening in the open air in early September.

Boringdon. 1 m N. The old home of the Parkers before they acquired Saltram. In their great 18c days John Parker took the title Baron Boringdon. The family came here in 1564 and by this means got a foothold in the squirearchy. They left for Saltram *c*. 1750. Only half the house remains, so that the central porch is at one end; it still has a fine hall with fireplace carving of 1640.

Old Newnham. 1 m NE. Former mansion of the Strode family (who built the Guildhall with the Trubys of Plympton House) with quite considerable remains of a Tudor building, but about 1700 a larger house was wanted and the family rebuilt at Loughton on the site of another Tudor House. *Newnham Park* just to the N. Tudor house of which only the cellars remain, rebuilt 1700 with later additions.

Wild Life Park at Sparkwell 3 m ENE.

Plympton St Maurice [27] Birth place of Sir Joshua Reynolds, and also Northcote, Eastlake and Haydon; why the sudden rash of painters in this ancient rotten borough? Disenfranchised in 1832 and now engulfed by Plymouth, but the heart of the village still has atmosphere. Remains of the Norman Castle stand on a tump W of the church. Just behind the church is *Plympton House*, built 1700 by Sir George Truby, now a hospital but still with its Queen Anne garden. In Fore St are the *Guildhall*, 1690, and the *Grammar School*, 1658. Both have a first storey resting upon a row of squat columns forming an arcade.

The church is usually dismissed in favour of Plympton St Mary, but in fact it has some interesting features and is well worth a visit. Tucked away in a dark corner by the N door is a beautiful early 18c font cupboard, octagonal, panelled, surmounted by a dome. Pulpit formed from 18c panelling with bands of older carving. Against the middle pier of the S aisle the stone base

and steps of an older pulpit: ridged and hexagonal.

Plymstock [27] Once an outlying village, now part of Plymouth. A few ancient houses but otherwise closely woven streets of suburban housing. Church has a Norman font and a 15c rood screen, the spandrels filled in with bits and pieces of carving from elsewhere; 17c pulpit with sounding board; Harris monument of 1677 has a curious sconce-like support for its central pillar: a naked-breasted woman swinging out from below like a ship's figurehead.

Plymtree [17] Cider apple country. Fine woodwork in the church: 15c screen with fan vaulting and bands of carving above, dense as guipure, painted panels below, best on the left, the style seems to change as you move right, possibly due to restoration; old pews and bench ends; 17c panels and reliefs in chancel surround; altar rails 17c; pulpit 18c; small alabaster relief, Flemish, early 17c in W wall.

Fordmore. Late 17c, now a handsome, working farmhouse.

Poltimore [29] Pretty village of thatched cottages built within the demesne of a great plain Georgian mansion now a private nursing home: once the house of the Bamfyldes, who have owned the manor of Poltimore since 1303. You drive through countryside which is essentially meadowy parkland carefully landscaped, planted with now mature oak trees, and grazed by fat cattle.

Church, *St Mary*, restored and enlarged 1880. Originally cruciform with three galleries until the S aisle was added. The gallery above the S transept was retained as squire's pew, it has a plaster ceiling and its own fireplace and must have been a pleasantly warm and private place whence to see and not be seen; 52 angel corbels; some ancient stained glass in the S window of the Sanctuary. 1604 monument to Sir Richard and Lady Bamfylde lying under a canopy, hands exceptionally fine and full of individuality; altar surrounded part of the 1880 refit, pew ends of 1883 with portraits of the then rector and his wife.

Bamfylde Almshouse, 1631, just N of the church.

Postbridge. *See* Dartmoor.

Poughill [13] Dull hamlet looking towards Dartmoor. Unassuming church, restored 1855, when it was given a painted "Glory" above the chancel; a Gothick plaster reredos picked out in gilt and colour; bands of painted decoration around arches and capitals; all this colour is now faded and rather charming. The restorers left the high 18c box pews, original wagon roofs and flooring.

Powderham [29] Grand and polyglot pile, home of the Courtenays, Earls of Devon. Oldest part is 14c but this has been built over and added on to. In 1755 the mediaeval Great Hall was made into a Staircase Hall with splashy plaster decoration in English rococo by Jenkins, of Exeter. In 1790 came the Music Room, very showy, by James Wyatt. And then *c*. 1840 the 10th Earl, having got a good price for allowing the railway to be built along the river bank on his E front, swivelled the main entrance to the W and there had Charles Fowler build him a new mediaeval banqueting hall and costly forecourt, romantic as a stage design by de Loutherburg. There is, too, a batch of portraits of the 9th Earl's thirteen daughters (three at a time) by Cosway, a Devon painter; also a magnificent pair of bookcases, rosewood inlaid with brass, made by Channon in 1740. Powderham stands in a deer park traversed by avenues; a grand avenue of cedar goes N and then changing to ilex, turns E to the church.

St Clement's is dullish except for an ancient S door which was already so old in 1645 as to need repair by Fairfax's Roundheads, who were attacking the castle and used the church as their base. Crudely painted screen.

Pigeon Vale, N of the castle, set in farmland between the Exeter road and the estuary: dovecote, now a cottage, unhappily its original thatch has gone.

Princetown [24] The vast prison with its workshops looks like some Lancashire millscape in the midst of Dartmoor were it not for the great rusticated gate with massy bell (shades of Dante), and the prison officers, in pairs, who eye you over walls. In the market square are gift shops and charabancs for those of us who come to gaze with such mixed motives. The prisoners, in grey uniform, may occasionally be seen. Originally built at the

Winscott Barton, **St Giles in the Wood**

suggestion of Sir Thomas Tyrwhitt, owner of granite quarries nearby, the name derived from the Prince of Wales, who gave the site. The prison was built in 1806 to the design of David Alexander and cost £130,000. One of the original buildings, the French prison, is said still to exist; it housed prisoners of the Napoleonic wars. At one time nearly 9,000 French prisoners were held in five two-storey buildings. These buildings had cast-iron pillars and the men slept in hammocks slung between them; the prisoners had previously been housed in hulks and the use of hammocks in the ships must have given someone the bright idea of how they could be packed into the prison. The prisoners provided labour for building new roads and generally opening up the moor at this time. After the Napoleonic wars the prison remained empty and unused until 1850, when it became the nucleus of the present vast establishment for long term prisoners.

St Michael's church has extremely narrow aisles with high wide arches. The interior was remodelled in 1908, and the arches run straight down into the pillars without interrupting capitals. Unstressed, self-confident and surprisingly modern.

Puddington [13] In upland country with occasional distant views of Dartmoor. Church much restored 1838, but the old bench ends were preserved with heavily incised abstract patterns in black oak.

Pyworthy [7] Dull, bleak and high with many bungalows; church restored 1885 but wagon roofs remain in N and S aisles. In the S porch a good mixture of 14c and Victorian bosses.

Rackenford [13] Church and manor house lie unusually far apart, the latter extensively renewed in 1928 but S front is good Georgian. In the village the Ebenezer Chapel, 1848, has a pretty Gothic window, and one of those pleasant, plain interiors, with a little gallery.

Rattery [31] Lying up hill and down dale with wide views from the churchyard. Parish dotted with mediaeval farmhouses; good example is *Venton Manor*, 1 m SE, but there are many others. 13c church with a covering of Victorian plaster, incised and coloured: Norman font; plain 18c pulpit; still lit by oil in pretty lamps. *Church House Inn* said to be 11c. *Syon Abbey*, formerly Marley House, is now a community of Bridgettine nuns, whose order was founded at Syon, Isleworth, 1415. The heavy Georgian house may be glimpsed through trees from the main Exeter–Plymouth road, or more clearly from the S.

Rewe [17] A small, flattish parish 5 m N of Exeter. Small 15c church, *St Mary*, with screen of the same date. Fine carved bench ends given by Sir Nicholas Wadham in 1495 and bearing his arms. Alms box, 1631, elaborately carved and painted. "Vinegar" bible, 1718, St Luke XX page heading has "The parable of the Vinegar" for "Vineyard". Near by a

141

Salcombe

little packbridge over the wandering Culm. Also a much restored village cross but the base is probably original.

Ringmore [27] Not being quite by the sea, it has remained a most peaceful and pretty old village of ancient rambling cottages with drooping thatch like old eiderdowns. Small church which has retained its original 13c plan; includes a tiny chapel with lancet windows. Heavily restored in 1863 by someone with a love of colour.

Overlooking the sea: *Castle Farm*, $\frac{1}{2}$ m N. Curious, ruined Victorian relic with tower, castellations, Gothick windows, barge boarded and slate hung. Pyramid dovecote in front.

Roborough [6] In high country far from any tourist route at the head of a side valley leading W to the river Torridge, and becoming ever prettier as it nears the parent valley. Village of old thatched cottages. Roborough church restored 1868 but the tower arch contains some bits of Elizabethan carving.

Rockbeare [17] Peaceful village tucked just off the main A30. Dormitory village for near by Exeter with a number of comfortable, cared-for, thatched houses. Church has a carved Elizabethan W gallery. Just by the church,

Rockbeare Court is dull Georgian. At the end of the village is the *Manor House*, built mid 18c but the front, and some of the interior, remodelled in 1820 and given a Doric colonnade between bow windows. *The Grange* is a charming late Georgian house with Doric porch and two Venetian windows.

Romansleigh [13] Village on a hill with views across South Molton to Exmoor. Some pretty thatched cottages.

Rose Ash [13] In the centre of a long, narrow ridge, or hog's back, 800 ft above sea level with views of Exmoor to the N and glimpses of Dartmoor S. Manor house, church and village school lie beside a tranquil green. Eight generations of Southcombs were rectors here from 1675 to 1949, and most are buried in the churchyard. The church has a (restored) perpendicular rood screen, and a Jacobean screen to the N chancel chapel surmounted by a Royal coat of arms of 1618, forming a pediment.

Rousdon. *See* Combpyne.

St Giles in the Wood [6] Little woodland now except around *Stevenstone House* just across the valley. This was carefully planted so as to improve the

view by the Hon. Mark Rolle *c* 1870 when he was rebuilding the family mansion. There were two former Rolle houses, the first Tudor, the second 18c (something remains of this). The present house is high Victorian Renaissance by Sir Charles Barry (who designed the Houses of Parliament). The church was rebuilt too and is pretty featureless: a few quaint Victorian embroidered pictures in gilt with gothick frames. The most attractive buildings in the village are the least pretentious: estate cottages, stone built with sentry box doorways, date stone M.R. 1877.

Winscott Barton, 1 m E. Enchanting house with dovecote, 18c exterior, set behind great buttressed barns.

St Giles on the Heath [19] Lying in a fold of the hills near the Cornish border, remote and with few dwellings. A small church the old vicarage near by is far larger; inside is a Norman font with a little decoration at the base; two bits of the old screen still in place but cut down to form reader's desk and rear of the pulpit; old bench ends, broad and crude; the old reredos

Honeychurch
(*see* **Sampford Courtenay**)

142

The Grand Western Canal near **Sampford Peverell**

c. 1800 finely carved in slate, gilt and painted.

Salcombe [34] Fishing and yachting centre in an idyllic setting. It lies snug at the head of a creek facing S. Steep hillsides keep out the winds and the place is luxuriant with palms, fuchsias and even oranges; it is as warm and exotic as the Italian Riviera but with an exquisite English greenness. Maze of streets at the town centre; no cars are allowed by the water's edge where there is a meandering quayside walk with fishermen's cottages, the *Customs House* and the *Shark Angling Club* Weighing Station. The area is thick with chic boutiques and small restaurants which show the kind of visitor expected. Dull church except for a little carving by Sedding in the choir (look at the arm rests particularly), and a pair of *Art Nouveau* chancel gates, bronze with coloured enamelling.

Fort Charles, ruined castle by the water's edge near North Sands, built by Henry VIII as part of his coast defences.

Sharpiter Gardens, $1\frac{1}{4}$ m SW. High up on the hillside a series of small gardens, some wild, some formal; blissfully peaceful, a Paradise Garden. Also in the gardens is the local *Overbecks Museum*.

Salcombe Regis [30] Salcombe was originally one of the manors of Alfred the Great. His grandson Athelstan gave Salcombe to the monastery he founded at Exeter. These are the royal connections which gave Salcombe its suffix. The parish runs as far W as the river Sid and takes in a good part of Sidmouth. Hence *Salcombe Lodge* and *Salcombe House*, exquisite Georgian houses in Sid Road, Sidmouth. But the village of Salcombe Regis nestles tranquilly in its own combe, protected on all sides save S, which is open to the sea 1 m away. The sea breezes have nibbled away at the 15c windows of the church tower. In *St Mary and St Peter* Norman work can still be seen in the pillars of the W aisle and the ghost of a door into the outside S wall of the chancel. Fragment of 15c stained glass in the N aisle window. In the exterior N wall of the chancel is a pig's snout carved in stone said to be three dimensional insult by a contemporary workman. 15c eagle lectern. Up on the old Sidmouth road a thorn bush has stood since Saxon times marking the boundary between the common land and the cultivated fields below. *Thorn Farm* has been worked since 750. Nearby is *Slade Farm*, Georgian with S porch having steps leading up to it. Smuggling was one of the principal trades here. Henry Northcott, labourer, tells in the parish records for 1819 that the brandy was strong and treacly, being condensed for shipment from France, and later watered down before sale. "Once they were in Slade cellar, but the King (*i.e. the Customs Officers*) called and they were only just started down the drains in time. It made the rats squeak."

Saltram. *See* Plympton St Mary.

Sampford Courtenay [9] Village street lined with thatched cottages winds across from one hill to another. *St Andrew's* church is plump and self-confident with high tower and much castellation; ancient hinged S door; Norman font; wagon roofs with fine bosses, particularly well lit in chancel; old communion rails, naïve country work (as at Honeychurch) re-used in choir and tower arch, present set 1831 as is the pulpit. Prayer book rebellion began in this church on Whit Monday 1549 in protest against the service being read in English instead of Latin, later spreading to the whole peninsula.

Honeychurch, 1 m N once a parish on its own, now amalgamated with Sampford Courtenay. It is poor and remote but these very factors have preserved *St Mary's* church: 12c. Hardly altered in the fabric, it remains a simple Norman building which time and the utmost simplicity have made beautiful.

144

Sandford

Norman work includes the font decorated with cable and zig-zag, and two mask-like heads in the S wall. Doors of extreme age, S door remounted with great care; wall painting in N wall badly damaged by damp said to be the arms of Elizabeth I. The parish was so poor that furnishings were only renewed when absolutely necessary: pews 15c with a few crudely carved ends, two patched up in the 18c to form box pews. Altar rails are 17c, crude country work. Ceiled wagon· roof. The name Honeychurch derives from Saxon: Huna's church. The countryside is so undisturbed that the farms recorded in Domesday occupy exactly the same area today (Hoskins). The *New Inn*, 16c ¼ m S of Sampford

Courtenay on B3216, worth a visit for a crowded collection of folk objects.

Sampford Peverell [74] The Peverells lived here in a castle "rebuilt and fortified" in 1337 but demolished in 1775. It stood on the mound just behind Sampford Barton (itself a pleasant, early Victorian, farmhouse). Sir Hugh Peverell was Lord of the Manor 1241–96, and went on a crusade to the Holy Land; it is probably his effigy that lies, much mutilated, in the church. The old rectory, square Victorian Gothic, stands on the site of a much older house built about 1500 by Lady Margaret Beaufort, mother of Henry VI, who lived in the castle. When the canal was cut it chopped through the gardens and

stables of the older house and so the canal company replaced the building in 1841.

Sampford Spiney [24] A snug Tudor farmhouse, once the manor house, lies just below the church. It is dated 1617 but parts are older. An unpretentious Jacobean gateway and a low wall frame a neat and pretty garden. The church is well placed but uninteresting. On the moor above are ancient crosses and the kennels of the Spooner's and West Devon Foxhounds.

Sandford [16] Attractive village of many humble 18c houses, and some less humble. The *Lamb Inn* is 16c or older. *Sandford School* built 1825 by Sir

145

Shaldon

Humphrey Davy of Creedy Park (the village is near Crediton) appears inspired by the Acropolis. Large church, *St Swithin's*, notable for a carved Jacobean W gallery, 1657; old oak pews, some child sized; brass 1604 to Mary Dowrich. Outside a painted sundial of 1818.

Dowrich House, $1\frac{1}{2}$ m N. Victorian but with a 16c gateway; this is very handsome: castellated with large central arch and lesser doorway each side.

Satterleigh and Warkleigh [6] Once two parishes, now joined, on a wooded plateau above the Mole. Two small churches both next to farmyards and far from any village. *Satterleigh* is 15c with a wooden bellcote instead of a tower; remarkable door, old as the church itself, with a crooked pointed frame; inside is a solid tympanum, usually a Georgian feature but here overpainted by the Victorians; 17c pulpit with sounding board; church well supplied with homely Victorian coat pegs. *Warkleigh* possesses a unique 15c pyx, $7\frac{3}{4}$ in high, delicately and gaily painted with flowers, sun in

circle and leaves in spandrels, the colours red, white, green and gold; the absence of blue gives a distinct flavour; discovered by Baring Gould in the parish chest. Plain 18c pulpit; at the base of the tower is part of a Renaissance carved screen probably removed from elsewhere.

Seaton [36] Exquisite coastal scenery expecially W with towering, delicately coloured cliffs. The town was once a few scattered fishermen's cottages on the coast with the village proper $\frac{1}{2}$ m inland around the church; now a dreary example of seaside development. A few interesting buildings: *St Elmo*, on the seafront; Victorian Gothic with castellations and mock embrasures, *Infants' School* 1840 in Sidmouth Rd, *Manor House School*, Fore St, late 18c with fanlight; restrained terraces around Major Terrace and Seafield Road, in "Builder's Georgian" – i.e. built around 1870 to an earlier pattern. *St Gregory*, well inland where the old village stood, is patched and botched: entrances, arches and chancel run into each other incoherently; yet the effect is a bit charmless possibly due to too much yellow varnish and cream plaster. Some good 13c and 14c windows.

Walks to *Hawksdown Camp*, $\frac{1}{2}$ m N,

Iron Age camp with views of the Axe valley. Also walks along the cliffs W to Sidmouth, and E to the Dowland Landslip. (See Axmouth.)

Shaldon [32] Dominated by a rearing red cliff the village lies along the Teign estuary. Low, modest Regency houses of great charm line the narrow village streets and are strung around the Green; garden walls overflow with fuchsias and palms. Gothick *Hunter's Lodge*, festooned with fox heads, antlers and rusticated stone, marks the entrance to the village from the main road.

Ringmore, $\frac{1}{2}$ m NW. In a pretty, sheltered setting along the Teign estuary with views across the water to Teignmouth. Demure early Georgian, slightly less extrovert than Shaldon. An eyecatcher on the main road is "*The Hermitage*", Gothick with wheel window.

Shaugh Prior [24] A stunning view towards Plymouth Sound has attracted a fringe of bungalows along its rim. The church, *St Edward*, has a fine font cover: octagonal and double decked, its tapering sides set with little monkish figures, a bishop crowns the whole. (*See also* Dartmoor – mining.)

Shaldon

Methodist chapel, **Sidbury**

Shebbear [5] Beautiful, peaceful and remote. The name comes from Old English: *sceaftbearu*, "the grove where poles were got". The houses are grouped around the village square on the Saxon plan. Even older is the *Devil's Stone*, a lump of stone identical to that brought from S Wales and used at Stonehenge. Each 5 November (no apparent connection with Guy Fawkes) it is turned to release the devil underneath and send him away for another year. The stone stands beneath an ancient oak just outside the churchyard. It seems likely that this has always been a sacred place, the piece of stone being purposely left in a sacred grove. The early Christians then built their church in the same druidical holy spot. Across the square is the *Devil's Stone Hotel* with date stones 1645, 1678 and 1782. It has been treated with tact and remains a charming 18c hostelry. The church has a Norman S doorway with row of heads and beaks as at Buckland Brewer, one beast with a fish in its mouth. Jacobean pulpit with carving of men and women holding eels, flowers, torches, and musical instruments.

Shebbear College, ½ m E. Theological

college; modern but built around an older building with early 19c details.

Sheepstor [24] Near by is the *Burrator Reservoir*, which supplies Plymouth with water; it replaced the original leats of Sir Francis Drake. The lake is now weathered and "natural" but the sheet of water surrounded by fir trees looks Scottish and alien to the small streams and oak, ash and thorn of Devon. There is a tall, splashy waterfall at the W end of the lake, well set off by dark rocks and overarching trees. You can see a fine view of the whole area from above the church. In the churchyard, underneath a slab of red Aberdeen granite, lies Rajah Brooke of Sarawak who ended an eventful life here in this remote moorland parish. Inside the church an endearing and domestic monument: Jacobean lady lying on her bed, her swaddled baby on her arms; by the bedside kneel three daughters, the bed curtains part on each side of the tablet.

Sheepwash [8] Enchanting hilltop village set around a small square on the Saxon plan; on one side is the *Half Moon Inn*, a fishing inn, low and

rambling; elsewhere there are pretty, thatched cottages. Church rebuilt 1881 by J. F. Gould, delicate painted decoration along the rafters; Norman font with carving of fruit and flowers. On the parish boundary with Highampton is a packhorse bridge of five blunt arches spanning a brown and splashy stretch of the Torridge.

Sheldon [15] Far away, hard to find and not much when you get there. Small church restored 1871 (tower older). Very plain Norman font; screen restored 1939 and incorporating a few pieces of mediaeval tracery.

Sherford [34] Remote parish, the narrow roads closely hemmed in by wooded hills and knolls. The area is littered with the remains of fine old buildings now reduced to farmsteads but still full of harmony and some distinction. *Keynedon*, *Malstone* and *Stancombe* were Domesday manors. *Homefield* has a 14c window in its garden, probably removed there when the church was restored. *St Martin's* is very attractive. It is clear that the parish is working to try and reveal the 14c

148

fabric of the church and doing so with care and tact. The rood screen, removed during the war, has been replaced; old and battered, it does not compare with the grand examples but is charming none the less with the spandrels filled up with a jumble of odd bits and pieces, mediaeval paintings of the apostles in the wainscot; pulpit made from pieces of the former rood loft.

Shillingford St George [29] Too near Exeter for comfort, a dormitory village of suburban buildings. Church has an ancient S door into which a spyhole has been later cut. Brass above a tomb chest in the chancel to Sir William Huddesfield, who enlarged the church and built its tower in the last quarter of the 15c; another more primitive brass to John Seaman, d 1664. Behind the church is the rectory of 1813; built upon the site of Sir William Huddesfield's Tudor manor house and partly using its materials.

Shirwell [3] High, flattish country intersected by steep wooded valleys. You pass the E gates to Youlston House on the main Barnstaple–Lynton road: little pedimented houses with urns in niches, decorated with cherubs. *St Peter's* church has pillars carved in the same style as East Down but better preserved here. Some wooden piers at the N transept: odd, awkward and botched. Loxhore church, not far away, has beautifully finished wooden arcading in comparable style. 15c effigy of lady in chancel. Lugg plaque on N wall has a rough little portrait of a man holding a book: Tudor, primitive, charming.

Shobrooke [16] Church has a Norman S door with carved capitals; it overlooks rich, fertile countryside. No village, but a handsome barton just below.

Shute [36] Shute Barton is the considerable remains of a very old and handsome house, now National Trust. The hall, 1380, was originally a single great room rising to the roof with collar beams and curved braces; an exterior newel stair led up to a gallery just below the rafters. At some time the hall was divided horizontally and an extra storey fitted in. In the 15c the great hall was bisected by a screen, which still survives, and a huge kitchen hearth cut into one wall. In the hearth hangs a vast spit capable of roasting two oxen – last used in 1829 for a coming-of-age. Later additions to the house include the tower, one of the newer rooms has 17c panelling. The gateway, Elizabethan and built to impress, has two wings with turrets meeting over a central arch and pavilion displaying the Pole arms. It was the Poles who built *Shute House*, 1787, ½ m beyond, now a girl's school. In *St Michael's* church: worldly statue of Sir William Pole, the stance courtly, holding a delicate wand of office – he was Master of the Household to Queen Anne.

Sidbury [30] Tranquil and unspoilt, it lies in a verdant, wooded bowl which forms the watershed of the river Sid, from here making its short journey to the sea. The village has many old cottages, including Spencer Cottage, 1614, and a Methodist chapel of 1820. Church, *St Peter and St Giles*, is a costly looking structure with turretted tower and embattled porch. Remains of a Saxon crypt 670. Tower is rebuilt Norman with two archaic figures (probably effigies of St Peter and St Giles) taken from the interior and placed here during rebuilding. Exterior

Gothick house at **Sidmouth**

E wall has Tudor chequerboard stone-work. Porch is vaulted with 15c central boss showing four angels carrying the soul of the donor to heaven by the corners of her shroud. Inside: Norman corbels in the room at the base of the tower; wagon roofs, well lit and low in the aisles so that you can easily see the carving; gallery 1749 with original colouring: soft blue and gold and simulated marble surmounted by a cherub with trumpet; traces of wall paintings. *Court House* overlooks the church; part Tudor, part 18c. *Sand Barton*, 1 m NE, late Tudor mansion may be glimpsed from the road.

Sidmouth [18] Gem of ravishing Regency architecture. Elegant, little villas sparkle with white paint, delicate ironwork and small panes of coloured glass. The town lies in the valley of the Sid, with the red cliffs of Peak Hill west and Salcombe Hill east. The seafront between the two was quickly filled in during the 1820s, so the buildings are much of a piece and exceedingly pretty. Later developments had to spread inland up the valley and are more or less out of sight.

The Esplanade has only a low parapet, in the brilliant air you feel the same sense of openness and exhilaration as if on a boat deck. It would be difficult to choose amongst the charming villas along the front, many of them now hotels and boarding houses, but *Beach House* is especially delightful. Standing back from the sea is *Fortfield Terrace*, with wooden balconies treated as wrought iron. The Grand Duchess Helen of Russia stayed in the central pedimented house with eagle crest. This overlooks the cricket field, laid out in 1820 and one of the oldest in the country. *Coburg Terrace*, two rows of Gothic houses face each other across the flower-edged bowling green. *Coburg Rd* has Gothic cottages with plump, colourful gardens. *Church House* is brick Georgian, rather more restrained.

The Duke and Duchess of Kent came here in 1819 with their baby daughter, Princess Victoria, during a period of retrenchment. They stayed at what was then Woolbrook Cottage and is now the *Royal Glen Hotel*, which sits in its little dell, a miniature Gothic castle. The Duke's sudden death, which made the infant princess heir to the throne, did nothing to diminish interest in the

town and was partly responsible for the rush of building about this time. Queen Victoria gave the great E window to the church, *St Nicholas*, when it was rebuilt 1860, in memory of her father.

N from Fortfield and Coburg Terraces is Station Rd, with *Pebblestone Cottage*, probably once a toll house. Also the *Woodlands Hotel*, an elaborate *cottage orné*, barge-boarded like a wedding cake, built by Lord Gwydyr in 1815. Further up are the remains of *Knole Cottage*, a little flint building now hidden behind the vast Knole Hotel, which has usurped its position looking out over the sea. On the opposite side of Station Rd is *Claremont*. A little further S is All Saints Rd, with *Powys* and *Cedar Shade*, the latter more Victorian in feeling with, sure enough, a lawn shaded by great cedars, and a polygonal conservatory. Elizabeth Barrett Browning and her family stayed here for some time (another of those genteel retrenchments).

Behind the church, near Coburg Terrace, is the *Old Chancel*, curious currant bun of a house built by the antiquarian Peter Orlando Hutchinson and incorporating various bits of the old church which he salvaged when it was restored. Vivid example of materials misapplied, an antiquarian's house; there is no sense of architectural fitness, the great 15c windows are stuck on like so many glacé cherries.

Apart from walks up Peak Hill and Salcombe Hill which give views of Lyme Bay and the Sid valley, there is an idyllic stroll to be made along the banks of the river Sid from the E end of the Esplanade and up through the Byes. It crosses *Sid Meadow* (National Trust) with early Victorian *Salcombe House*, *Salcombe Lodge* (River Sid is the Salcombe parish boundary) and Sid Abbey. The walk finishes at *Sidford* where there are a few 16c cottages.

The main beach in front of the Esplanade at Sidmouth is pebbly. But just W, below Peak Hill and the *Connaught Gardens* (a series of ornamental gardens with sheltering walls and views of the bay), is a bathing beach with sand and rocky pools, good for children. Large car park nearby.

Silverton [17] Parts of the village are exquisite, particularly Fore St, where Nos 3, 27 and 29 have Georgian doorways each different and all attractive. Church has 17c wooden gallery with

carved stone pilasters; also an early iron bound chest.

Silverton Park, 1 m. E. Decayed Georgian mansion of the Earls of Egremont: severe lines of classical pediments are softened by ivy and warmed by terracotta brick where the plaster has flaked off. The surrounding country is rich and soft, and the gardens have long since reverted to pasture: the whole place romantic and derelict.

Slapton [34] Very flat with a lagoon behind the shingle beach. In the centre of the strand is an obelisk commemorating the American troops who rehearsed the Normandy landings here in 1944. On a rise N overlooking the sea is *Brockholt Hotel*, early Victorian. Slapton Village, quiet and interesting, is inland. Beside the parish church, 1318, is an 80 ft ruined tower, the remains of a collegiate chantry founded by Sir Guy de Brien, 1372; tucked behind is the old church house now an inn. *St James's* church: large screen, only the upper part is original; Victorian pulpit but the goblet stem looks much earlier; in the vestry two quaint wooden figures in Tudor dress barely a foot high. On the edge of the village is Slapton Ley Field Studies Centre.

Sourton [21] Hamlet on the N of Dartmoor: the higher, bleaker side; legend has it that the Devil died of cold on Sourton moor. Apart from the beauty of the situation Sourton is remarkable for the *Highwayman's Inn*, a rollicking piece of *kitsch*, the loving fantasy of many years, every nook indescribably quaint.

South Brent [3] In a broad, shallow bowl looking towards Dartmoor. *Ugborough Beacon* is a landmark W. Some suburban building near the main road dated by such names as *Mons Avenue*. The heart of the village is untouched; in Church St the old toll house still displays a board with tolls payable at fairs and markets. Church has a Norman font with cable, zig-zag and scroll patterns, the carving more lush and skilful than most Norman country work; altar rails incorporate fragments of 15c carving, probably from the old screen; carved chest with arms of Charles I. Outside the lych gate has a delicate piece of wrought iron for its latch. Just S of the churchyard is an old *Priest's house*.

Hope Cove, **South Huish**

Lydia bridge, $\frac{1}{2}$ m N: romantic little packhorse bridge with dark and bearded waterfalls, a few pretty cottages near by.

South Huish [34] Rocky coves at the coast, narrow twisting lanes inland, a few ancient cottages gnarled as rams' horns. This coast must have been idyllic until about 1900, but now the villages are smothered by inter-war building and the roads choked with cars. Nothing remains of South Huish church but a great creeper-covered stump and tombstones swallowed by brambles and rough grass. This must have been a fine old church with much 15c work, but it was abandoned as unsafe in 1866, to the deep resentment of the 400 parishioners, mostly fisherman and agricultural labourers, who were told to find the £300 needed for repair themselves if they wanted to keep the old building. The Vicar, squirearchy and Earl of Devon were determined to have a new church and raised £1,053 to build one, peculiarly ugly and featureless, at Galmpton. From the old church the Earl of Devon got the 15c bench ends; some of the materials went to Dodbrooke in 1886 for the new N aisle; Mr W. R. Ilbert of Bowringsleigh paid 20 guineas for the 15c screen.

Hope Cove. Sheltered double cove at the east end of Bigbury Bay. Good walks over Bolt Head (National Trust) and fine views W of the bay. *Outer Hope* is trippery and suburban, only a few ancient cottages patched and like old lobster pots give the place any flavour. *Inner Hope* is much more attractive: a few hundred yards inland, in a cleft of the cliffs, protected from sea and gales, are two little squares of fishermen's cottages set around patches of grass and cobble.

Southleigh [18] A dull church in a beautiful situation warmly folded in the hills above a tributary of the river Coly. Plain Norman S door. Nearby is *Blackberry Castle*, large Iron Age hill fort, oval in shape and now grassy and tree-shaded. Easily reached from the road, a good spot for picnics and ball games.

South Milton [34] A few old houses, the spaces between filled with suburban mess. Church stands high with a glimpse of the sea SW; tall graceful tower rather like Ashburton, its height emphasised by slender stepped buttresses and narrow twisted turret stair. Inside some fine Norman work, notably an unusual bronze crucifixion *c* 1150, scarcely six inches high, dug up

at Trendwell farm in 1961; in the S chancel chapel. Norman font with large zig-zag pattern haphazardly interspersed with heads and above a band of birds and beasts with an odd, crouching human figure; screen wainscot painted with monkish figures, coving still carries remains of painted curtaining, probably Georgian; exquisite parclose screen of unusual design, early 16c in feeling; ceiled and painted wagon roof with dates 1792–7 painted on, but the carving is much earlier; "Vinegar" bible of 1719 (Luke 22).

Across the valley is *Collaton Barton*, thatched farmstead probably as old as the church itself.

South Molton [13] Busy little market town with many pleasant Georgian and Victorian houses, as far removed in feeling as in geography from the chic London street that bears its name. Broad St has two island sites: the *Medical Hall*, iron balcony supported on Ionic pillars, looks across to the *General Post Office*, 1888, and already foreshadowing the neo-Georgian of so many post offices since. On the S side of Broad St, *Market and Assembly Rooms*, 1863, the Assembly Rooms have a remarkable roof of arched iron beams, the gap between beam and roof filled

Staverton Bridge

with fancy ironwork. Next door the *Guildhall*, 1743. Interesting to compare the two, especially since the Market Hall was clearly intended to echo the Guildhall; both are Civic Architecture, but the 18c building is lighter, gayer, more wayward.

The churchyard lies behind and between streets, a secret green place, entered from Broad St through handsome iron gates and avenues of plane trees. Inside the stone carving, mostly 14c, is very fine, particularly pulpit, font, chancel capitals and corbel to chancel arch.

In East St is *Paradise Lawn*, enclave of Victorian houses with balconies and balusters carved in wood, grouped round three sides of a treey lawn and divided from the road by a pretty iron railing, all rather demure and enviable. It seems to have been taken over by the town's medical profession.

Hugh Squiers School, 1684, further E still, arched doorways and three Gothic windows. Three old mills at the E end of the town, standing by the river Mole and now put to baser purposes.

South Pool [34] Prettily dispersed along an unspoiled valley, mill stream running down through the village with stepping stones at the bottom. Church has Norman font with red sandstone and key decoration as at Rattery. Screen wainscot painted with Renaissance arabesque. 14c effigy of lady in S transept; Easter sepulchre with damaged carving of Resurrection and sleeping soldiers, later used to house 16c effigy of Sir Thomas Bryant, rector; wall tablet: Leonard Darre and wife d 1615, her face carved with unusual sensitivity.

South Tawton [9] Hillside village where the Taw flows down from Dartmoor. Handsome church for so small a place: 18c pulpit inlaid with figures of the evangelists, fine workmanship and romantic style. Two good monuments: John Wykes, tomb of 1592, lying beneath a low tester in N chancel chapel, his feet supported by a duck; Robert Burgoyne, d 1651 and wife: father and mother in effigy above ten children on incised slate tablet below. Outside is the

Church House, 1572, a complicated exterior stairway leading to the first floor.

South Zeal, $\frac{1}{2}$ m S. Strung along what used to be the main Okehampton–Exeter road before it was rerouted through Sticklepath. In the middle is *St Mary's* chapel looking curious and archaic but said to date from 1713. The *Oxenham Arms* is superb early Tudor with two-storey porch and mullioned windows.

Sticklepath, $\frac{3}{4}$ m WSW. Athwart the main Okehampton–Exeter road. Notable for non-conformism and with early Industrial Museum of exceptional historical interest. The Finch Foundry made farm tools here for the west country from 1814–1960. This fascinating old works, with its pair of trip hammers, old machinery and timber acqueduct has been preserved by local enthusiasts. Behind is the crowded Quaker Burial Ground: many Friends from Sticklepath went to found the Settlement of Pennsylvania, and it was Quakers who first welcomed Wesley to the village. John and Charles Wesley preached regularly from a rock W of

152

the town. Another industrial survival is *Cleave Mill* down by the river; it made serge, including cloth for troops of the Nizam of Hyderabad, in the early 1800s.

South Zeal. *See* South Tawton.

Sowton [17] Thatch and red brick: workaday and unself-conscious. Church has good carving on capitals: angels hold shields or scrolls in long, squarish hands. *Bishop's Court* nearby was said to be the home of Bishop Bronescombe, one of the builders of Exeter Cathedral; his chapel remains *c* 1276. The house was rebuilt 1863 in Ecclesiastical Gothic by William White, great-nephew of Gilbert White of Selborne and intrepid restorer of churches.

Spreyton [9] Comely thatched cottages face each other across a street so broad as to be almost a square. Tom Cobley lies buried in the churchyard and the village takes credit in a quiet way (Widecombe is about 15 m away, just the right distance to knock up a horse). The church is approached by an avenue of limes planted 1802 and now immensely high. Present building is 15c with fine, well lit wagon roofs. In the chancel a long inscription meanders over the beams, indecipherable to me but said to record the name of the vicar, Henry le Maygne "a native of Normandy who caused me to be built 1451 and wrote all this with his own hand". Two fonts: one Norman with jolly outlined figures, the other Saxon; a few fragments of the old screen on the W wall.

Staverton [31] Church lies between the village and river Dart with wooded hills on the far side. It has a two-storey, embattled S porch and scratch sundial. Inside are several primitive brasses to the Gould family and tucked behind the organ the Worth monument, 1629, with kneeling figures. Chained copy of Fox's *Book of Martyrs*.
  Staverton Bridge, 1413: six arches and six bays for pedestrians on each side, its length, narrowness and the deep indentations give it much elegance.

Sticklepath. *See* South Tawton.

Stockland [36] *St Michael and All Angels*, large church for so small a vil-

Stoke Canon: detail of font

lage and a tall spire for E Devon. It rises behind and above an orchard with pleasantly wild churchyard overlooked on the SW by ancient cottages; very light inside because of three large lancet windows. Good manor house W of the village, Tudor with 18c facelift.
  Stockland Great Castle, 2 m SW. Iron Age hillfort through which the road runs.

Broadhayes House, 1½ m SSW. Georgian domestic at its most attractive: warm red brick and beautiful proportions.

Stockleigh English [13] Deepest Devon, no village. The big house, just by the church, is *Stockleigh Court*, late 18c. Charming churchyard: path leads down between clipped yews to the

153

modest church; the tower has lightly carved pinnacles like ears of wheat. Inside restored but with many Bellew monuments; they lived at Stockleigh Court until 1952.

Stockleigh Pomeroy [17] Scattered village with some neat 18c houses. Church full of 16c bench ends, the pulpit too is formed from them; remains of the old rood screen below the tower arch; Norman S doorway. *Great Gutton,* 1 m SW. Large, mellow, Tudor farmhouse still with its original mullioned and transomed windows.

Stoke Canon [17] Approached from S by a long, low bridge crossing water meadows, originally 13c but altered since. Church, rebuilt 1835 except for W tower, has a primitive Norman font: dragons bite the heads of men below, monks and strapwork, very attractive. Graceful Jacobean pulpit.

Stoke Fleming [35] The coast road from Stoke Fleming to Start Point is a true *corniche* winding up, round and down, always within sight of the sea, with the pines and conifers giving a Mediterranean feeling. You pass *Blackpool Sands,* a curve of white shingle beside (on a good day) the emerald sea framed by shelving wooded headlands. Stoke Fleming church stands high overlooking the sea. It has a brass, almost life size, to John Corp, d 1361, and his granddaughter Elyenore d 1391 a petite, elegant figure standing on a small pedestal to make her as tall as her grandfather. Another brass to Elias Newcomen, 1614, with punning rhyme. 13c effigy to Elinor Mohun.

Stoke Gabriel [31] In a deep cleft by a side creek of the Dart, a large, winding, hilly village with several fine old houses. It has a lakeside feeling: about 60 years ago the then squire built a weir preventing the upper part of the creek from being tidal; you can walk across the weir at low water. Church S porch has interesting, ugly corbels. Inside 15c carved wood pulpit (renewed); screen with painted wainscot; "Vinegar" bible; caseful of old parish documents.

Stoke Rivers [3] On the edge of a plateau. Church has tall W tower with stair turret and broad outlook over the valley. Interior restored but pulpit has early Renaissance panels, the carving a

little crude compared with, say, Swimbridge; font with 17c cover and some mediaeval tiles around base.

Stokeinteignhead [32] Village lying in a wooded and sheltered valley. Church has a very early screen; small brass in S chancel to Sir Thomas Taggel, d 1375 (earliest in Devon); another brass, heart shaped with French inscription, to Elizabeth Furlong, d 1647.

Stokenham [34] Coastal parish including *Start Point,* immemorial lookout, and a few small resorts and fishing hamlets. *Torcross* is one of the most attractive: simply a row of pleasant, old-looking houses fronting the sea and a comfortable hotel, no cars on the front, it must have been almost the same 100 years ago. Behind is the lagoon, *Slapton Ley,* and between lagoon and sea a road runs past Slapton Sands to Dartmouth.

Stokenham is a large village with large church. Pulpit of 1874 with small shields painted with various scenes and emblems: a cow, some soldiers, a ship etc.

Stoodleigh [14] Parish set high on a ridge cut through by the River Exe, with deep wooded gorges on each side; from *Stoodleigh Beacon* there are amazing all-round views. Church forms a group with school and school cottages. Norman font, plain except for two primitive heads on stem and claws below; 15c wagon roof with band of barbaric painted carving. *Stoodleigh Court:* "Tudor" of 1882, now a school.

Stowford [2*] A pretty village in a fold of the hills above the River Thrushel with a number of snug Tudor farmhouses; in springtime the churchyard is spangled with wild flowers. The church, *St John the Baptist,* restored wholeheartedly, and well by Sir G. Gilbert Scott, 1874. Best fun of the monuments is that to Christopher Harris as desired by Mrs Harris in her will of 1726; he stands dressed as a Roman foot soldier in the glory of a full-bottomed wig, but painfully short in the leg, like a harpy in Greek sculpture. Romano-British stone just by the church gate. *Hayne* (the family home of the Harris's) lies 1½ m W. Tudor house considerably altered *c.* 1810 by Wyatville.

Strete [34] Village of old, stone houses lying in an open, wooded valley beside the sea. Most seaside parishes are bleak and bony but these few valleys between Dartmouth and Start Point run NW–SE sheltered from the prevailing winds. Parish was carved out of Blackawton in 1881 but the simple church is 1836. N is the vicarage, 1831 (i.e. the parson kept an eye on the church during building) with a beehive porch S. *Kings Arms Hotel* has Victorian wrought-iron balcony and awning of elaborate delicacy.

Sutcombe [4] Compact village near the Cornish border far from tourist routes, but offering its individual pleasures. *St Andrew's* church is basically Perpendicular but with vestiges of the earlier Norman building: plain Norman doorway to S porch; Norman head mounted in a blocked-up Tudor doorway in the exterior S chancel wall. Inside is much good Renaissance carving: pulpit, base of screen, bench ends and carved ribs and bosses of the wagon roof. Many old Barnstaple tiles gnarled like fossils. Well kept chapel of 1868 with magnificent yew and, like the school, fretted with rich bargeboarding. *Thuborough Barton,* 1 m S, mentioned in Domesday, is now Georgian: built of granite blocks, with a pillared portico.

Swimbridge [3] Large, attractive village with Georgian houses and Baptist chapel, 1837, with graceful Gothick windows. John Russell was Rector of Swimbridge for 48 years from 1833, famous hunting parson and breeder of the Jack Russell Terrier. Reverend Jack's church has beautiful furnishings: font made like a cupboard with folding doors with cover and canopy above, exquisite Renaissance carving; particularly fine screen, bold and lavish; pulpit *c* 1490 with figures in niches, traces of gilt and paint; marvellous roofs: N transept, behind the organ, has roof bosses with delicate faded paint, low and well lit so they can be seen easily. On the S wall hang two old photographs showing the church before restoration in the '80s, essentially the same, but with box pews and a W gallery but above all the Georgian air of simplicity and plainness, now gone.

above Torcross and Slapton Ley (*see* **Stokenham**)

below **Strete**

Tawstock: Bath family memorials

Sydenham Damarel [23] NW of Tavistock in pleasantly wooded country on the banks of the Tamar. Church burnt down and rebuilt in 1957, half its original size; interior now so plain that the very radiators look like abstract art; it's strange to see a church with no monuments or decoration.

Horsebridge, 1 m SW. At the Cornish border a massy pack bridge of seven arches with recesses for foot travellers. Enticing vistas along the river which tempt one to walk along the water's edge but both banks are privately owned and strongly worded notices proclaim the fact. The *Royal Inn* has Gothick windows rather large for an inn; perhaps it was once a toll house. The whole group is prettily set amongst the wooded slopes of the Tamar.

Barnstaple tiles,
Sutcombe

Talaton [30] Hillside village, a pretty one, of cob and thatch, built on different levels with the church at the bottom. Even so there is a pleasant broad outlook from the churchyard. *St James:* tower stair turret niches still complete with figures of saints; 15c S door with "sanctuary" knocker; fine screen; wagon roof with gilt bosses; Norman font; old bench ends.

Tamerton Foliot [23] Plymouth oozes ever N inland creeping up the hillsides and trickling down into the valleys beyond. The old village of Tamerton Foliot has been engulfed by new housing built in the last five years. Still some Georgian houses – notably *Wadlands,* unpretentious, overlooking the churchyard and a few stone built cottages. Church has good monuments: a mediaeval 1400 knight and lady recumbent; Coplestone Memorial, 1617, man and wife kneel facing each other, their children below, at either side babes in

cribs their heads cushioned on tiny skulls. Susan Calmady, 1617, stands in her shroud against a black shell. Coplestone Bamfyld, 1669, aged 9, seated at a table of books.

Maristow. 2½ m N. An ugly, great house in a beautiful park. You can share the view over the river to Plymouth as there is a public road running past the house, which is now a school. Private chapel, open to the public for Sunday services, an interesting example of the social arrangements in these private Victorian chapels. The Family entered by a private door from the house and sat at the rear on individual thrones in a carpeted pew; lesser breeds were provided with wooden pews in front and below. Decor is richly gilt Victorian Gothic, a little too reminiscent of pit and boxes.

Maristow Barton. Near by is a beautiful weathered farmstead with a great old barn and hexagonal winnowing shed.

Tavistock

Tavistock [23] Built on several hills so that as you walk about you see changing vistas of Georgian shops and houses. Gothick villas and tree-lined streets. The town is divided below by the river and canal and above by a dramatic railway viaduct that strides across the town, rickety houses leaning up against its legs. The two main phases of the town meet in Bedford Square. The Abbey was founded in the 10c and became one of the most important in Devon. But in 1539 came the Dissolution when the Abbey lands were given to the Russells, who thereafter took charge. Hints of the Abbey remain to show its size. If you take the Bedford Hotel and the road in front of it as occupying the main portion and line of the Abbey building, you will find the Abbey's *Gatehouse* to the W, housing an old sarcophagus. In front of the hotel, N, is the churchyard with fragments of the Abbey wall, a decorated arch and also a little original paving.

Near Tavistock
above Morwell Barton
below Morwellham Quay

Across Bedford Square, incorporated in the Civic buildings of 1860, is the *Town Gate of the Abbey.* (Nestling within it a charming little reading room, one of the oldest in the country, founded in 1799.) Just behind the Bedford Hotel, near the river, is the *Abbey Dining Hall for the Sick*, now a Unitarian chapel. A carved braced roof truss preserved in the garden clearly shows the original method of construction with oak pins. Nearer the river stand remains of the *Abbey Wall* and the *Still Tower*.

The hand of the Bedfords is everywhere in the town, notably that of the 7th Duke. During the first half of the 19c his local mining interests, developed during the previous 50 years of the industrial revolution, were at their most productive and profitable. The Bedfords have left an impression of care and paternalism: they remodelled the centre of the town in castellated Gothick, which was fashionable when they started with the Bedford Hotel in 1820, and retained it for the civic buildings of 1860; the style recalls a little the feeling of an Abbey township. The dining room of the Hotel was the ballroom of the original 18c house and remains today. In the late 1840s

the Bedfords built a model estate for their miners. *Wisbridge Villas*, to the W of the town.

Cornmarket, West Street 1830 in a plain classical style (since it was not in Bedford Square); now a supermarket, but sufficient of the exterior remains to show it very pleasing in its plain and unselfconscious way.

St Eustace Church 15c and *not* built by the Bedfords but by the clothworkers of Tavistock, upon the proceeds of Devon serge. (Cloth gave the town its prosperity between the Abbey and the mines.) High and spacious church. W tower has great openings N and S probably used for processional purposes since the S arch led directly to the Abbey: stained glass E window in N aisle by William Morris; tomb of Sir John Fytz, his wife and son; in 1605 this young man killed three others, then ran himself through with his own sword. Fine tomb, with very good portrait figures of John Glanville and his wife, d 1600; also a little parish collection: Churchwarden's roll of 1385, 17c pewter flagons, chained book, old ecclesiastical chest probably 14c, etc.

Workhouse N of the town at the top of Bannawell Street, great classical

Teignmouth

in, but the exterior very little altered. Sign marks the house on the road from Bere Alston to Culworthy and you pass it on foot as you walk through to the woods beyond on your way to Morwell Rocks, magnificent rocky outcropping above the Tamar valley.

Morwellham Quay, 4 m SW of Tavistock. The Tamar is navigable to this point and in 1802 the Tavistock canal was cut and through it came all the rich ore from the Bedford mines. For 50 years the little place boomed and prospered. Now it lies like some forgotten Klondike with dirt roads, a few old stone cottages and one or two more handsome houses built for the leading workmen. The quays (they were surprisingly large) may still be traced by the lines of great stone bollards. Abandoned arsenic furnaces down by the river. The place feels poignant and marvellously romantic, the quietness all the more intense because it was once so full of clatter. Work has recently started to reinstate Morwellham Quay as a piece of industrial archaeology.

See also Whitchurch.

Tawstock [3] Snug and pretty countryside of cosy valleys and wooded hills. From the 15c onwards it belonged to the Earls of Bath as a glance in the church will show and then, through their heirs, to the Wrays. Their great mansion was burned down in 1787. Only the Tudor gatehouse survives, date plate above the coat of arms 1574. The present house, Gothick in style, stands in an enviable position looking S over a delicate view. Now a school.

The church has an extraordinary collection of memorials, mostly to the Bath family. Cheek by jowl these nobles stand squashed and jumbled as in a depository; the most splendid, in the chancel, is to the third Earl with kneeling, standing, reclining figures (the gentlemen wearing their coronets), the whole gilt and painted. Amongst them is a strange bust: a man turns his head at right angles to his naked shoulders, his eyes disturbed, long hair and beard, the inevitable coronet and above it a tasselled cap. The fifth Earl is remembered in the S chancel chapel crowded in with his relations: a heavy affair of bulbous sarcophagus supported by four enormous dogs, an obelisk at each corner and with coronets thrown over the obelisks like so many quoits: tinny and battered. 14c

building with huge walls to frighten the paupers, an early work by Gilbert Scott and now converted into flats.

St Mary Magdalene dominates the town from the W. Large church built by the Bedfords for their R.C. tenants in 1865.

Boehm Statue of Sir Francis Drake, 1883, stands at the head of Plymouth Road. Drake was born near Tavistock.

Replica on Plymouth Hoe.

Morwell Barton, 3½ m SW of Tavistock, 15c house once a country residence of the abbots of Tavistock. Fine two-storeyed porch, the pillars on each side surmounted by jolly pinnacles with crockets and castellations, leading to an inner courtyard. Now part farm, part farm workers' cottages. Some of the windows have been roughly bricked

wooden effigy of a lady in the chancel. The church, even without its monuments, is interesting; most of it dates from 1340; the arches of the arcades rest on corbels with painted and sculpted heads; transept roofs have delicate plastered flowers and tendrils in a star design; a gallery, now in the N chancel, but it looks out of place; Hoskins dates it late 16c and considers it may have come from the old house after the fire. In the S chancel chapel is an altar cloth of 1697, faded crimson and gilt with a countess's coronet and the initials R.B. A curious pew-like object in the W transept, like a large sedan chair but probably dating from before the mid 16c, panelled, the ceiling being carved with rosettes and painted. Inside one of the panels low down is a crafty little cupboard which one hopes used to hold something a little cheering or perhaps a chamber pot.

Tedburn St Mary [28] Two villages in fact; the new village has grown at the confluence of pub, Methodist chapel and school room (with Georgian roundheaded windows) and main road; the original village stands $\frac{3}{4}$m W around the church. *St Mary's* is restored but has remains of 14c tomb in S transept chapel; brass in S chancel wall to Jane Gee, d 1613; capital of first pier in N aisle has charming carved naked figures.

Teigngrace [31] Vainly struggling to resist the dislocating effect of nearby Newton Abbot. Pretty church lies back behind weeds and houses and approached by a grass-grown carriage drive with turning circle round an old yew. *St Peter and St Paul* was rebuilt 1786; only the 17c tombstones from the earlier church remain in the floor. Some interesting details: W door square Georgian, lintel supported by three slender columns each side, a 14c influence; the same column beneath the organ loft but here marbled. A number of monuments, of considerable taste and refinement to the Templars of Stover House.
   Stover House, $\frac{3}{4}$m W. Built 1776, handsome but not overstated; (the same taste as in the church): porch supported on Doric columns added 1820. Now a school.

Teignmouth [32] Archetypal seaside resort of much charm; fishing village

Tiverton: St Peter's

and small port before it became a watering place late in the 18c. In 1826 Teignmouth staked its claim to gentility with *Den Crescent* by Patey of Exeter, a sequence of houses with the Assembly Rooms in the centre, just a little too grandiose, now a cinema surrounded by ice cream slogans and boarding house signs. The Promenade is gay and open, fronted by a narrow beach of coarse, reddish sand with a diminutive lighthouse of 1845 at the S end. Shaldon Cliff rises S, and the *Parson and Clerk* rock stacks N. Behind the promenade are small Regency streets, such as Northumberland Place; Keats stayed here in 1818 at No. 20. Running off Northumberland Place pretty narrow streets, Ivy Lane, Teign St etc., lead down to New Quay built

1821 for shipping Dartmoor granite to rebuild London Bridge. This overlooks the *Salty* lagoon lying behind the bar of land at the estuary mouth; here fishing boats are drawn up on the coarse shingle, absolutely sheltered if winds rake the promenade; two good riverside pubs, and *Salty Cottage*, a boat's hull framing the door; also a ferry to Shaldon and boat trip up river to Newton Abbot. Returning to the town centre W. H. Smith in Regent St is housed in the *Royal Library*, early 19c and Egyptian in feeling. Further W is *Bitton House*, now U.D.C. offices: large Regency house with views across the estuary, easily approachable through pleasure gardens; entrance hall and council chamber retain much of the feeling of the original mansion.

Having once been two parishes Teignmouth has two churches which, if not old, stand on ancient sites. *St James* with Norman W tower is an unusual octagonal church of 1820: an elegant vaulted roof is supported on tapering cast-iron pillars and lit by a slate-hung lantern; Victorian pulpit of translucent amber marble, very seaweedy when the sun shines through. Right down by the shore is *St Michael's*, on a Saxon site, built 1823: Norman in style, Early Victorian in proportion, by Patey of "The Den".

See also Shaldon.

Templeton [13] Lost and decrepit village in wildest Devon standing on a ridge between deep valleys. Original church was built by the Knights Templar in the 14c but nothing remains; except for the W tower the whole fabric was heavily restored in 1877. Printed poster below the bell tower, gay as a playbill, advertising the re-opening in 1878.

Tetcott [7] Featureless village above a side valley leading down to the Tamar; but nearby is *Tetcott House*, 1603, with additions *c.* 1700. Picturesque and romantic, the house rambles below a spreading, sunken slate roof exquisitely speckled with amber lichens and punctuated by buttress-like chimneys. Around it weathered farm buildings and to the S just across a courtyard is the church. *Holy Cross* is interesting for the Arscott pew in the S chancel with

lavish carving *c.* 1700, and a Norman font with band of saltires.

Thelbridge [13] Scattered hamlet in the very centre of Devon. Church has fierce gargoyles on the tower. Interior restored 1872 and without artistic interest. A small pleasure is a Victorian screen below the tower in different shades of green glass; worthless if it doesn't appeal to you as it did to us.

Thornbury [5] Scattered village in remote, dull upland country not far from the Cornish border. Church S door has a carved Norman arch in good preservation. Spicott monument *c.* 1641, family affair with kneeling figures.

Thorverton [17] Lying below a ridge of hills, pretty and carefully kept village. Wide streets some with broad cobbled shoulders; runnels of water refresh the streets and join the village stream as it crosses the green. Thatched, colonnaded house of 1763, now a butcher's, hung with baskets of flowers and many more pretty cottages of many dates in the local stone; *Jessamine Cottage* has a Tudor doorway and screen. Church over-restored, but jewel of a S porch: fan vaulted, central boss with allegorical representation of Trinity; bosses of four evangelists shows each seated in front of little chair back, or screen, books spread before them.

Throwleigh [9] With Gidleigh, its neighbouring parish, one of the most peaceful and beautiful of Devon parishes. Lying on a hilltop at the head of The Teign valley NW of Dartmoor; there is a pleasant view of the moor if you stroll through the churchyard to the W. At the head of the village is a group of amiable thatched cottages with the old Church House. The church itself has a fine priest's door to the S chancel given importance by the Perp. carving. Sundial 1663 over S porch. Interior much restored but pulpit includes bits of the 1544 screen; mutilated remains of an Easter Sepulchre.

Many fine mediaeval farmhouses remain in the area including *Shilston*, *Wonson* and *Clannaborough*, the latter $\frac{1}{2}$ m NW perched at the very shoulder of the moor.

Thrushelton [20] Deep in rural Devon, peaceful and remote. Church stands

above a stream in a quiet valley. Not very notable inside although it has an original wagon roof. Ghoulishly preserved in the porch is wagon wheel, small, but lethal looking, that killed a man in 1788.

Thurlestone [26] Exceptionally balmy air and fertile soil have given the village its particular character. The curving main street is lined with low thatched cottages, the garden walls tumbling over with flowers and luxuriant with fuchsia hedges, palms and fig trees. The *Old Rectory* has a fine and fondly kept garden overlooking Bigbury Bay, open to the public. Churchyard filled with the sound and smell of the sea. The most striking architectural feature is probably the early 15c S porch. Inside a fine Norman font; fragments of a 15c rood screen used in Lady Chapel altar; in the chancel four small carvings probably mediaeval Flemish. By the church an old barton surmounted by a dovecote of 1882, grand as a campanile.

Thurlestone Sands SSE: good stretch of beach with golf links, hotels, cafés and every other commercial amenity. Offshore is the *thurled* (pierced) rock from which the village takes its name.

Tiverton [14] Standing where the rivers Exe and Loman meet the name means "two fords". Its first great period of prosperity was based upon wool and its chief employers are still textile manufacturers.

The town is divided by the Exe, each half being of a distinct character. The W bank is a very unusual example of an early 19c workers' housing estate; the buildings as seemly and pleasing as anything comparable in Bath or Cheltenham. The E bank is now the shopping centre elbowing the remains of a fine market town. Most of the earlier buildings disappeared in a catastrophic fire of 1731; the character of what remains is threatened by a vile one-way traffic system. If you enter the E end of the town by a bridge over the Loman, on your left are the old buildings of *Blundell's School*, founded 1599, during the town's wealthiest period by Peter Blundell, wool merchant. The buildings date from 1604, the cupola is 1740. The Rev. Samuel Wesley, brother of John and Charles, was a headmaster. John Ridd, hero of *Lorna Doone*, went to school here and gives a vivid description of a fight on the "ironing box", an

Topsham

163

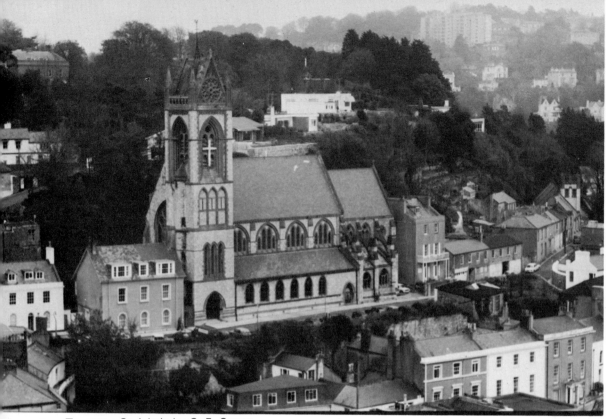

Torquay: St John's by G. E. Street

odd shaped lawn, still to be seen, and the traditional "ring" at Blundell's. In 1880 the school moved further out to a new building by Hayward (well known as a West Country church architect). Leaving Blundell's you come to Fore St with a number of good early buildings including *Greenway's Almshouses* 1529. The main roads of the town are now seen to form a square. It is fun to walk along Fore St; many small alleys run off S (e.g. Stafford Place and South View). Leaving the traffic and strident shop fascias you enter calm, cobbled felicities of little 18c houses and cottage gardens. At the W end of Fore St is *St George's* church built 1714–30 by John James. Georgian exterior with some Georgian fittings inside. A small diversion left down St Andrew's St will bring you to the old school with an extremely interesting local and folk museum (an open air exhibit of the museum is an old tank engine set up on the main road E of the town centre).

The pivot of the town centre is the *Town Hall*, a bastard born of High Renaissance and olde Rome. Right into St Peter's St, you find a group of ancient

buildings which escaped the fire of 1731. The *Slee Almshouses* are on the raised pedestrian way to the right. Opposite is the *Chilcot School*, 1611, with its original door. Thence, continuing N a number of good 18c houses.

At the N end of St Peter's St is the church standing high above the River Exe but the view is now hidden by overgrown trees. The S exterior is thickly encrusted with rich mossy carving. Principal donor was John Greenway who built the S porch and chapel; the work here is very fine and the motifs, such as armed merchantmen, intimate and vivid. The interior of *St Peter's* is much restored. The old screen went to Holcombe Rogus where it is now the chancel screen. Norman door in N wall. In the chancel are the tombs of John Walrond, d 1579, and George Slee, d 1613. These names will be familiar also as the donors of almshouses. Two large pictures: Gaspar de Crayar "Adoration of the Magi"; Richard Cosway "Delivery of St Peter", 1784. Cosway was born in Tiverton, *Mayor's Pew*, with lion and unicorn of 1615, has splendid set of prayer books, 1750 and 1758.

Greenway's Chapel, by the S door, divided from the church by a low stone screen and entered from the S porch by a 16c door. Chapel restored 1829 and 1952.

Just NE of the church is the *Castle*. Built 1106 by Richard de Redvers, 1st Earl of Devon. Much of the castle was destroyed by Fairfax in 1643 but what remains is still impressive including a massy 14c gatehouse. SW tower with fine early 14c window; round SE tower; also parts of the Tudor mansion.

Across the river on the W bank are the large *John Heathcote Textile Works*. Heathcote came here from Loughborough in 1816 after his lacemaking machinery had been burned by Luddites. The factory he then built was burned in 1936, presumably by less violent cause. The original lodge gates remain, very dignified, and incorporated in the new building are several fine, broad Georgian fanlights. By the gates the factory school of 1841 is in quite different 15c style. All around the works stands the monument to Heathcote's paternalism, taste and breadth of soul; these are the streets and squares of cottages Heathcote built for his workers. Many are double fronted, with seemly detailing, none are mean. In sharp contrast are the later Victorian factory cottages: much more in the style of "workers' dwellings".

Chevithorne Barton, 3 m NE. House dates from *c* 1600 but stands on the site of a Saxon dwelling. It retains the original lines and detail, but wall surfaces etc. are much altered. Approached by an avenue of beeches with charming view sloping away S. To visit Chevithorne on an early July day is to see the English countryside at its most attractive: great trees black-green against the pale gold of ripening barley and cut hay.

Knightshayes Court, 2 m NNW. 1870–3, essay in high Victorian Tudor by William Burgess. The gardens of both houses are periodically open to the public.

Topsham [29] Lying on the broad Exe estuary, the Romans established a port here and built a road leading into Exeter. In 1290 Countess Wear throttled Exeter's navigable river and Topsham became the city's vital outlet to the sea. It is a charming little town, not so much unspoiled as cunningly tarted up by affluent commuters who want to keep it charming. Down on the Strand are handsome 18c houses built in Dutch style by merchants trading with the Low Countries; they look inwards to private courtyards and gardens shielded from view by high walls, but through open doors you catch enticing glimpses of cobbles and mimosa; on the other side of the road, by the waterside, are more gardens, the glittering river beyond dotted with small boats. All the houses are attractive, the most distinguished is probably the *Shell House*, 1571.

Within the town, Fore St lies parallel to the Strand; at the corner of Station Rd is *Broadway House*, *c*. 1700: Corinthian doorway and gates, contemporary with the house, of springy looking wrought iron. Follet St, almost opposite, with Clara Place, 1841, a group of pedimented houses looking on to a tree-shaded lawn protected by demure iron railings. Returning to Fore St and heading S you reach the *Salutation Inn*: Tuscan portico over the pavement, massive studded door with postern, above a showy Venetian window set below a broken pediment. Beyond is

All Saint's, Babbacombe: pulpit by Butterfield (*see* **Torquay**)

the church rebuilt 1869–78 by Ashworth who also did Bideford; the tower is old. Chancel roof has Victorian carving; raised design of formalised twigs in graceful diamond patterns; Duckworth monument, *c* 1817 by Chantrey, of naval battle in relief; Norman font with crouching beasts looking backwards. Churchyard has a famous view.

Beyond the church, where Fore St and the Strand begin to converge is *Cromer House*: red brick William and Mary, Tuscan doorway, wrought-iron paling surmounted by small urns. One of the attractions of Topsham is its pubs. A favourite by the river at the N end of the town is the *Passage Inn*, with slate hung date stone 1788, but the inn is much older. Its waterside garden has, to my mind, a more attractive view than that from the churchyard. Another ancient pub is *Bridge Inn* at the E approach to the town, overlooking plump water meadows, probably 16c or earlier, a picturesque wandering building with oddly angled roofs and chimneys. Museum of local history is in an old sail loft at 25, The Strand.

Torbryan [31] Charming hamlet in a sheltered hollow: church, a few cottages and *Church House Inn*, this dated *c*. 1500 with Tudor screen, the ideal of an old country pub modernised. Exceptionally interesting church: exquisite fan vaulting in S porch; screen, little restored and stretching across church; well preserved wainscot paintings; pulpit very narrow and high made from parts of a screen; Jacobean font cover; 15c oak pews encased to make box pews in Georgian times; Vinegar bible 1717; reredos *c*. 1820: icing sugar Gothick.

Denbury, 1¼ m N. The massive garden walls of the manor house take up a quarter of the village; it is a 17c house with Georgian façade and another restoration 1825. At the centre of the village is an 18c water conduit converted to war memorial. Church still preserves its aisleless 13c form (but with a dormer window inserted above S porch). Simple furnishings: Norman font in red sandstone with palmettes; screen (restored) across N transept. Monument to John Taylor, d 1733, by Weston, showing naval battle.

Torcross. *See* Stokenham.

Torquay [32] From Teignmouth the limestone cliffs rise sharply and the *corniche* traces the indented headlands, one of the finest stretches of coast in the county. As the premier resort of Devon Torquay can boast endless amenities but the oldest is unquestionably *Kent's Cavern* on the heights NE of the town proper: two main caves in which tools of Stone Age man and bones of extinct animals were found early in the 19c. *Tor Abbey* was founded 1196 and built on the level ground W only 500 yds from the sea. Some parts of the old building remain: Gatehouse 1320, great 124 ft Tithe Barn and Abbott's Tower; the W side of the house retains its mediaeval look and great chunks of masonry fallen from the Abbey Church lie N of the house. It became a ruin after the Dissolution and in 1662 passed to the Carys, who added a Georgian S front. The house now belongs to Torquay Corporation who use it as a museum and recreation centre.

Early in the 19c the village of Torquay began to attract some attention as a minor watering centre and haven for the families of naval officers during the Napoleonic Wars. The Carys and, more particularly, the Palks, seized their opportunity and began to develop the town. Sir Robert Palk was one of those young men who during the 18c set out for India to claim a fortune or die of cholera. He returned in 1768 not with one fortune but two, a friend having made Palk his beneficiary; Palk's newly acquired estates included the village of Tor Quay and thus he started his family upon their third, and greatest fortune. Two generations of Palks and of their architects, the Harveys, made Torquay as we see it. Many of their streets and terraces were planned as a whole, and since they were aimed at a select and high-class family clientele the houses have style and solidity, and are surrounded by gardens which flourish in the temperate winters; *Hesketh Crescent*, 1846, now the Osborne Hotel, is perhaps the most conspicuous example but there are many others. But geology imposed itself upon the plan; the great strains of limestone shoulder up through the town thrusting the houses aside. The terraces cannot shroud this landscape they must conform to it; if you stand and look down upon the town, from Warren Rd perhaps, you will see that Torquay is two thirds rocks, trees and gardens.

Churches. Torquay once was three parishes: Tormohun, Babbacombe and Cockington. With the enormous expansion during the 19c came the Victorian churches, some by the best architects of the period and very fine. However St Michael's Pimlico has disappeared beneath a supermarket, its stained glass by Morris and Co is now in the care of St John's Montpelier Terrace.

St Saviour's, original parish church of Tor Mohun, said to incorporate a Norman church but now mainly 15c. The Victorian restoration came early when it was realised that the parish at the gate was mushrooming. The old church has a warm atmósphere: Torquay is obviously still a church-going community. Fine 15c font: three angels link arms at the base, with panels of rippling leafy forms above. Monuments to Thomas Cary, d 1567; brass to John Gifford and wife, d 1581, and elaborate wall monument to Thomas Ridgeway, d 1604, reclining figure in armour. *St Mary's* church, Babbacombe, parish church destroyed by bombing, the rebuilding poor. Fortunately an exceptional Norman font survived: panels show bear walking, hound crouching, man drinking (?) etc. *St George and St Mary,* Cockington, lying just beside the big house, a charming, much visited 15c church. A graceful early Renaissance pulpit painted and gilt saved from St Saviour's in 1825, as were the misericords; altar rails 17c; a few old bench ends; etc. *All Saint's,* Babbacombe, 1865–74 by Butterfield. A promising exterior: the S porch steeply pitched with pagoda roof patterned with Butterfield's variegated tiles, richly diapered and trellissed. Inside, the basic shapes and masses are quite simple but the surfaces sumptuously rich. It forms an interesting contrast with *St John's,* Montpelier Terrace, 1861–71, by G. E. Street, with glass by Morris and Burne Jones. St John's is high, light and airy, the surface decoration a little fussy with much wrought iron and brass, all adding to the light, twinkling effect.

Cockington. Torquay Corporation is now the principal landowner in these parts, and has shown itself tactful and farsighted. In 1935 the municipality bought the village of Cockington for £50,000 and now maintains it as yet another amenity. It's a very pretty village: *Cockington Court* is Elizabethan, slightly Georgianised; the forge and surrounding cottages preserve an immaculate finish. The *Drum Inn* 1934 by Lutyens is one of those fine, thatched, Bedford Parkish buildings, fitting into the village but maintaining its integrity.

Totnes [31] The Saxon town of Totnes covered barely 10 acres. Its walls run N past the Guildhall and Ramparts Walk (reached by steps below Eastgate), thence along the line of South St, and back to the Castle. After the Norman conquest the town soon spread down Fore St to the river, and the heart of Totnes is the walk up Fore St, under Eastgate and on into High St. Start at the bridge (Charles Fowler, 1826) with *Bridgetown,* full of Early Victorian, behind you. L is *The Plains,* still Bridgetown in feeling; memorial to Wills, native of Totnes, d 1861 exploring the Australian Outback with Burke. On up Fore St, past houses dated 15c onwards, all attractive and gaining from being close packed. Of particular interest: *Gothic House* 1783; on the same side the former *King Edward VI Grammar School,* founded 1553 but now in a handsome Georgian house with hooded doorway and Corinthian pilasters. No. 70 *The Museum,* in a house dating from 1575 and 1630: interesting local collection including material on Charles Babbage, b Totnes 1792, inventor of the first computer. Then Eastgate, with cupola and oriel window; R parish church set back from the road and once faced in by houses; opposite is Nicholas Bak's house of 1589 (his daughter m. Thomas Bodley, founder of the Bodleian Library), somewhat touched up. Now come the *Butterwalk* and the *Poultrywalk,* set on pillared arcades of granite, cast iron and wood. Opposite is the new Civic Hall.

Castle. Commanding the navigable reaches of the Dart where three valleys meet, fine Norman motte and bailey built 1086 by Judhael de Totnes, follower of Norman William.

Guildhall. Tucked away N of the church, unpretentious and domestic, basically 13c but given a new frontage 1611 with sturdy granite pillars. Interior furnishing mostly Victorian but in Council Chamber is a plaster frieze and arms 1624; underneath is the town lockup, looking 13c indeed.

Church. Elaborate exterior with fine red sandstone tower as at Ashburton and Cullompton. One of the image niches houses the supposed head of Bishop Lacy of Exeter and text "I made this tore". Inside a magnificent stone screen 1459–60 painted and gilt and very free in style; rood loft removed 1862 by Sir G. Scott during his restoration, but an unusual rood stair remains, entered from behind a stone screen in N chancel. Tomb chest in S chancel chapel to Walter Smith, d 1555, insensitive carving. Wall tablet in N aisle to Christopher Blackall, d 1633, and four wives. Popular tablet to Walter Venning, d 1821, prison worker who died of fever caught in a St Petersburg gaol; epitaph in Russian means "I was a prisoner and you visited me".

Civic Centre. Shops line a broad piazza on the E side and opposite are the stalls of the Friday market; a low stone wall gives seat bays with raised flower beds between. Behind is the Hall, slate hung like the Butterwalk opposite (Jellicoe, Ballantyne and Coleridge 1960).

Trentishoe [3] A church and a farm stand at the end of a rough road, extraordinarily hidden and remote in feeling yet only $\frac{1}{2}$ m from the sea: no wonder this was a centre of smuggling. Church, very small, has a musician's gallery with a hole cut in the front to accommodate the bass viol.

Heddon's Mouth is an unspoilt combe, thickly wooded and leading to the sea. Old limekiln on the beach; limestone was ferried across from Wales, burnt here and used on surrounding farms. The road across Knap Down to Combe Martin gives a panoramic view across the Bristol Channel to Wales; on a clear day the whole S side of the Principality lies before you. Good, well marked walks.

Hunter's Inn. Brewer's Tudor replacing a much older thatched hostelry burnt down in the middle of the last century.

Trusham [28] Wandering village in Teign-side valley, set with hummocky hills. Church has a double view. Two interesting monuments: in N chancel recess 16c painting of Staplehill family, primitive brass below; E end N aisle

The Guildhall, **Totnes**

large wooden tablet: John and Mary Stooke 1697, classical style but country execution, painted, marbled and gilt with two portrait medallions; she wears a homely kerchief about her decent head.

Twitchen [10] On the very edge of Exmoor, exquisite hidden country with steep twisting roads where bracken fronds brush the sides of the car. Dull church; Norman font with bold chevron pattern.

Two Bridges. *See* Dartmoor.

Uffculme [14] Sloping down to the River Culm. Large village with the usual unassuming Georgian houses, but also *Ayshford House* W of the Square. A medallion records that Nicholas Ayshford endowed a school here in 1701; the whole is much altered and added to but it looks more 17c than 18c. *Bengal House*, Fore St, has a sensitive 18c doorway with pediment and pilasters. Dominating the start of the High St, a factory with date stone 1838 in red brick with octagonal tower and roundheaded windows.

A handsome church, *St Mary*, early 15c screen, exceptionally wide: 67 ft. Parts of the Jacobean W gallery incorporated in tower screen. Pulpit dated 1719 but with 16c Flemish carving of the Ascension. The *Walrond Chapel* has carving from Bradfield house and an altar incorporating 16c carving recently painted and gilt. Huge Walrond tomb chest of 1663, crudely carved and boldly coloured; set upon it are life size, free-standing busts of a man, a woman and a boy, the faces ugly and full of vitality; a life-size, full-length figure of 1689 in armour and full-bottomed wig reclines along the window sill.

The Walronds lived 2 m SSW at Bradfield where they established themselves in the 13c, but their house as it stands is 16c. The exterior has been altered later although it still looks very fine seen from the S. The interior has a magnificent hall with hammer-beam roof and much 16c carving and plaster work.

Ugborough [27] The village square has a conduit dated 1887 but in an earlier style; above is an ancient earthwork with the church set plumb upon it to demonstrate its superiority over earlier faiths. The N door with date 1731

studded in nails. An interesting interior: carved Norman font in red stone; early 16c screen with painted panels, cut down in the centre to improve sight lines. Lively, well-lit bosses in the N aisle; brass in N transept, discovered 1862, of a lady in 15c dress, the surface cushioned and not flat like most brasses.

Up Exe [17] A scattered hamlet in the lowlands of the Exe valley. The little chapel, very like that at Nether Exe, stands down a country lane, its deserted churchyard shoulder-high in knot grass and thistle.

Uplowman [14] 14c church built by the mother of Henry VII who lived nearby at Sampford Peverell; restored to the teeth in 1864; stone above the porch may be the head of an early capital. *Widhayes* has a splendid door built into its barton wall: a great 17c stone arch and below it the original massive wooden door, fan shaped above and iron-studded below; large dovecote outside. Pleasant orchardy countryside.

Uplyme [36] Undulating village in a dip of the hills behind Lyme Regis; old cottages and some suburban in-filling attracted by the nearness of the sea. Church is on a hill with a pleasant view to W. Jacobean pulpit; memorial in engraved glass to two children by Laurence Whistler 1970 (switch below illuminates the case). In the new churchyard NW two complementary tombstones by the same artist.

There was a Celtic settlement at Holcombe, *c* AD 44, ¾ m WSW where an engraved bronze mirror was found, now in the British Museum. A Roman villa was built on the same site between 1c and 4c growing progressively larger until it had a quite elaborate octagonal bath house. Excavated 1967–70 but now filled in.

Upottery [15] Pleasant but not notable country and the village likewise. Viscount Sidmouth, sometime Prime Minister, built a mansion here in the early 19c, and some almshouses in much the same style; bargeboarding and many coats of arms (he was the 1st Viscount).

Upton Hellions [16] Village scattered along a sunny S slope. Church has a

plain Norman S door with rich carving on capitals. Old bench ends, a lion crouches on top of one; 15c roof bosses; monument 1631 to Richard Reynell and wife: kneeling figures face each other.

Upton Pyne [17] Sloping village with view N. The church lies beyond a quiet cobbled enclave of old cottages. Ancient cross by the S porch. Tower variously decorated with carving and images. Interior equally attractive, though restored 1867–8 by Rhode Hawkins. S aisle has Larder monument with man in 16c armour; 17c altar rails now form a gallery in tower arch.

Venn Ottery. *See* Ottery St Mary.

Virginstow [20] Bleak, poor, remote parish on the Cornish border. The hamlet overlooks wooded valley of the Carey threaded by the now grassy track of the old Launceston railway. Church has a Norman font with a little flattish decoration round the bowl.

Walkhampton [24] Church stands alone on its hill. The tower, very large and out of all proportion to the church itself, provides a landmark for miles around. *Huckworthy Bridge*, ½ m N, is a pretty spot on the Walkham; weathered old houses and mediaeval bridge.

Warkleigh. *See* Satterleigh and Warkleigh.

Washfield [14] Large parish in the bosomy valley of the Exe. *St Mary's* church has a splendid Jacobean screen, 1624, surmounted by Royal coat of arms. Carved Victorian stone pulpit which would look good in St Pancras station but is all wrong here; Norman font; good brass tablet to Henry Worth, d 1606, in N chancel.

Washford Pyne [13] Isolated hamlet, quite remote from any through road, lying 9 m W of Tiverton. There have been rectors here since 1257, but the present church is Victorian (1887), very small and snug, all tiles and wood and polished brass. Tucker Memorial (1922) is a screen richly carved in the old style.

Weare Giffard [5] Looking across the water meadows of the broad Torridge valley: *Weare Giffard Hall*, now an hotel, lies just behind the church; 15c it still has a fine mediaeval hall and much Renaissance panelling and carving. The exterior is little altered: the Gatehouse still stands with double doors, studded and diamond braced, surmounted by twin lions (very similar to those at Mycenae – effigies of fierce beasts placed to guard a door being, as you might say, continuously popular). Good view of the hall from the main Bideford–Torrington road.

Church has early 14c effigies: knight in N aisle, lady in chancel; mediaeval wall painting: martyrdom of St Edmond; monuments to the Fortescues who lived in the hall.

Welcombe [4] Furthest corner of Devon, the unvisited quarter, remote and "foreign". The hills are bleak but the valleys snug and thickly wooded; Tudor cottages, and small Georgian houses keep their heads well down against the wind; very little new building. There is a reputed holy well S of the church. *St Nectan* is tiny and interesting; W tower (?12c) low and stumpy; original paving stones on the floor; plain and early Norman font in its original position, judging by the arrangement of the stones on which it stands. The screen, below the cornice, probably the oldest in Devon, with primitive, almost barbaric carving; pulpit with Renaissance panels; Jacobean lectern. Fascinating collection of windows of different periods.

The coast here is rocky and spectacular, as at Hartland. A rough beach at Welcombe Mouth is accessible by car, and there is a cliff walk to the N.

Wembury [27] The church stands on the cliff edge fronting the elements, a challenge and a landmark; from its tower you look over the flecked sea to the *Great Mew Stone*. Tiny, romantic churchyard crammed full and inclining to the sea. The S porch has part of a Norman pier above the door. Inside two grand monuments: to Elizabeth, Lady Narborough, who died 1678 "Mightyly Afflicted with a Cough and Bigge with Child". She had only been married ten months and the family did their memorial best by her: kneeling figure, flanked by contemporary paling, theatrical and Venetian in feeling. Hele monument *c* 1608: a riot of busty ladies.

The village is much dispersed: to the

NE of the church is *Wembury House*, 1803, its central niche enshrining a full length figure, and at its gates the *Hele Almshouses*, 1682, with central chapel. W is the village proper, with much modern overflow from near by Plymouth. The cove itself is National Trust.

Langdon Court, 1 m W. Elizabethan 1577, altered 1668 and again 1886. What remains is a broad, dignified, rather heavy house ornamented with pilasters and with satyrs' heads above the doorways. Once the home of the Calmadys (the last of the family lies in Wembury churchyard) and now an hotel.

Wembworthy [6] Sprawling, not over distinguished village in rolling upland country in mid Devon. Church has a wagon roof with good bosses: grotesque head, armed head, mermaid, male head bearded and ringleted like a tragic mask etc.

Rashleigh Barton, 1 m. NW of Eggesford, but in Wembworthy parish, is a farmhouse, once a Jacobean manor, with two exquisite plaster ceilings.

West Alvington [34] Dominating site above Kingsbridge. Ancient parish from which others were carved as the population grew; dull village with main road running through. Church stands above and has bits of a mediaeval rood screen in the aisles, also an ancient parclose screen; tomb chest and Easter sepulchre of great charm with early 16c carving, it originally had brasses but these have disappeared.

Bowringsleigh, ¾ m NW. Considerable remains of a 15c mansion, rebuilt in Elizabethan times and again in the late 19c. In 1869, the old parish church of South Huish being abandoned, Mr W. R. Ilbert paid 20 guineas for the 15c screen and installed it in his house. Good plaster ceilings in hall and dining room. Fine carved Elizabethan screen.

West Anstey [13] Remote, semi-moorland village on the edge of Exmoor. Church has fine Norman font with palmettes and saltire; a few Renaissance carved bench ends at the back of the church.

West Buckland [3] Large school building: Devon County School 1861. But otherwise no compelling reason to come here.

West Down [2] Open rolling country; relaxed village of wide streets and pleasant houses. Old vicarage is early Victorian, manor house E of church, late 16c and said to contain fine plaster overmantel and frieze. Cruciform church: painted Isaac monument with two half figures holding hands; Norman font in rough condition; chief interest is N transept with open wagon roof of trefoil section; lying in a recess a wooden effigy, probably Sir John Stowford, *c.* 1290–1372; this ancient effigy has recently been painted with horrible crudity in white, red and blue.

West Ogwell. *See* East and West Ogwell.

West Putford [5] Unspectacular country. *St Stephen's* is one of those churches away from a village but close to a farm; lying low, hidden, tree-shaded in a pretty churchyard. Iron-studded door with the date 1620 exquisitely incised; Norman font: bulbous irregular bowl with worn cable moulding; chancel entirely floored with old Barnstaple tiles; 18c pulpit and altar rails with barley sugar balusters; Tudor windows in N wall. Nearby is *Churston Manor*, *c.* 1600, Elizabethan manor house with a weather vane perched on a bit of 15c polygonal pinnacle.

West Worlington. *See* East and West Worlington.

Westleigh [5] A high, hilly, wooded village above the Torridge. Church has old bench ends; ceiled wagon roof with gilt bosses and angels with spreading wings; two large undistinguished paintings by Lord Leighton and Harlow.

Tapeley is a Georgian house once owned by John Christie, who founded Glyndebourne Opera House. Gardens open to the public.

Westward Ho! *See* Northam.

Whimple [17] Whiteway's cider factory is here. The railway still runs and the village is not far from Exeter; understandably there is much suburban housing. Nucleus of the old village is set around The Square with streams running through. In the church, restored 1845 by J. Hayward, are a few painted panels from the old screen preserved in the tower arch, looking like playing card figures.

Whitchurch [23] Two ancient crosses mark the Abbot's Way from Tavistock, which lies 1½ m WNW. There are more of these old crosses on the moors around punctuating the trackless waste like so many early English telegraph poles. *St Andrew's* church: 15c with traces of Norman—the unadorned S door, and a Norman capital in the N wall; Alleyn Monument, in slate, has ten kneeling children wearing hats or caps, according to sex, and all carrying a skull. The inn has a 17c sign plastered above its door. *Honour Oak* stands by the side of the Tavistock road, marking the boundary for French prisoners of war on parole from Princetown. It was also the place where money was left for food during an outbreak of cholera in 1832.

Whitestone [16] The landscape rises sharply from the main A30 and looks over the Exe estuary; some of the hillsides are so steep that it is like looking down from a helicopter; much new overflow from Exeter set to catch the views. The church, *St Catherine of Alexandria*, has Jacobean carving on the front of the W gallery and parclose screen; a little mediaeval glass in the N aisle; in the vestry are instruments from the old church band.

Widecombe-in-the-Moor [31] In high summer the coaches converge. Widecombe is known because of the song but remains popular because it manages to keep some of its character. Dominated by a high, slender church tower it rides in a dip of Dartmoor like a raft amidst waves. Centre of the village is the Square with *Glebe House*, 1527, now a gift shop, and *Old Church House* (National Trust) with colonnade of granite pillars. The moor billows out beyond the church with which it forms a grand contrast. Church interior surprises by its space; screen is cut down to wainscot but paintings remain; panelling in N aisle: mixed bits of various periods, Jacobean and 18c; reredos now in tower with large, primitive paintings of Moses and Aaron; small work in same sort of style by S door: Abraham sacrificing Isaac.

Widworthy [18*] Late 14c church, built by Sir William Rouz, whose effigy it may be that lies there, figure armoured in exact detail. The three co-heiresses of Sir William are remembered by their shields carved in stone above the ex-

terior W door. Otherwise this intimate church is filled with monuments to the Marwood family, mostly 18c and richly lachrymose, including one to Thomas White, d 1838, "who lived in the Marwood family 40 years as steward and confidential agent". *Manor House* nearby well preserved with plaster fireplace dated 1591.

Willand [14] If you approach from the water meadows of the Culm you come to the old part of the village first: pleasant enough with some Georgian porticos and other pretty details. To the W is suburbanised sprawl. The church, romantically low and sunken, is nearly 700 years old. Some of the drip stones to the windows have small carved heads, probably of the same period. Inside: a simple 14c screen, its flat surfaces painted with gilt scrolls; two-decker Victorian pulpit not out of sympathy with the screen.

Winkleigh [6] On a windswept hilltop, the town was once a stronghold and had two castles. *Castle School*, 1840, stands on the site of one, the other is now only a great tree-covered mound. Few houses of real distinction, except perhaps *Linden House* with portico and delicate Georgian fanlight; otherwise pleasant cob and thatch. An *obelisk* in the market place, 1832, built as a monument to William IV, later became the village pump. The church has a strongly carved head, probably Norman, built into the exterior S wall.

Witheridge [13] Lying half way between Tiverton and South Molton this was once an important little town. Markets and fairs have been held here since 1248. It still has its vast market place, large as a lake whose edges lap peacefully at the walls of cottages in cob and thatch and village Georgian. Some pretty houses in the streets behind; best are probably *Cyprus House*, West St, and *Mitre House*, Fore St, also a Victorian frontage with porch of stained glass and ornamental joinery at No. 10 West St. Church, *St John the Baptist*, is built of local stone, and large. 16c pulpit with carved figures including a crucifixion.

Woodbury [17] Woodbury Castle is an Iron Age hill fort overlooking the Exe estuary, a commanding site re-used in the Napoleonic wars. Woodbury Common: a similar view, heathy

plateau, good for picnics. *St Swithin's* church: consecrated 1409, but restored during the 19c by an over zealous, amateur incumbent. Some woodwork remains: screen; Elizabethan altar and font rails; bench ends.

Woodland [31] Church has one interesting feature: part of an altar cloth formed from an Elizabethan cope, grey-green damask embroidered with flowers.

Woodleigh [34] Hamlet above the Kingsbridge estuary. Church has an Easter Sepulchre erected by Sir Thomas Smyth, rector from 1492–1527: three crude carvings, the faces mutilated.

Woolacombe. *See* Mortehoe.

Woolfardisworthy. (Nr Bideford). [4] Large thatched village on a plateau. *Holy Trinity* church has a fine Norman S door arch (as at Buckland Brewer); and some old bench ends. Down a steep winding combe is *Buck's Mills*, 2½ m NE, a picturesque fishing village which has not become as popular as Clovelly and, because of the scarcity of land, has escaped modern building. The cottages perch above the rocky shore looking N. Down by the water's edge is an old lime kiln like a moated fortress; the limestone was ferried across from S Wales, burned here on the shore and then carried to the inland farms.

Woolfardisworthy. (Nr Crediton). [13] Towards the edge of a plateau looking across Dartmoor but hardly even a hamlet. Unpretentious church entirely restored by Hayward, 1845, with a few 19c monuments: Victorian Gothick and *Art Nouveau*.

Yarcombe [36] Village lies on a long steep curve of the A30, a very beautiful stretch of road with the Yarty valley beyond. The Inn is almost within the churchyard, and may once have been the Church House. Inside the church, *St John*, 15c, a little restored, is some good carving: pulpit with linenfold panels, lectern made from 15c pulpit, bench ends in choir topped by beasts and monks in thinking attitudes, angel corbels on the transept arches wearing Elizabethan dress; N transept has some 15c stained glass; there is a Breeches bible (Gen. III.7.) printed Geneva 1595. *Sheafhayne House* nearby is an Eliza-

Widecombe-in-the-Moor

bethan Manor House with terrace overlooking the wide sweep of the valley.

Yarnscombe [6] On a plateau to the W of the Taw in an area of bosomy, green hills. Village is undistinguished but *Langley Barton*, 1 m NNE, is a low rambling farmhouse with Georgian façade and a pillared portico, said to contain traces of earlier work. *St Andrew's* church has a 15c wall tomb in the chancel, and some mediaeval Barnstaple tiles at the E end of the S aisle.

Yealmpton [27] One of the most interesting Victorian architects, Butterfield, completely rebuilt the church in 1849–51. It was one of his earliest works and

is a little austere and perhaps tame compared with his later style. All the same, his characteristic bold use of colour shows itself in the alternating bands of light and dark grey in the piers, in the pattern of inlaid marble echoing the shapes of the windows and in the richly veined marbles in the chancel. Brass from the former church in the N transept to Sir John Crocker, d 1508; double wall tablet to two members of the Bastard family of Kitley. Tower is 1915.

Some attractive buildings NE of the church including a square handsome 18c house now the Kitley Manor Estate Office. *Kitley* is a mansion dating from the time of Henry VIII but largely

remodelled by Repton *c* 1825, when it became whole-hearted Gothick revival. It was here that Miss Sarah Martin, sister-in-law of Squire Bastard, wrote "Old Mother Hubbard", said to have been based upon the then Kitley housekeeper.

Zeal Monachorum [16] Hillside village on a S facing slope looking across fields and orchards to Dartmoor. Canute gave this land to Buckfast Abbey and a cell of monks was founded. In the churchyard by the S door is a huge block of stone weighing about a ton, believed to have been the altar of the Norman church.

Index

"Breeches" bible see Loddiswell, Malborough, Marldon and Yarcombe
Brerewood, Dr T. see Colyton
Brewer family see Hemyock
Brewer, Lord William de see Dunkeswell
Bridgettine nuns see Rattery
Bridgetown see Totnes
Bridgman, G. S. see Paignton
Bristol Channel see Trentishoe
Bristol pottery see Plymouth p 136
Bristol Steamer Service see Martinhoe
British Museum see Uplyme
Brixham see p 17
Broadhayes House see Stockland
Broadnymet see North Tawton
Broadway House see Topsham
Brockholt Hotel see Slapton
Bronescombe, Bishop see Sowton
Brooke, Rajah see Sheepstor
Broomfield see Jacobstowe
Brown, Capability see Ashprington and Mamhead
Browning, Elizabeth B. see Sidmouth
Brunel, I. K. see p 32
Bryant, Sir Thomas see South Pool
Byron, Lady see Exmouth
Buck's Mills see Woolfardisworthy (nr Bideford)
Buckfast Abbey see Zeal Monachorum
Buckland Abbey see Buckfastleigh and Buckland Monachorum
Buckland Court see Buckland in the Moor
Bude canal see Canals
Budleigh Salterton see p 17
Bull Point lighthouse see Morthoe
Buller, Sir Redvers see Crediton
Burke, see Totnes
Burdon Manor see Highampton
Burgess, William see Tiverton
Burgh Island see Bigbury
Burgoyne, Robert see South Tawton
Burrator Reservoir see Sheepstor
Bury Barton see Lapford
Bury family see Chulmleigh
Burne-Jones, Sir E. see Culmstock and Torquay
Bushell, Zachariah and William see Down St Mary
Butterfield, W. see p 26, Abbotskerswell, Exeter pp 88, 91, Ottery St Mary, Torquay and Yealmpton

Cada's Burgh see Cadbury
Cadbury family see Culstock
Cadhay see Ottery St Mary
Calmady family see Tamerton Foliot and Wembury
Calmady, Susan see Wembury
Canals see p 32, Burlescombe, Exeter p 90, Great Torrington, Halberton,

Holsworthy, Mary Tavy, Pancrasweek, Sampford Peverell, and Tavistock
Canonsleigh see Burlescombe
Canute, King see Buckfastleigh and Zeal Monachorum
Capern, Edward see Heanton Punchardon
Caravan Club see Bradford
Carew family see Bickleigh (nr Tiverton)
Carey, River see Virginstow
Carey, Will see Clovelly
Carminow, Thomas see Ashwater
Caroe, see Exeter p 91
Carpenter, R. C. see Bovey Tracey
Cary family see Torquay
Cary, Thomas see Torquay
Castle Drogo see Drewsteignton
Castle Farm see Ringmore
Castle Hill see Filleigh
Castles, mediaeval see Berry Pomeroy, Bickleigh, Dartmouth, Exeter p 89, Gidleigh, Kingswear, Lundy, Lydford, Marldon, Okehampton, Plympton St Maurice, Powderham, Salcombe, Tiverton, Totnes and Winkleigh
Catherine of Aragon see Plymouth p 136
Cattewater see Plymouth pp 133, 136
Celtic settlement see Uplyme
Chagford see p 17
Chambercombe Manor see Ilfracombe
Channon, see Powderham
Chantrey see Topsham
Charles I see Holsworthy and Honiton
Charles II see Plymouth p 133
Chaucer see Dartmouth
Chelfham viaduct see Goodleigh
Chelves Hayes see Clyst Hydon
Chevithorne Barton see Tiverton
Chichester family see Arlington
Chichester, Sir Francis see Plymouth p 133
Chichester, Lord see Eggesford
Chichester, Sir Robert see Pilton
Chichester, Rosalie see Arlington
Chilcot School see Tiverton
China clay see Dartmoor and Ivybridge
Cholwich Town see Cornwood
Christie, John see Westleigh
Chudleigh, Sir George & Lady Mary see Ashton
Church House Inn see Torbryan
Churston Manor see West Putford
Cider see Plymtree and Whimple
Cistercians see Buckfastleigh, Buckland Monachorum
Civil War see Kingswear, Membury and Plymouth p 133
Clapper bridge see Dartmoor
Cleave see Bere Ferrers

Cleave Mill see South Tawton
Clocombe House see Axminster
Cloister Hall Farm see Frithelstock
Clovelly see p 34
Clyst valley see Broadclyst, Clyst St George, Farringdon
Cobley, Tom see Spreyton
Cockerell, C. R. see Broadclyst
Cockington Court see Torquay
Cockington parish see Torquay
Coffin, Richard see Heanton Punchardon
Coleford see Colebrooke
Coleridge, see Totnes
Coleridge, Lady see Ottery St Mary
Coleridge, S. T. see Ottery St Mary
Collacombe Manor see Lamerton
Collaton Barton see South Milton
Colleton Barton see Chulmleigh
Columbjohn see Broadclyst
Coly, River see Farway and Southleigh
Colyford see Colyton
Combe Barton see Gittisham
Combe-in-Teignhead see Haccombe with Combe
Combe Martin see p 35
Combe Royal see Churchstow
Commonwealth see Ashwater, Bovey Tracey, Dittisham, Exeter pp 84, 86 and 87
Compton Castle see Marldon
Compton-Smith, Mrs see Brixham
Cookworthy, William see Plymouth p 136
Coplestone Chapel see Colebrooke
Coplestone family see Offwell
Coplestone memorial see Tamerton Foliot
Copper Castle see Honiton
Copplestone see Colebrooke
Corp, Elyenore and John see Stoke Fleming
Coryton Park see Kilmington
Cosway, Richard see Powderham and Tiverton
Countryside Act, 1968 see p 34
Courtenay, Elizabeth see Meshaw
Courtenay family see Molland and Powderham
Courtenay, William see Plympton St Mary
Coverdale Tower see Paignton
Cowick Barton see Exeter p 90
Crabadon Court see Diptford
Crealock, General Hope see Littleham (nr Bideford)
Crediton see p 19
Cremyll Ferry see Plymouth pp 133, 137
Crocken Tor see Dartmoor
Crocker, Sir John see Yealmpton
Cromer House see Topsham

Croyde *see* Georgeham
Crusades, the *see* Dartmouth
Cubitt, William *see* East Allington
Culm, River *see* Butterleigh, Clayhidon, Cullompton, Rewe, Uffculme and Willand

Damage Barton *see* Morthoe
Damehole Point *see* Harland
Dampier-Wetton, W. C. *see* Ottery St Mary
Danes *see* Vikings
Darre, Leonard *see* South Pool
Dart, River *see* pp 11, 34, Ashburton, Ashprington, Buckland in the Moor, Cornworthy, Dartmouth, Dittisham, Harberton, Staverton, Stoke Gabriel
Dart, Little, River *see* Chulmleigh and East Worlington
Dart Valley Railway *see* Buckfastleigh
Dartington Arts Trust *see* Beaford
Dartington Glass Factory *see* Great Torrington
Dartmoor, *see* pp 11, 19, 32, Ashbury, Belstone, Bere Ferrers, Bickington, Bishopsteignton, Bratton, Clovelly, Brentor, Broadwood-Kelly, Broadwoodwidger, Buckland Filleigh, Burrington, Cadbury, Chagford, Chawleigh, Clannanborough, Coldridge, Down St Mary, East Portlemouth, Halwell, Harford, Hatherleigh, Holcombe Burnell, Holne, Iddesleigh, Ilsington, Inwardleigh, Ivybridge, Lydford, Merton, Morchard Bishop, Moretonhampstead, North Molton, Poughill, Princetown, Puddington, Rose Ash, Sourton, South Brent, South Tawton, Teignmouth, Widecombe-in-the-Moor, Woolfardisworthy (nr Crediton) and Zeal Monachorum
Davies, *see* Hockworthy
Davy, Sir Humphrey *see* Sandford
Dawlish *see* p 17
de Brien, Sir Guy *see* Slapton
de Gomme, Bernard *see* Plymouth p 133
de Redvers, Richard *see* Tiverton
Deer Park *see* Buckerell
Denbury *see* Torbryan
Dennis, Sir Robert *see* Holcombe Burnell
Devey, G. *see* Jacobstowe
Devil's Lime Kiln *see* Lundy
Devil's Stone *see* Shebbear
Devil's Stone Hotel *see* Shebbear
Devon, Earls of *see* Powderham and South Huish; *see also* Beaufort, Margaret
Devon & Friendship Mine *see* Mary Tavy

Devonport *see* Plymouth, pp 133, 137 and 138
Devonport Leat *see* Dartmoor
Dirham family *see* Kingskerswell
Dissolution of the Monasteries *see* Buckfastleigh, Buckland Monachorum, Dunkeswell, Exeter pp 84, 90, Ottery St Mary, Plympton St Mary, Tavistock and Torquay
Dodbrooke *see* Kingsbridge
Doderidge, Sir John and Lady *see* Exeter p 87
Dolbury Hill *see* Broadclyst
Domesday *see* Jacobstowe, Sampford Courtenay, Sherford and Sutcombe
Dominicans *see* Plymouth p 136
Dorset, Marchioness *see* Ottery St Mary
Dowlands Landslip *see* Axmouth
Downes *see* Crediton
Dowrich House *see* Sandford
Dowrich, Mary *see* Sandford
Drake family *see* Meavy and Musbury
Drake, Sir Francis *see* Plymouth pp 133, 136, 138, Sheepstor and Tavistock
Drake's Island *see* Plymouth p 133
Drewe family *see* Broadhembury
Drewe, Francis *see* Broadclyst
Duckworth monyment *see* Topsham
Dunkeswell Abbey *see* Hemyock
Dunsland House *see* Bradford

East Leigh Manor *see* Horwood
"East-the-Water" *see* Bideford
Eastlake *see* Plympton St Maurice
Ebenezer Chapel *see* Rackenford
Eddystone rock *see* Plymouth p 133
Edge Barton *see* Branscombe
Edgecumbe, Mt *see* Plymouth p 133
Edward the Confessor *see* Ottery St Mary
Egremont, Earls of *see* Kentisbeare and Sidmouth
Elizabeth, Queen *see* Honiton
Elmhirst, Leonard & Dorothy *see* Dartington
Endsleigh *see* Milton Abbot
Erme, River *see* Ermington and Ivybridge
Essex, Earl of *see* Honiton
Eveleigh, Nicholas *see* Bovey Tracey
Exe, River *see* p 17, Bickleigh (nr Tiverton), Bradninch, Butterleigh, Dartmoor, Farringdon, Kenton, Mamhead, Nether Exe, Pinhoe, Stoodleigh, Tiverton, Topsham, Up Exe, Washfield, Whitestone and Woodbury
Exeter Airport *see* Clyst Honiton
Exeter, Dukes of *see* p 19, Dartington and Littlehempston

Exhibition of 1851 *see* Monk Okehampton
Exmoor, *see* p 11, Atherington, Bampton, Burrington, Cadbury, Challacombe, East Anstey, Morchard Bishop, Morebath, North Molton, Romansleigh, Rose Ash, Twitchen, and West Anstey
Exmouth *see* p 17
Exmouth, Viscount *see* Christow
Eyston, John & Margaret *see* Morchard Bishop

Fairfax, General *see* Tiverton
Fairs *see* Bradninch, Brentor and Witheridge
Fallapit *see* East Allington
Fardel *see* Cornwood
Fellowes Monument *see* Eggesford
Feoffees *see* Colyton
Ferrey, B. *see* Huntsham
Field strip system *see* Braunton
Field Studies Centre *see* Slapton
Finch Bros foundry *see* p 34 and South Tawton
Fingle Bridge *see* Dartmoor
Fishacre, Sir Peter *see* Moreleigh
Fishing *see* Brixham and Dartmouth
Five Mile Act *see* Culmstock
Flaxman *see* Buckland Filleigh, Dawlish and Kingsbridge
Fletcher, Barminster *see* Ottery St Mary
Flete House *see* Holbeton
Forbes, James *see* Bovey Tracey
Ford, John *see* Ilsington
Forde House *see* Newton Abbot
Forde, Nicholas *see* Blackawton
Fordmore *see* Plymtree
Fordton House *see* Crediton
Forestry Commission *see* Huntshaw
Forster, E. M. *see* Exeter p 84
Fort Charles *see* Salcombe
Fortescue family *see* East Allington, Filleigh and Weare Giffard
Fortescue monument *see* Lamerton
Fortescue, Ann *see* Buckland Filleigh
Fosse Way *see* Axmouth
Foulston, John *see* Plymouth pp 137, 138
Fowler, Charles *see* Honiton, Powderham and Totnes
Fowler, Dymond & Charles *see* Exeter p 91
Frere, Mary *see* Newton Abbot
Frogmore *see* Charleton
Fry family *see* Culmstock and Membury
Fry, Frances *see* Membury
Fulda monastery *see* Crediton
Fulford family *see* Dunsford
Furlong, Elizabeth *see* Stokeinteignhead

175

176

Knap Down *see* Combe Martin and Trentishoe
Knights Templar *see* Templeton
Knightshayes Court *see* Tiverton

Lacy, Bishop *see* Totnes
Ladram Bay *see* Otterton
Lady Modyford School *see* Buckland Monachorum
Lambert's Castle *see* Hawkchurch
Lana *see* Pancrasweek
Lancet, The see Membury
Lane, John *see* Cullompton
Langdon Court *see* Wembury
Langley Barton *see* Yarnscombe
Langton, William *see* Exeter p 87
Larder family *see* Upton Pyne
Lascaze, *see* Dartington
Launceston railway *see* Virginstow
Lawrence, General Stringer *see* Dunchideock and Kenn
Lawrence, T. E. *see* Plymouth p 133
Leach, Sir Simon *see* Cadeleigh
le Maygne, Henry *see* Spreyton
Le Notre *see* Bicton
Lee *see* Ilfracombe
Lee Abbey *see* Lynton
Leigh *see* Churchstow
Leighton, Lord *see* Westleigh
Leofric, Bishop *see* Exeter pp 84 and 88
Lime *see* Trentishoe, Woolfardisworthy (Nr Bideford)
Linden House *see* Winkleigh
Lister, Barbara *see* Dolton
Lloyd's signal station *see* Chivelstone
Loman, River *see* Tiverton
Longlands *see* Hennock
Lorna Doone see Brendon and Tiverton
Loughwood Farm *see* Dalwood
Lower Cadham *see* Jacobstowe
Loxhore church *see* Shirwell
Lugg plaque *see* Shirwell
Lundy *see* Morthoe
Luscombe Castle *see* Dawlish
Lutyens, Sir Edwin *see* Drewsteignton and Torquay
Lyd, River *see* Coryton, Lydford and Marystow
Lydford Gorge *see* Dartmoor
Lydia bridge *see* South Brent
Lyn, River *see* Lynton
Lyndale *see* Budleigh Salterton

Mackrell almshouses *see* Newton Abbot
Mallet, Catherine *see* Petrockstow
Malstone *see* Sherford
Marisco Castle *see* Lundy
Marisco, Sir William de *see* Lundy
Maristow *see* Tamerton Foliot
Maritime Museum *see* Exeter p 91

Martin, the Rev Keble *see* Newton Abbot
Martin, Miss Sarah *see* Yealmpton
Marwood family *see* Widworthy
Marwood House *see* Holsworthy
Marwood, John *see* Holsworthy
Marwood, Thomas *see* Honiton
Mayflower Stone *see* Plymouth p 136
Meavy, River *see* Meavy
Mendips *see* Hawkchurch
Merton College *see* Merton
Merton, Walter de *see* Merton
Middle Ages *see* Braunton and Exeter pp 89, 90
Milber, St Luke's Church *see* Newton Abbot
Millais *see* Budleigh Salterton
Milton Combe *see* Buckland Monachorum
Milton Green *see* Milton Abbot
Minerals and mining *see* p 11, Bere Ferrers, Dartmoor, Mary Tavy and Tavistock
Mint towns *see* Barnstaple, Exeter and Lydford
Mohun, Elinor *see* Stoke Fleming
Mole, River *see* George Nympton and South Molton
Moore, Henry *see* Dartington
Moreton Hampstead *see* p 17
Morris, William *see* Barnstaple, Monkton, Okehampton, Tavistock and Torquay; Morris & Co. *see* Torquay
Morte Point *see* Morthoe
Morwell Barton *see* Tavistock
Morwhellham *see* pp 32, 34
Mount Pleasant *see* Clovelly
Mudge, Zachary *see* Plymouth p 136
Museums, p 34, Brixham, Buckfastleigh, Buckland Monachorum, Dartmouth, Exeter pp 84, 90, 91, Honiton, Lynton, Salcombe, South Tawton, Tiverton, Topsham, Torquay and Totnes

Napoleonic Wars *see* Dartmoor, Lynton, Moretonhampstead, Princetown, Torquay and Woodbury
Narborough, Lady *see* Wembury
Nash *see* Dawlish
National Trust *see* Arlington, Bideford, Bradford, Branscombe, Brendon, Broadclyst, Clovelly, Dartmoor, Georgeham, Lydford, Lynton, Malborough, Martinhoe, Meavy, Newton Abbot, Shute, Sidmouth, South Huish, Wembury and Widecombe-in-the-Moor
Naval telegraph stations *see* Awliscombe
Nelson, Lady Horatio *see* Exmouth and Littleham (nr Exmouth)

Netherton Hall *see* Farway
Newcomen, Elias *see* Stoke Fleming
Newcomen, Thomas *see* Dartmouth
Newcourt family *see* Georgeham
Newnham Abbey *see* Axminster
Newnham Park *see* Plympton St Mary
Newton Ferrers *see* Newton and Noss
Normans *see* p 19; Norman Conquest *see* Totnes
Norris, Dom Charles *see* Buckfastleigh
Northam Burrows *see* p 7 and Northam
Northcote *see* Plympton St Maurice
Northcote, John *see* Newton St Cyres
Northcott Theatre *see* Exeter p 91
Northcott, Henry *see* Salcombe Regis
Northernhay, Gardens of *see* Exeter p 90
Noss Mayo *see* Newton and Noss
Nunneries *see* Abbeys
Nutcombe Manor House *see* Clayhanger
Nymet *see* Bishop's Nympton
Nymet Barton *see* Bow

Oaklands *see* Okehampton
Okehampton, Lord of *see* Baldwin de Brionne
Okement valley *see* Broadwood-Kelly, Dartmoor, Exbourne, Monk Okehampton and Okehampton
Old Barrow Hill *see* Countisbury
Old Canonteign House *see* Christow
"Old Mother Hubbard" *see* Yealmpton
Old Newnham *see* Plympton St Mary
Old Noss Church *see* Newton and Noss
Oldstones *see* Blackawton
Orchard Hill *see* Northam
Oriel College *see* Offwell
Orleigh Court *see* Buckland Brewer
Osborne, Julian *see* Clyst St George
Otter, River *see* Awliscombe and Colaton Raleigh
Overbecks Museum *see* Salcombe
Oxenham Arms *see* South Tawton
Oxton *see* Kenton

Pack of Cards *see* Combe Martin
Paignton *see* p 17
Painsford *see* Ashprington
Palk family *see* Torquay
Palk, Sir Robert *see* Dunchideock, Kenn and Torquay
Palmer House *see* Great Torrington
Palmer, John *see* Great Torrington
Pannier Market *see* Barnstaple and Great Torrington
Parker family *see* Plympton St Mary
Parliament Cottage *see* Berry Pomeroy
Parminter, the Misses *see* Exmouth
Patey of Exeter *see* Dawlish and Teignmouth

177

Smeaton's Lighthouse *see* Plymouth p 133
Smith, Walter *see* Totnes
Smuggling *see* Trentishoe
Smyth, Sir Thomas *see* Woodleigh
Sortridge House *see* Horrabridge
South Huish *see also* West Alvington
South Zeal *see* South Tawton
Southcomb family *see* Rose Ash
Southcote, Walter *see* Bridford
Southernhay *see* Exeter pp 84, 91
Spark, Richard *see* Blackawton
Sparkwell *see* Plympton St Mary
Spence, Jane *see* Berrynarbor
Spencer *see* Colebrooke
Speke, Sir George *see* Exeter p 87
Speke's Mill Mouth *see* Hartland
Spicelands *see* Culmstock
Spicott monument *see* Thornbury
Spinster's Rock *see* Drewsteignton
Spitchwock Nature Reserve *see* Buckland in the Moor
Spooner's and West Devon Foxhounds *see* Sampford Spiney
Squiers, Hugh, School *see* South Molton
Stafford, Bishop *see* Exeter p 87
Stafford, Henry *see* Littleham (nr Exmouth)
Stanborough fort *see* Halwell
Stannary Parliament *see* Lydford
Stannary towns *see* Ashburton, Chagford and Lydford
Staplehill family *see* Trusham
Starcross *see* Kenton
Start Point *see* Halwell and Stokenham
Staverton Bridge *see* Dartmoor
Stedcombe House *see* Axmouth
Stevenstone House *see* St Giles in the Wood
Sticklepath *see* South Tawton
Stockleigh Court *see* Stockleigh English
Stockridge House *see* Oakford
Stoke Point *see* Newton and Noss
Stonehouse *see* Plymouth pp 133, 137 and 138
Stonelands *see* Dawlish
Stoningcross *see* Hatherleigh
Stooke, John & Mary *see* Trusham
Stover House *see* Teigngrace
Stowford, Sir John *see* West Down
Street, G. E. *see* Ashburton, Huish and Torquay
Strip-field, mediaeval *see* Braunton
Strode family *see* Plympton St Mary
Strode, Richard *see* Plympton St Mary
Stuckeridge House *see* Bampton
Stucley family *see* East Worlington
Stuer, Grace *see* Blackawton
Sully, Sir John *see* Crediton
Sumaster, Wylliam *see* Ashprington
Sutton Pool *see* Plymouth pp 136, 138

Sutton Prior *see* Plympton St Mary
Sydenham *see* Marystow
Syng, John *see* Beaford
Syon Abbey *see* Rattery

Taddington *see* Little Torrington
Taggel, Sir Thomas *see* Stokeinteignhead
Tamar, River *see* p 11, Bere Ferrers, Brentor, Bridgerule, Dunterton, Germansweek, Luffincott, Milton Abbot, Plymouth p 133, 138, Sydenham Damarel, Tavistock and Tetcott
Tapeley *see* Westleigh
Tavistock Abbey *see* Hatherleigh and Milton Abbot
Tavistock Canal *see* Mary Tavy
Tavy Cleave *see* Peter Tavy
Tavy, River *see* Bere Ferrers
Taw Estuary *see* Ashford, Bondleigh, Burrington, Dartmoor, Heanton, Punchardon, High Bickington, Horwood, Instow, Monkleigh, Northam, Nymet Rowland, South Tawton and Yarnscombe
Tawstock Court *see* Bishop's Tawton
Taylor, John *see* Torbryan
Taylor, John Coleridge *see* Feniton
Taylor, Mary *see* Ottery St Mary
Teign, River *see* p 17, Ashton, Bishopsteignton, Dartmoor, Doddiscombsleigh, Drewsteignton, Dunsford, Haccombe with Combe, Hennock, Shaldon, Throwleigh and Trusham
Teignmouth *see* p 17
Templar family *see* Teigngrace
Thomson, Lt J. H. *see* Hatherleigh
Thorn Farm *see* Salcombe Regis
Thushel, River *see* Bratton Clovelly and Stowford
Thuborough Barton *see* Sutcombe
Tiles, mediaeval *see* Barnstaple, Buckland in the Moor, Cheldon, Coldridge, Cookbury, Haccombe with Combe, Landcross, Little Torrington, Marwood, Stoke Rivers; *see also* Barnstaple tiles
Tipton St Johns *see* Ottery St Mary
Tobacco trade *see* Bideford
Tome Stone *see* Barnstaple
Toplady, Rev Augustus *see* Harpford
Topsham Barracks *see* Exeter p 91
Tor Abbey *see* Torquay
Torcross *see* Stokenham
Tormohun parish *see* Torquay
Torquay *see* pp 17, 26 and 34
Torre Abbey *see* Hennock
Torridge, River *see* Bideford, Black Torrington, Burrington, Cookbury, Dowland, East Putford, Frithelstock, Great Torrington, Heanton Punchardon, Highampton, Horwood, Idde-

sleigh, Landcross, Little Torrington, Merton, Northam, Roborough, Sheepwash, Weare Giffard and Westleigh
Totnes *see* p 11
Totnes Museum *see* Harberton
Tremayne family *see* Lamerton
Trendwell farm *see* South Milton
Truants *see* Aylesbeare
Truby, Sir George and family *see* Plympton St Mary and Plympton St Maurice
Tuckenhay *see* Ashprington
Tucker Memorial *see* Washford Pyne
Tucker, Mr *see* Ashprington
Tucker's Hall *see* Exeter p 90
Tuckfield, John & Elizabeth *see* Crediton
Two Bridges *see* Dartmoor
Tyrwhitt, Sir Thomas *see* Princetown

Ugborough Beacon *see* South Brent
United Services College *see* Northam
Upcott Barton *see* Cheriton Fitzpaine

Valley of the Rocks *see* Lynton
Vaughan, *see* Combpyne
Veale, Walter *see* Iddesleigh
Venn Ottery *see* Ottery St Mary
Venning, Walter *see* Totnes
Venton Manor *see* Rattery
Victoria & Albert Museum *see* King's Nympton
Victoria, Queen *see* Sidmouth
Vikings *see* Crediton, Exeter pp 84, 89 and Lundy
"Vinegar" Bible *see* South Milton, Stoke Gabriel, Torbryan
Voysey, C. F. A. *see* Halwill

Wadham family *see* Branscombe
Wadham, Sir Nicholas *see* Rewe
Wadlands *see* Ashbury, Tamerton Foliot
Wakeley, Thomas *see* Membury
Walkham, River *see* Dartmoor and Walkhampton
Walrond Chapel, Walrond family and Walrond, Hugh *see* Uffculme
Walrond, John *see* Tiverton
Walrond, Mrs *see* Beer
Walronde *see* Cullompton
Walshe, Thomas *see* Alverdiscott
Walters, F. A. *see* Buckfastleigh
Warelwast, Bishop *see* Exeter p 84
Wakleigh *see* Satterleigh
Warryings, Robert *see* Broadhempston
Waterhouse Farm *see* Membury
Waterman, Richard *see* Instow
Watermouth Castle *see* Berrynarbor
Watersmeet *see* Lynton
Way Barton *see* Bideford

179

Wear, Countess *see* Exeter p 90 and Topsham
Webb, Sir Aston *see* Dartmouth
Weber, Mary *see* Loxhore
Welcombe Mouth *see* Hartland
Wellington, Duke of *see* Clayhidon
Wembury *see* p 35
Wesley, John & Charles *see* South Tawton
Wesley, Rev Samuel *see* Tiverton
Westcott Barton *see* Marwood
Weston, *see* Torbryan
Westward Ho! *see* p 7
Weycroft Hall *see* Axminster
Whistler, Laurence *see* p 35, Dolton and Uplyme
Whistler, Rex *see* Dolton
White, Gilbert *see* Sowton
White Lady Waterfall *see* Lydford
White, Thomas *see* Widworthy
White, William *see* Sowton
Whitehall *see* Hemyock
Whiteway's Cider Factory *see* Whimple
Whitty, Thomas *see* Axminster
Whyddon, John *see* Chagford
Widhayes *see* Uplowman
Wier Quay *see* Bere Ferrers

Wild life park *see* Plympton St Mary; *see also* Okehampton
William I *see* Totnes
William III *see* Brixham
William IV *see* Winkleigh
Williams, Thomas *see* Harford
Wills, W. J. *see* Totnes
Willsworthy *see* Peter Tavy
Winscott Barton *see* St Giles in the Wood
Winsford Hospital *see* Halwill
Winslade Estate and Winslade House *see* Clyst St Mary
Wistleigh *see* Burlescombe
Wolborough, St Mary's church *see* Newton Abbot
Wolf, River *see* Broadwoodwidger and Germansweek
Wollan, Robert *see* Broadwood-Kelly
Wonson *see* Throwleigh
Wood, William Henry *see* Bradstone
Woodleigh, Rector of *see* Moreleigh
Woody Bay *see* Martinhoe
Woodyer *see* Ottery St Mary
Woodleigh, Rector of *see* Moreleigh
Woody Bay *see* Martinhoe
Woodyer *see* Ottery St Mary

Wool trade *see* Barnstaple, Cullompton, Ottery St Mary, South Molton, South Tawton and Tavistock
Woolacombe Sands *see* p 7 and Morthoe
Woolbrook Cottage *see* Sidmouth
Worth, Henry *see* Washfield
Worth monument *see* Staverton
Wortham Manor *see* Lifton
Wray family *see* Tawstock
Wyatt, James *see* Powderham
Wyatville, Sir John *see* Milton Abbot and Stowford
Wykes, John *see* South Tawton
Wylde Court *see* Hawkchurch
Wyse, Sir Thomas *see* Marystow

Yarty chapel *see* Membury
Yarty valley *see* Yarcombe
Yealm, River *see* Newton and Noss
Yeo, River *see* Bishop's Nympton, Crediton, East Down, King's Nympton, Lapford, Littleham (nr Bideford), Nymet Rowland
Yeo Vale House *see* Alwington
Yes Tor *see* Dartmoor
Yonge family *see* Newton and Noss

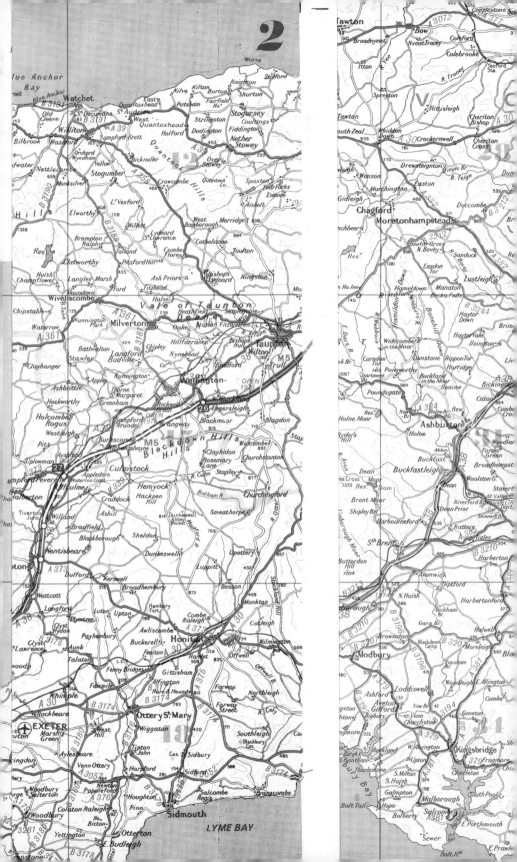